THE VICTORIAN CONSTITUTION

THE
VICTORIAN
CONSTITUTION

Conventions, Usages and
Contingencies

G. H. L. LE MAY

St. Martin's Press
New York

© G. H. L. Le May 1979

ISBN 0–312–84145–0

Library of Congress Cataloging in Publication Data

Le May, Godfrey Hugh Lancelot.
  The Victorian constitution.

  Includes bibliographical references and index.
  1. Great Britain – Constitutional history.
  2. Great Britain – Politics and government – 1837–1901.
  3. Great Britain – Politics and government – 1901–1910.
  I. Title.
JN223.L45   1979   342′.41′029   79–18072

ISBN 0–312–84145–0

To
MICHAEL ROBERTS

Contents

Acknowledgments

I should like first to express my thanks to Her Majesty the Queen for her gracious permission to make use of material in the Royal Archives at Windsor. I should like also to thank Sir Robert Mackworth-Young and Miss Jane Langton for their help.

Many friends and colleagues have been generous with their time and their advice. I should like to thank in particular Professor George Brauer, Lord Briggs, Mr James Campbell, Professor Richard Chowan, Professor Charles Coolidge, Mr Gordon Lawrie, Professor Michael Roberts and Mr H. G. Pitt. I am particularly grateful to Penelope, my wife, who has patiently read every page, and has saved me from many infelicities. For the errors that remain, the responsibility is my own.

The first draft of this book was written when I was the guest of the Rockefeller Foundation at the Villa Serbelloni. By those who have experienced the delights of that experience, my deep appreciation will be well understood. I should like to thank Dr and Mrs William Olson for their kindness.

G. H. L. Le M.

Abbreviations

RA	Papers in the Royal Archives at Windsor
Add. MSS.	Additional manuscripts in the British Museum
H. of C.,	Hansard's Parliamentary Debates; Official
H. of L.	Reports of Parliamentary Debates
LQV	Letters of Queen Victoria: 1st series, 1837–61; 2nd series, 1862–85; 3rd series 1886–1901
EHR	*English Historical Review*
TRHS	*Transactions of the Royal Historical Society*

I

Introduction

No one, at that time was taught, by a wide survey of society, that governments are not framed after a model, but that all their parts and powers grow out of occasional acts, prompted by some urgent expediency, or some private interest, which, in the course of time, coalesce and harden into usage; and that this bundle of usages is the object of respect and the guide of conduct long before it is embodied, defined, and enforced in written laws.

Sir James Mackintosh (1765–1832)

This book attempts to examine the conventions of the English constitution between the end of one era, in the 1830s, and the end of another, in the years immediately preceding the outbreak of war in 1914. By 'conventions' I mean the general agreements among public men about the 'rules of the game' to be borne in mind in the conduct of political affairs.

James Bryce wrote in 1901:

That which we call the Constitution of the Roman State, that which we now call the Constitution of the United Kingdom, is a mass of precedents, carried in men's memories or recorded in writing, of dicta of lawyers or statesmen, of customs, usages, understandings and beliefs bearing upon the methods of government, together with a certain number of statutes, some of them containing matters of petty detail, others relating to private just as much as to public law, nearly all of them presupposing and mixed up with precedents and customs, and all of them covered with a parasitic growth of legal decisions and political habits, apart from which the statutes would be almost unworkable, or at any rate quite different in their working from what they really are.[1]

This book, then, is concerned only with a part of constitutional history—with customs, usages, understandings and beliefs, and with contemporary statements about them. Thus, its subject matter is vague and slippery. It is also concerned with politics.

English politicians have been readier to work their system of government than to analyse it in its full complexity; Maitland suggested that they had substituted the authority of the Crown for a theory of the State. Political debate in the nineteenth century was mainly concerned with what ought to be done and who ought to do it; the political machinery was accepted as more or less adequate for its task by most of the serious parties to the argument. One generation could find security in what was believed to be a self-adjusting balance between 'what we may fairly call a monarchic, an aristocratical, and a democratic element'.[2] The idea of a balance of power as something to be regarded as desirable is usually held, in domestic as in international affairs, by those who are conscious that they have something to lose. A description of the constituents of government as existing in balanced harmony might be extended to the assertion that there was a similar condition among the classes of society—a comfortable doctrine that might, with luck, become a self-fulfilling prophecy. The idea of balance can be found in the writings of Blackstone, Paley and de Lolme (to mention only three of the more notable contributors to the doctrine), sometimes in a form which, in its American version, became the theory of checks and balances. To de Lolme, indeed, balance or 'equilibrium' was a desirable condition of deadlock: 'the chance that no changes will be made is greatly increased.'[3]

Prescriptive assertion from one side could always be met by counter-assertion from another. Park, in 1832, talked about a

---

[1] James Bryce, *Constitutions* (1901), p. 13.

[2] E. A. Freeman, *Growth of the English Constitution* (1872), passim.

[3] Quoted in M. J. C. Vile, *Constitutionalism and the Separation of Powers* (1967), p. 106.

constitution that was celebrated but unreal, 'a theory upon which Blackstone, and Montesquieu, and de Lolme have descanted with as much rapture as Petrarch did upon his Laura, who is believed by some to have been an imaginary person also'.[4] As for Paley's mutual checks supposed to be exercised by King and Parliament each against the other— Parliament kept in check by a royal veto which was too dangerous a power for the King to use—, that was a circle such as Mr Puff had described in Sheridan's *The Critic* :

> There's situation for you! there's an heroic group! You see the ladies can't stab Whiskerandos; he durst not strike them for fear of their uncles; the uncles durst not kill him, because of their nieces. I have them all at a dead lock; for every one of them is afraid to let go first.

The eighteenth-century idea of balance might be attacked, but it was never quite destroyed. National harmony was an attractive aim; it emphasised the virtues of patriotism, of a reconciliation of opposing interests, of a middle way between extremes. Its reiteration, and its association with the notion of perpetual compromise in a continuing conflict in which there should be no outright winners or losers, helped to shape a common outlook on the limitations of political warfare among its habitual practitioners. Balfour was preaching a doctrine of peace when he said that 'our whole political organisation is arranged in order that we may quarrel'.[5] Cairns, a Conservative Lord Chancellor, wrote, during the franchise controversy of 1884 : 'In our temperate and balanced Constitution, a contest resulting in the defeat and humiliation of one of the component parts is a bad thing, and a thing to be avoided if possible.'[6] Twenty-five years later Loreburn, a Liberal Lord Chancellor, said of the House of Lords' determination to reject the budget :

---

[4] J. J. Park, *Dogmas of the Constitution* (1832), pp. 60–1.
[5] Speech at Fulham, 19 July 1902.
[6] Quoted in C. C. Weston, 'The Royal mediation in 1884', 82 *EHR* (1967), p. 300.

The power in this country is divided between King, Lords and Commons. To the Crown belongs the supreme authority over all, checked by the doctrine of ministerial responsibility, and by the power of the House of Commons to refuse Supplies. To the House of Commons belongs the control over the purse and therefore the control over Ministers of the Crown, checked by the Royal prerogative of dissolution residing in the Crown. To the Lords belongs the supreme jurisdiction in the administration of justice . . . together with a full share in all legislation except finance. There is no check on this House, except the creation of Peers. Such is the ancient and famous balance of power known to our Constitution, the envy of other nations, which your Lordships are now being invited to overthrow.[7]

The action of the House of Lords in 1909 upset, if not an ancient balance, at least an established convention, and set in motion a reaction that produced a legal definition of the powers of the Lords in the Parliament Act, 1911; it also produced precedents in the relations between the King and his Ministers which tended to define not only what the King might do of his own accord but also what he must do at the demand of the Cabinet. It is these redefinitions of what had been customary relationships that, from the constitutional aspect, characterise the period between 1909 and 1914 as a new era. This process had been completed by 1914, by forces acting in time of peace. From then onwards, 'balance' could be no more than an aspiration or a metaphor : the reality was a cruder preponderance of force, to be expressed in some clumsy phrase such as 'supremacy of the Cabinet within the majority party within the House of Commons'.

It was commonplace, among commentators, to eulogise the English constitution for its antiquity and its continuity; indeed, by comparison with the states of western Europe, it was remarkable how much that was new could be accommodated within old forms. But much of the continuity was formal only : old institutions were worked in new ways, by new men with changing aspirations. (A more rewarding comparison might have been with the United States of America, where new forces were being accommodated within what appeared

[7] H. of L., 22 Nov. 1909, c. 754.

to be a rigid framework. It is among Bagehot's many merits that he was one of the first Englishmen to perceive this, and much of the point of his *English Constitution* is missed by those who do not recognise that it is essentially a comparative work. 'The practical choice of first-rate nations,' he wrote, 'is between the Presidential government and the Parliamentary; no State can be first-rate which has not a government by discussion, and those are the only two existing species of that government.'[8]) There was a period of intense political turmoil between 1827 and 1832, when the repeal of the Test and Corporation Acts, the granting of Catholic Emancipation and the enactment of the Reform Bill seemed to have swept away the settlement of 1688 and with it all the defences of the old order: Wellington, in 1833, thought that there would be 'no blow-up, no bloodshed' but that 'all our ancient institutions will be destroyed by due course of law'.[9] That did not happen; instead, there followed seventy-five years of high constitutional stability. Whereas in the United States political quarrels found their focus and determination in decisions of the Federal Supreme Court (with one cataclysmic exception after the Dred Scott judgment), in Britain the emphasis was upon access to the machinery of government, which could be achieved indirectly by the acquisition of the franchise. Many diverse purposes could be coalesced under the slogan of 'parliamentary reform'.[10] The most radical claims put forward in the nineteenth century were those of the Chartists, made in a form which would enable them to change society from within the parliamentary system—universal male suffrage, abolition of property qualifications, annual elections, equal representation, payment of M.P.s, vote by ballot.

The Chartists might believe (as Thomas Attwood said, when introducing their petition to the House of Commons in 1839) that they were 'endeavouring to recover those ancient privileges which they believed to form the original and constitutional

[8] Walter Bagehot, *The English Constitution*, p. 310. (The edition used is that in Cornell Paperbacks, a republication of that in the Fontana Library, 1963.)

[9] Quoted by Norman Gash, 'From the origins to Sir Robert Peel' in *The Conservatives*, edited by Lord Butler (1977).

[10] Asa Briggs, *The Age of Improvement* (1959), passim.

right of the Commons of England'; there was no chance whatever that Parliament would capitulate to what was seen to be a challenge to the rights of property. Nor would favour have been found with their interpretation of 'Commons', which was in the law and custom of parliament taken to refer to communities rather than 'common people'. By conventional wisdom, the House of Commons represented interests and opinions rather than numbers. There was little support, either, for the claim that 'the only authority on which any body of men can make laws and govern society, is delegation from the people'. The sovereignty of Parliament was regarded as a self-evident truth, but it related to the supremacy of statute law and the axiom that no particular parliament could be bound by decisions of any kind taken by its predecessors. But Parliament was a trinity of King, Lords and Commons; and there was still, in the 1830s, a residue of opinion that the peculiar functions of the House of Commons were to grant supply, after redress of grievances, and thus to control the exercise of power by the Crown. A clear distinction could be drawn between legislation, 'enacted by the King's Most Excellent Majesty, by and with the Advice and Consent of the Lords Spiritual and Temporal, and Commons, in this present Parliament assembled', and governance, which drew the greater part of its authority from the prerogative of the Crown. The strength of the prerogative lay in its indefiniteness; it was known to the common law, but consisted in all powers regarded as necessary and proper for the defence and good ordering of the realm which were not covered by statute. For the most part, the prerogative was exercised in the King's name by his Ministers; the dividing line between what the King could do of his own and what he could do only upon advice was clearer, perhaps, to those who confected the literary theory of the constitution than it was either to King or Ministers. Dicey, in 1885, wrote that 'the conventions of the constitution are (in the main) rules for determining the exercise of the prerogative . . .'[11] The conventions expressed 'the constitutional morality of modern England', and he produced a

[11] A. V. Dicey, *Introduction to the Study of the Law of the Constitution* (1885; 8th edition, 1915), p. 424.

catalogue of maxims by way of example. 'The King must assent to, or (as it is inaccurately expressed) cannot "veto" any bill passed by the two Houses of Parliament.' 'The House of Lords does not originate any money bill.' 'A Ministry which is outvoted in the House of Commons is in many cases bound to retire from office.' 'A Cabinet, when outvoted on any vital question, may appeal once to the country by way of a dissolution.' 'If there is a difference of opinion between the House of Lords and the House of Commons, the House of Lords ought, at some point, not definitely fixed, to give way, and should the Peers not yield, and the House of Commons continue to enjoy the confidence of the country, it becomes the duty of the Crown, or of its responsible advisers, to create or to threaten to create enough new Peers to override the opposition of the House of Lords, and thus restore harmony [*sic*] between the two branches of the legislature.'[12]

The flaw in Dicey's argument was that it was related entirely to the past; his list of maxims (though it did not pretend to be exhaustive) was no more than a codification of previous practices. Many conventions could, indeed, be described as originating in accidents which it had been found convenient to allow to crystallise into precedents; but Dicey did not, then, make sufficient allowance for time and circumstance. He, like Bagehot, came to question some of his own assumptions. Bagehot wrote just before the pattern of politics was altered by Disraeli's 'leap in the dark' of 1867, and Dicey wrote before passions had been aroused by Home Rule for Ireland. In his introduction to the second edition of *The English Constitution*, in 1872, Bagehot warned that the existence of an enlarged electorate might have a pernicious effect upon politicians. 'The leading statesmen in a free country have great momentary power. They settle the conversation of mankind. . . . In plain English, what I fear is that both our political parties will bid for the support of the working man; that both of them will promise to do as he likes if only he will tell them what it is . . .'[13] In 1885, Dicey wrote that 'the underlying principle of all modern constitutionalism' was 'obedience to the will of the

---

[12] Dicey, op. cit., pp. 25, 416–17.
[13] Bagehot, op. cit., pp. 274, 277.

nation as expressed through Parliament . . .'[14] By 1914, Dicey
was less certain that the House of Commons was an accurate
reflector of the national will, since it acted more and more
exclusively under the influence of party interests. He saw
merit in the referendum. 'Its strongest recommendation is that
it may keep in check the inordinate power now bestowed on
the party machine.'[15]

To confine discussion of conventions to maxims or to
customary rules of procedure is to take too narrow a view.
In one sense, conventions are habits of political behaviour,
and it is necessary to ask how those habits were formed, and
what purposes they served. Changes in rules of procedure
might have unexpected consequences. The adoption of the
closure as part of the standing orders of the House of Commons
made it necessary for whips to keep a substantial number of
party members within the House, with a consequential
strengthening of their powers. Political habits are formed in
association, and they may be affected by ideas.

The predominating intellectual influence on English politics
in the eighteenth century was that of John Locke; in 1765,
the Lord Chief Justice could echo Locke's argument from the
bench by stating flatly: 'The great end, for which men
entered into society, was to secure their property.'[16] In the
nineteenth century, Locke was supplanted by Bentham.
Bentham's own writings were essentially destructive of conventional wisdom—'Talk of balance: never will it do: leave
that to Mother Goose and Mother Blackstone.'[17] It was
ironical that his disciples should transform the ideas of this
most resolute of individualists into a justification of the increase
of the power of the state. Dicey pointed out the contradiction.
'The patent opposition between the individualistic liberalism
of 1830 and the democratic socialism of 1905 conceals the
heavy debt owed by English collectivists to the utilitarian

---

[14] Dicey, op. cit., p. 450.
[15] Ibid., p. xcvii.
[16] Lord Camden in *Entick* v. *Carrington*.
[17] Jeremy Bentham, *Plan of Parliamentary Reform in the Form of a
Catechism, with an Introduction showing the Necessity of Radical, and the
Inadequacy of Moderate Reform* (1817); quoted in Alan Bullock and
Maurice Shock, *The Liberal Tradition* (1956), p. 41.

reformers. From Benthamism the socialists of to-day have inherited a legislative dogma, a legislative instrument, and a legislative tendency.'[18] The dogma was the principle of utility, usually coarsened for public consumption into the slogan that the purpose of government was to promote the greatest happiness of the greatest number. The legislative tendency was the constant extension and improvement of the mechanism of government. The legislative instrument was the transformation of parliamentary sovereignty into 'democratic despotism'. Bentham himself had the profoundest contempt for the doctrine of natural rights:

> Right . . . is the child of law : from real laws come real rights; but from imaginary laws, from laws of nature, fancied and invented by poets, rhetoricians, and dealers in moral and intellectual poisons, come imaginary rights, a bastard brood of monsters . . . Natural rights is simple nonsense : natural and imprescriptible rights, rhetorical nonsense—nonsense upon stilts.[19]

But logical exactitude is no necessary ingredient of persuasive rhetoric, and politicians acknowledging the name of Utility found the doctrine compatible with assertions of claims which could be expressed as natural rights. To the dismay of that upright utilitarian John Morley, Joseph Chamberlain was among the heretics: 'Now that we have a Government of the people by the people, we will go on and make it for every man his natural rights—his right to existence and to a fair enjoyment of it.'[20] Morley was at pains to explain that 'claims to right must depend not upon nature but upon the good that the said rights are calculated to bring to the greatest number'. Chamberlain's references to nature, Morley said, 'dismayed me as if I had seen a deinotherium shambling down Parliament Street to a seat in the House of Commons.'[21]

[18] A. V. Dicey, *Lectures on the relation between Law and Public Opinion in England during the Nineteenth Century* (1905; 2nd edition, 1914), p. 303.
[19] Bentham, *Anarchical Fallacies*, Wks. vol. II, pp. 501–2, 523; quoted in S. I. Benn and R. S. Peters, *Social Principles and the Democratic State* (1959), p. 376.
[20] Speech at Warrington, 8 Sep. 1885; quoted in Bullock and Shock, op. cit., p. 207.
[21] John Morley, *Recollections* (1917), vol. I, p. 158.

Benthamism was not, of course, the only doctrine at large; J. S. Mill thought that Coleridge shared with Bentham the distinction of being one of the two great seminal minds of their age: '. . . they have been the teachers of the teachers; there is hardly to be found in England an individual of any importance in the world of mind, who . . . did not first learn to think from one of these two . . .'[22] Bentham had a singular capacity of becoming the avatar of the singleminded; his disciples were to be found strategically placed at many levels of government.

Writing in 1820, Lord John Russell argued that the English public schools were part of the constitution: they produced a 'democracy of the aristocracy' by giving a rough experience to those not accustomed to it, and they produced a common intellectual climate for those who would become public men. 'Upon the whole, there is perhaps no point from which a man can start in any profession or pursuit so advantageous as a complete and thorough knowledge of what is known by other young men. among whom he wishes to excel.'[23] Indeed, the public schools made their own contribution to the complicated web of circumstances that thwarted the fulfilment of the prophecies of Karl Marx: '. . . the great social divide of the 1840s between landlords and businessmen was bridged. The public school, consequently, provided for the gradual fusion of classes and their drawing upon a common store of values.'[24] It was by way of Harrow and Eton, respectively, that Peel and Gladstone took their places, as of right, amid the governing class. The doors of preferment might be hard to open, for new men not endowed with uncommon talents, but they were never locked; they opened into a small and exclusive theatre, where the actors (and actresses) knew intuitively their own roles and those of the other protagonists. In no other country, perhaps, did the dinner party play so significant a part in politics. Constitutional historians have generally overlooked this informal, but essential, part of the political network, though

---

[22] J. S. Mill, *Dissertations and Discussions.*

[23] Lord John Russell, *An Essay on the History of the English Government and Constitution* (1821; 3rd edition, 1873), p. 161.

[24] Asa Briggs, *Victorian People* (1954; Pelican edition, 1965), pp. 152–3.

it was perfectly well understood by contemporaries, and emphasised in the novels of Disraeli and Trollope. Josef Redlich, almost apologetically, drew attention to the importance of Society in 1908 :

> It may perhaps appear to many a teacher of constitutional law inconsistent with the dignity of science, not merely to recognise, but even to enter upon a serious analysis of the effect upon the life of the state produced by this element, with its mixture of all the weaknesses, both great and small, of human nature. But it must be done if we are to grasp the anatomy and physiology of English public life in all its entirety.[25]

Disraeli was speaking only partly in jest when he talked of 'majorities collected God knows how, voting God knows why' and suggested that they were the product of Lady Palmerston's judicious distribution of her invitation cards. Sidney Low, in 1904, emphasised the significance of what he called 'the socio-political connection' in preserving the cohesion of the governing class and in co-opting new members to its ranks (fifty years later, this phenomenon would be christened 'The Establishment'). There was never, in nineteenth century England, that division between the worlds of politics and high society that characterised the Third Republic of France or the United States of America in its Gilded Age.

> The governing cliques can govern because they see one another daily : they are always calling on each other, or lunching, or dining, or attending receptions together; they have been at the same schools and colleges; they have shot together, hunted together, yachted together; they stay at the same country houses, when they leave the dozen or so of streets and squares in London in which they all live; and about half of them are more or less closely connected by the ties of blood or marriage . . .
> Society in England, however, has always exhibited a wide liberality in its recognition of personal ability. The selective

[25] J. Redlich, *The Procedure of the House of Commons* (1908), vol. II, p. 126.

process, by which it winnows out a certain number of capable men, and admits them to the socio-political connection, is really an important, though of course quite unacknowledged, element in our political system . . . Addington was the son of a physician, Canning's father was an obscure barrister and his mother an actress, and the elder Disraeli was a Jewish literary man, of foreign descent, with a name which most Englishmen were unable to pronounce correctly. The successful outsiders had made their way, by luck or their own cleverness, into the select circle. Addington, whose father had been medical attendant to the great Earl of Chatham, was put into Parliament for a close borough when he was six-and-twenty. Canning, after attracting attention to himself in his brilliant career at Eton and Christ Church, was no more than twenty-four when Burke and Pitt introduced him into politics as member for Newport.[26]

Gladstone, one might add, was not quite twenty-three when he was elected to Parliament for Newark, which the Duke of Newcastle regarded as a family borough.

The world of politics, then, remained essentially aristocratic at the top without ever shrinking into a closed circle. England, it might seem, had been markedly skilful, or markedly fortunate, in combining within the body politic the elements of permanence and of progressive improvement.[27] 'Improvement' was a Victorian dogma; furthermore, in innumerable material things, it was a demonstrable fact. Belief in it was a solvent of class bitterness, more important for social peace than the 'deference' postulated by those who regarded the working-classes through rose-coloured spectacles. Bagehot did much to popularise the myth of deference, but he also gave full weight to social improvement when he wrote of the English 'system of *removable inequalities*, where many people are inferior to and worse off than others, but in which each may *in theory* hope to be on a level with the highest below the throne, and in which each may reasonably, and without sanguine impracticability,

[26] Sidney Low, *The Governance of England* (1904; revised ed., 1914), pp. 187–8.

[27] S. T. Coleridge, *On the Constitution of the Church and State according to the Idea of Each* (1830).

hope to gain one step in social elevation, to be at last on a level of those who at first were just above them'.[28]

One reason why political warfare never broadened into class warfare was that the governing class exhibited diversity as well as unity; the great political quarrels—parliamentary reform, free trade, Ireland, the Church of England, the expansion of the Empire and, at the end of the period, tariff protection—cut across social lines. Bernard Cracroft, writing in 1867, described the fragmentation of aristocratic opinion on many issues.

A and B are cousins, landowners, county Members. Both are Etonians, both Guardsmen, both have married daughters of peers. But one is a member of the Carlton, the other of Brooks's. One is a Protectionist, the other a Freetrader. One hugs primogeniture, the other thinks that land should be as saleable as a watch. One is an enthusiastic defender of the Protestant faith in Ireland, the other thinks that the Irish Church would be best swept off the face of the earth. One hates America and all that is American, drawing all his arguments from New York; the other shrugs his shoulders, says the Americans are kindest people in the world, and points with a landowner's pride to the conduct of the Western farmers in the late war.[29]

Common enmities, too, had their part in preventing a polarisation of classes. Mill owners and mill operatives had conflicting economic interests, but they could find points of agreement in hostility to parsons, squires and the Corn Laws which were believed to sustain them. Nonconformity did not make for quietude—indeed, it produced some very angry middle-aged men indeed—but it could bind men together against the Church of England. John Morley described the 'tobacco parliament' which Joseph Chamberlain gathered around himself in Birmingham in the 1870s. 'One of the company was an ardent expounder of Ruskin. Another was a

[28] Bagehot, 'Sterne and Thackeray' (1864), *Collected Works,* vol. ɪɪ (1965), p. 308.

[29] *Essays on Reform*; quoted in W. L. Burn, *The Age of Equipoise* (1864), p. 319.

clear-headed Baptist divine, and a third a broad-minded Unitarian divine . . . The traditional feud between Churchman and Unitarian was still alive and deep in the town that had been the home of Priestley; it went so far as to check even intermarriage and commensality, so the Church of England was unrepresented.'[30]

It was commonly asserted that the English people enjoyed liberty and rejected equality; it was also asserted that lords were dearly loved. Thus Gladstone, with all the qualifications of which he was a supreme master, could write:

> The love of justice, as distinguished from equality, is strong among our countrymen; the love of equality, as distinguished from justice, is very weak . . . The love of freedom itself is hardly stronger in England than the love of aristocracy . . .[31]

This view of the constitution (or of the distribution of power within its framework) was certainly not that of Colonel Rainborough, or Tom Paine, or William Cobbett, or the Anti-Corn-Law League or the Birmingham Caucus, still less that of the Chartists or the Syndicalists. It was essentially a Whiggish view; and the Whigs took their politics from John Locke and their economics from Adam Smith. In consequence, government was regarded as a limited function, from which economic and social matters could be excluded on theoretical grounds, or included on grounds of national interest, as might be found convenient. *Laissez faire* was a general guide, not a defining principle. The smallness of the governing class meant that it was relatively easy to agree, in outline at least, upon a national interest; hence the exercise of power was seldom permitted to degenerate merely into the distribution of advantages—' Who gets what, when, how.' Patronage was very important, both as a motive for entering politics and as a necessary condition of its practice; but it was kept in place as a means to an end. Economy was important, too. One of Locke's maxims (echoed by Burke) was that government was a trust; thus Lord John Russell could reconcile the concepts

---

[30] Morley, op. cit., p. 149.
[31] 'The county franchise and Mr Lowe thereon'; 2 *Nineteenth Century* (1877), p. 547.

of trusteeship and inequality in the claim that the welfare of
the people, but not its will, was the supreme law.[32] In the
same vein and direction, Nassau Senior could advance from
Adam Smith in extending the functions of government. He
did not agree with those who would confine them to protecting
the subject against internal or external violence and fraud.
' The only rational foundation of government . . . is expediency
—the general benefit of a community. It is the duty of a
government to do whatever is conducive to the welfare of the
governed.'[33] It was no great step from this to the contention
that the object of government was to promote the greatest
happiness of the greatest number (though, as G. M. Young
pointed out, 'the greatest number' was still unborn), and from
that to the assertion that the will of the majority should prevail. Classical economics was no more static than classical
politics. The arguments of Nassau Senior are reconcilable with
those of Russell, but there is a subtle difference of language
and tone in their expression: that is some measure of the
extent of the invasion of the kingdom of Locke by the epigoni
of Bentham. It was a cautious invasion, but it led in the end
to a permanent occupation. It is a remarkable example of what
might be accomplished by a small but intense minority, conscious of its purpose and armoured in certainty. It succeeded
by employing techniques which Professor Finer (using language
of which Bentham himself might well have approved)
christened Irradiation, Esuscitation and Permeation.

> *Irradiation* was the process by which small knots of
> Benthamites attracted into their salons, their committees and
> their associations a much wider circle of men whom they
> infected with some at least of their enthusiasms and thereby
> turned into what I might call Second-Degree Benthamites.
>   *Esuscitation* needs a little more explanation. I had originally
> chosen the word *Publicisation*; but on consulting the Oxford
> Dictionary, I found that such a word as *Esuscitation* did exist.
> It exactly conveys what I mean: 'To stir up; to excite [a
> rebellion, a feeling etc.]; to raise out of inactivity; to quicken,

---

32 Russell, op. cit., p. 244.
33 Quoted in M. Bowley, *Nassau Senior and Classical Economics* (1937),
p. 265.

vivify, animate.' *Esuscitation* was the process of arranging public inquiries or the press or both together in such a way as to create a favourable public opinion, of a temporary kind, amid influential groups in the country.

Permeation was the process of securing official employment of oneself and thereafter using this position for further *irradiation*—on one's supporters and subordinates; and for further *esuscitation* also.

Irradiation made friends and influenced people. Through them, *esuscitation* proved possible. Esuscitation led to official appointment and hence *permeation*. And permeation led to further irradiation and esuscitation; and so on, *da capo*.[34]

Thus, below the 'socio-political edifice' of politicians there existed a sub-edifice of intellectual administrators, 'statesmen in disguise'[35] exercising power but concealed from public scrutiny by the convention of exclusive Ministerial responsibility to Parliament. It was they who welded Utility to Whiggism.

Two premises were assumed in the Whig interpretation of the constitution : that the economic system was largely self-regulating, and that equality was proportional and not numerical. From these it could be inferred that the business of government was to protect special rather than general rights. The 'empirical tradition', when translated into action, meant that the individual would be regarded in his capacity as property-holder, or rate-payer, or lodger or office-holder. Rights were dependent on antecedent rules; they entailed corresponding duties, and they were neither general nor indefeasible. In the cant of the times, one talked of the rights or liberties of Englishmen, not of the Englishman; and rights and liberties, as they had been over the centuries, were sometimes interchangeable terms.

[34] S. E. Finer, 'The dissemination of Benthamite ideas, 1820–50' in Gillian Sutherland (ed.), *Studies in the Growth of Nineteenth-century Government* (1972), p. 13. I am grateful to Professor Finer for permission to quote this passage. Since it was first published, he has amended 'Suscitation' to 'Esuscitation'.

[35] The phrase was coined by Sir James Stephen, who was arguing against competitive examination because it would produce candidates with qualities not needed by a civil servant. 'You stand in need not of statesmen in disguise, but of intelligent, steady, methodical men of business.' *Parliamentary Papers* (1854–5), xx, pp. 71–80.

Whig doctrines died hard, but they died none the less. But, since they formed a cluster rather than a single concept, they did not die as a whole; here and there, one of them displayed a capacity for survival, and sometimes an idea that had seemed to be moribund was suddenly repossessed of vigour. In classical orthodoxy, the business of Parliament, and especially of the House of Commons, was not to govern but to control the Crown. After 1832, even the most devoted Whig could hardly regard the royal power as a source of oppression. A shrewd French observer could remark that 'England is in reality a republic wearing the semblance and invested with the forms of a monarchy'.[36] Once it was generally recognised that Ministers held office at the pleasure of Parliament, and had in their hands the substance of the prerogative, an attitude of perpetual wariness towards the Crown became an anachronism. Sir Robert Peel, in the Bedchamber crisis of 1839, was the last prime minister to demand an overt sign of confidence from the monarch as a condition precedent to taking office. Those who did not have directly to deal with her tended unduly to minimise the extent to which Queen Victoria attempted to influence politics. Sir George Cornewall Lewis, in 1863, put into the mouth of one of his disputants in *A Dialogue on the Best Form of Government* the judgment that: 'Still life, as a term in painting, is analogous to limited monarchy, since it originally denoted dead animals; that is, animals which were alive, but are so no longer.'[37]

Changes in attitude to the Crown as a reservoir of powers may be seen in the evidence given to the select committees on the procedure of the House of Commons, which met once every decade or so after 1832. The idea became firmer that, since the government of the day was by definition representative of the House of Commons, therefore no conflict of interest between them was possible; later, the majority could be substituted for the House as a whole. This presumed identity of interest could be used as an argument for simplifying pro-

---

[36] Emile Boutmy, *The English People: A Study of their Political Psychology* (English translation, 1904), p. 180.
[37] George Cornewall Lewis, *A Dialogue on the Best Form of Government* (1863), p. 18.

cedure, on grounds of utility. Speaker Denison, in evidence before Robert Lowe's committee in 1871, wanted financial procedure to be streamlined: he thought that the old safeguard, that the redress of grievance should precede the granting of supply, was no longer needed, since the Government had become the servant of the House. (Denison argued in vain; the formal distinction between the Committees of Supply and of Ways and Means was not obliterated until nearly a century later.) At the same time, there was current the older idea that the principal business of the House of Commons was to control the executive, especially at the price of inefficiency. The two ideas can be seen in conflict in an exchange between Campbell-Bannerman and Joseph Chamberlain in 1902, during a debate on Balfour's proposals for radical changes in procedure. To Campbell-Bannerman (then in Opposition), the House of Commons was pre-eminently the 'grand inquest of the nation', the forum in which Ministers were called to account.

> This is not a mere factory of statutes; not a mere counting-house in which demands on the public purse are being checked, approved and provided for; it is something much more . . . Efficiency in the conduct of business is merely secondary . . . Facilitate the progress of business as much as you like; make it as reasonable as you like; but do not do anything which will have the effect of placing the House of Commons more and more at the mercy of the Government of the day.

This was not Chamberlain's conception of the House of Commons; to regard it as a censor of government was to deny the right of the majority to rule.

> I often hear some . . . on both sides of the House endeavour to distinguish between the Government and the House . . . After all, the Government are the servants of the House. They are chosen practically with the approval of the House. Of course, when we speak of the House, we always mean . . . the majority for the time being . . . Therefore, when you talk about curtailing the powers of the Government, what you mean . . . is curtailing the powers of the majority . . . I believe that the people who elect the majority of the House have a right to see that that majority has power to carry out

what is *ex hypothesi* the will of the majority of the nation; and our elections and our representative system are a perfect and absolute farce if with one hand you pretend that the majority elects a Government, and then with the other hand prevent that Government from doing its proper work.'[38]

This was good Birmingham radicalism, but it was encased within a fiction. There was a gap between the Treasury bench and the Opposition, and another gap between Ministers and their own supporters. Once invested with the powers of the Crown, Ministers were as concerned to preserve them intact as any Sovereign had been. What the Ministry came increasingly to demand from the House of Commons was a general confidence, unaccompanied by any special surveillance. It was not preposterous for Bagehot to describe the Cabinet as a committee of the House of Commons, considering the contemporary rhetoric that was intended to convey precisely that fallacious impression. The Duke of Devonshire could follow Bagehot in interpreting parliamentary supremacy as meaning 'the direct government of these Islands by Parliament through a Committee'.[39] Sidney Low was nearer to reality: 'The English Cabinet is a Party Committee; and it is a Secret Committee.'[40]

There was one attitude shared by all those who had come to maturity in politics before mid-century—fear of the mob. No one who was conscious of events between the end of the Napoleonic Wars and the failure of the Chartist demonstration of 1848 could forget that England might be a dangerous place. Tennyson, who was a remarkably accurate reflector of 'respectable' opinion, wrote in *Locksley Hall*:

Slowly comes a hungry people, as a lion creeping nigher
Glares at one that nods and winks behind a slowly-dying fire.

There were many reasons why England achieved the transition from aristocracy to democracy without violent upheaval; one of them was the conscious prudence of the governing class.

[38] H. of C., 6 Feb. 1902, 550–2, 568.
[39] H. of L., 5 Sep. 1893, 34.
[40] Low, op. cit., p. 34.

One day, in my hearing, a noble lord of the Whig party compared Parliament to a traveller in a sledge, pursued by a band of famished wolves. From time to time he throws them quarters of venison to distract their attention and keep them back, so that, half-satisfied, they may be less ferocious when they gain the horse's head. Of course, it is necessary to husband the venison, and make it last as long as possible by cutting it up into little pieces. Part of our nobility, he said, meritoriously devote themselves to this ungrateful task.[41]

In the same mood *The Times*, in one of its spasms of self-congratulation, complimented England on being able to enjoy a wise conservatism because it had displayed a timely liberality. Lord Palmerston, defending himself in the House of Commons in the Don Pacifico debate in 1850, talked about unconscious revolutionaries, 'blind-minded men who dam up the current of human improvement'. There were plenty of blind-minded men in England, but they were seldom the men who mattered in politics. Gladstone, writing in 1865 to a peer who had criticised him as a fomenter of change, said :

> Please to recollect that we have got to govern millions of hard hands; that it must be done by force, fraud or good will; that the latter has been tried and is answering; that none have profited more by this change of system since the Corn Law and the Six Acts, than those who complain of it.[42]

This attitude may be seen in the work of those who framed the Great Reform Bill of 1832, in the restraint which Wellington preached to the House of Lords, in Peel's timely retreats over Catholic Emancipation and the Corn Laws, and in Gladstone's finance (a coherent theory of social peace may be extracted from his great budget speech of 1853).

One corollary of the idea of the balanced constitution was that of limited government, with each of the co-ordinate branches having the capacity to confine the others to moderation. At the same time, in de Lolme's phrase, it was assumed that Parliament could do anything except change a man into

41 Boutmy, op. cit., p. 146.
42 Morley, *Life of Gladstone*, vol. II, p. 133.

a woman. The inconsistency was resolved by a prudent auto-limitation of sovereignty. This in turn depended upon the assumption that there were many aspects of daily life that were not regarded as within the political arena. When Samuel Wilberforce became Bishop of Oxford in 1845, Prince Albert sent him a letter of advice on how he should conduct himself in the House of Lords.

> He started with the obvious point that a Bishop should abstain completely from politics but that he should speak 'boldly and manfully' on the interests of Humanity. These he specified as Negro emancipation, improvement of the health of towns, measures for the recreation of the poor, against cruelty to animals, for regulating factory labour. This shows the extent to which, in the 1840s, 'the condition of the people question' was regarded as being outside politics . . . A Bishop ought likewise to be ready to admonish the public, and the Prince instanced the duty of Bishops to reprove the wickedness of railway speculators.[43]

It became increasingly difficult to keep 'the condition of the people question' outside politics once a substantial minority of the people had acquired the vote.

The conventions of the constitution, then, have meaning only when they are looked at against a background of continuous political change. It is very difficult to say with certainty what they were at any particular moment. Above all, they cannot be understood 'with the politics left out'.

[43] Roger Fulford, *The Prince Consort* (1949), p. 186.

2

The Inheritance of Queen Victoria

No compact or agreement, it is evident, was expressly formed
for general submission; an idea far beyond the comprehension
of savages; each exertion of authority in the chieftain must
have been particular, and called forth by the present
exigencies of the case : the sensible utility, resulting from his
interposition, made these exertions become daily more frequent; and their frequency gradually produced an habitual,
and, if you please to call it so, a voluntary and, therefore,
precarious acquiescence in the people.

David Hume, *On the Original Contract*

It was argued in the previous chapter that there was general
agreement, at least in the governing class, that the constitutional machinery of England was appropriate to its purpose.
But agreement on the merits of a piece of machinery does not
obviate quarrels about how it should be operated, and by
whom. The authority of the Crown might be seldom
questioned, but there was uncertainty about which decisions
taken in the name of the Crown entailed acts of volition by
its wearer. One might ask to what extent the King was regarded
as bound to agree with his principal Minister, and what would
happen if disagreements arose that could not be reconciled.

The authority of the Crown, at the beginning of Queen
Victoria's reign, was going the way of other high offices of
state in the past : it was being placed in commission. The
functions of the Lord High Admiral and the Lord High
Treasurer had been absorbed by the Boards of Admiralty and
of the Treasury; there was now a tendency to diminish the
role of the King and exalt that of the King-in-Council. The
King, as a corporation sole, should be dissolved in his Ministry.

By the second quarter of the century, a great deal of prerogative power had moved from the Court to Whitehall; it will
be convenient to refer to this as the prerogative of the Crown,
as distinct from the prerogative of the Sovereign. Ministers
had already concentrated in their own hands, either singly or
collectively, the making of appointments under the Crown to
all but the highest offices of state; they had acquired the
initiative in raising the public revenue and enjoyed a wide
discretion in the spending of it; it was under the authority
of the Crown and not of the King that dependencies were
governed and corporations created. However, prudence, if not
the law, required that Parliament should be consulted, or at
least kept informed; a declaration of war was a prerogative
act, but wars could not be waged without money raised by
Act of Parliament. But, although the general direction of the
movement was evident, it could seldom be asserted with
definitive clarity at any particular moment just where the
prerogative of the King ended and that of the Crown began.
The process and the quarrels that accompanied the transfer
of functions from one category to the other were spasmodic.
The movement could, perhaps, never be completed; as
Boanerges reminded Pliny, in Bernard Shaw's *The Applecart*,
a living person is not a rubber stamp.

During the period covered by this book, Ministers almost
invariably had the last word in conflicts with the Court, but
that did not mean that victory could be taken for granted
in any particular engagement. At no time was the monarch
willing, without argument, to concede to Ministers exclusive
control over the army, or the conduct of foreign affairs, or the
appointment of bishops, or access to the fountain of honour,
or the timing of a dissolution of Parliament. Lord Beaconsfield
was certainly describing an unbroken practice when he told
the Queen in 1881, when he was out of office and close to
death, that she had 'a right, which it would be wise always to
exercise, to express your Majesty's opinion on every point of
the policy of your Ministers, and to require and receive
explanations';[1] he was providing her with reassurance rather

---

[1] 2 LQV III, p. 181.

than with reminder. Queen Victoria did not need to be incited to claim what she regarded as her rights. If she did not like a Minister, she ignored him; if she loathed a Minister, as she came to loathe Gladstone, she did her best to harass him into retirement. She was a continuing point of friction even when Ministers of whom she approved were in office. It was understandable enough that Gladstone should once cry out: 'The Queen is enough to kill a man'; Lord Salisbury, who stood very high indeed in royal favour, complained that he had four ministries where one would have been enough—the premiership, the Foreign Office, Lord Randolph Churchill and the Queen.

In his Romanes Lecture for 1952, the late Sir Lewis Namier pronounced *ex cathedra* a definition of constitutional monarchy; the essential elements were:

> A Sovereign placed above parties and policies; a Prime Minister and Government taking rise from Parliament and received rather than designated by the Sovereign, yet as 'H.M. confidential servants' deriving from the Royal Prerogative that essential executive character which an elected legislature could not impart to them . . .[2]

Namier's conclusion was that the Prime Minister replaced the King as head of government when the element of discretion had been removed from the King's choice of Prime Minister: this happened after the appearance of political parties sufficiently popular with the electorate to form a majority of the House of Commons, and sufficiently united to be able to agree to follow a leader of their own choice and no other. The King rose above politics only when the parties pushed him there. It follows from the logic of this argument that Namier's constitutional monarch was constrained by the necessity of events to be neutral towards measures as well as men. Cautiously, Namier did not say when precisely all this was supposed to have happened: it was 'a process that can be logically defined, but eludes precise dating'. The process was

[2] L. B. Namier, 'Monarchy and the party system'; *Crossroads of Power* (1960), p. 213.

certainly not completed before 1914; no theorist of the time, and certainly no practitioner of government, asserted anything of the kind. The Prince Albert came nearest to Namier's viewpoint, when he said in 1850: 'The circumstances which led to a change of Ministry almost always pointed out also the men to succeed.'[3] But the Prince tried to couple partisanship towards measures with neutrality towards men: he thought that the Sovereign had 'an immense moral responsibility upon his shoulders with regard to his government and the duty to watch and control it'.

If the Prince had written his memorandum a few years later, he might well have modified his opinion that Ministers were automatically designated by events. An era of stable ministries was about to give way to nearly a decade of positively Gallic fluidity, between 1851, when Russell resigned and then had to resume office because no alternative government could be formed, and 1859, when the *prominenti* among the Peelites finally threw in their lot with Palmerston. The eye of hindsight may see some comparison with the Third and Fourth Republics; indeed, the activities of the Queen and the Prince often resembled those of a conscientious French President assisting at a cabinet reshuffle. From time to time, the Queen allowed a weary note to sound in her journal, as she set out once more to ensure that her government should be carried on. Her correspondence shows how closely involved she was, almost to the day of her death, in the day-to-day stuff of politics. In these middle years of her reign, she can be seen discouraging Lord Derby from yet another *nolo episcopari*, soothing Lord John Russell, reassuring Lord Aberdeen, and trying unavailingly to avoid Lord Palmerston. There were others, besides Russell and Derby, who were disposed to hand back the poisoned chalice of office: Lord Hartington declined three times to attempt to form a government—in 1880, in July 1886, after the defeat of the first Home Rule Bill, and in December 1886, after the resignation of Lord Randolph Churchill as Chancellor of the Exchequer. The Queen used her own discretion when she chose Lord Rosebery rather than

[3] F. Eyck, *The Prince Consort* (1959), p. 138.

Sir William Harcourt in 1894, just as George V used his when he chose Stanley Baldwin rather than Lord Curzon in 1923.

Once in office, it was the recognised duty of a prime minister to offer advice, but it was by no means settled that the sovereign was bound to accept it in all circumstances. Two generalisations may be ventured. First, when there was a disagreement with Ministers, the Court usually thought not in terms of doctrines or even of precedents but of the likely consequences that particular actions would have upon its own prestige. Secondly, where precedents were sought and cited, the primary purpose was to provide a justification that could protect the Court from a public accusation of partisanship. Queen Victoria could be reckless, and there were several occasions when her Ministers seemed more concerned than she herself to preserve such reputation for impartiality as she possessed in the 'Westminster community'.

An example of this essentially pragmatic approach to political problems may be seen in Lord Liverpool's handling of the question whether King George IV had a right to exclude a particular person from a Ministry. On 27 June 1821, Liverpool wrote to Bathurst :

> Upon the abstract question . . . it is very difficult to give any general opinion . . . the effect of it will generally be to exalt the individual and to lower the King . . .
> It is not Mr Canning out of office, but Mr Canning out of office by the personal exclusion of the King, agreed to by his Government, which is the question. Can anyone doubt that he would become an object of compassion in the first instance, and afterwards of popularity?[4]

The royal power to exclude men from office, which entailed the power to dismiss them once they were there, was regarded, then, from the standpoint of expediency and not of disputed right. No one seriously questioned the proposition that George III was well within his constitutional rights when, in 1807, he rid himself of the Ministry of All the Talents because he objected to their pressing upon him a measure of Catholic

[4] H. J. Hanham, *The Nineteenth Century Constitution* (1969), p. 42.

relief which went further than he had agreed to go.[5] The Whigs, when out of office, raised the matter in the House of Commons, but concentrated upon the point that the King, by requiring a pledge that Ministers would not bring forward the Catholic question again, was demanding something which conflicted with a privy counsellor's oath and was thus denying the responsibility of Ministers. Mr Brand, moving the resolution, said that the King had the right to select his Ministers but not to restrict the range of their advice or the free exercise of their judgment.[6] Sir Samuel Romilly argued that the demanding of pledges was a dangerous principle, subversive of the maxim that the King could do no wrong: royal immunity depended upon ministerial responsibility, but Ministers could not be called to account for advice that they had not given, and they could not give advice where they stood pledged to withhold it. Mr Wharton came down solidly on the side of the prerogative. The House, he said, should not discuss abstract propositions, which might be considered as incontrovertible until they were applied to new cases; 'and surely no case could be more new, than that an administration should lend its weight in parliament to measures which had not only not received the concurrence of the King, but to which his majesty had expressed an absolute repugnance.' Spencer Perceval, the new Chancellor of the Exchequer, assumed a hesitant responsibility:

> He said that his majesty was not censurable, but his advisers. Now, it was contrary to the fact, that his majesty acted in this case, in consequence of any advice; he denied that any advice was given to him on this point . . . But he [sc. Perceval] approved of what had been done, and was ready to be responsible for it; though he was obliged to state the fact exactly as it was.

Perceval's action was a precedent for Peel's more robust assumption of responsibility, after the event, for William IV's dismissal of Melbourne in 1834, which occurred while Peel

---

[5] Michael Roberts, *The Whig Party, 1807–1812.*
[6] H. of C., 9 April 1807, cc. 285 sqq.

was in Italy. Clearly, however, opinions differed according to whether men regarded themselves as the victims or the beneficiaries of the King's decision. Bathurst thought that there was at least one exception to the doctrine that there was no act of the Crown for which Ministers were not responsible, and that was when the King had dismissed his Ministers: 'unless the exception to responsibility be allowed in that case, the King's prerogative of choosing his own ministers must be nugatory.' Canning was more jauntily sceptical of the extreme Whig doctrine, when he referred to himself as 'in a state of retrospective responsibility for counsels which he could not be acquainted with, and for that dismissal which was the consequence of his own suicidal act'. Whitbread found the big battalions against him when he tried to formulate a doctrine which would bring the Crown constantly under the surveillance of the House of Commons by asserting that 'there was not a moment of the King's life, from his accession to his demise, that there was not a person constitutionally responsible for his actions'.

In March 1810, Whitbread returned to the theme of responsibility, this time by arguing that Lord Chatham, by secretly handing to the King a narrative of the naval and military operations at the Scheldt, had violated the constitution. This was a confused accusation, in part that Chatham had dissociated himself from other Ministers, and in part that he had made accusations in private against officers of the Royal Navy. Brand talked about secret influence, and Brougham found a flaw in the doctrine of ministerial responsibility when Ministers were not collectively aware of what one of their number was doing. W. Adam, in a long speech filled with citations of authorities, contrasted ministerial responsibility with the evils of secret councils and 'double government'; in the maxim that the King could do no wrong he discerned the efficient secret of 'this mixed and limited monarchy':

I assert, that the grand and fundamental principles on which we have combined . . . civil and political freedom on the one hand, and a powerful executive government on the other, rest mainly and principally upon the maxim that the King can do no wrong—out of which the responsibility of the King's advisers—the necessity of public documents—the absence of all secret advice and secret councils—the obligation of all executive officers to make their communications to avowed ministers—and the great superintending inquisitorial authority of this House, necessarily and unquestionably arise.[7]

Ministers, with a solid majority at their backs, could comfortably afford to reject these assertions.

It was a landmark in the development of ministerial authority when, in March 1829, King George IV accepted what amounted to an ultimatum from his Prime Minister, the Duke of Wellington, and allowed the Cabinet to take up the matter of Catholic Emancipation. Before then, attempts to bring Catholics within 'the pale of the constitution' had been blocked by royal opposition. In 1801, George III had taken refuge behind his coronation oath, and had told Pitt that 'I shall regard any man my enemy who shall propose any such measure'.[8] Pitt felt that he was so deeply committed that he preferred retirement to acquiescence, but the Tory coalition remained intact and Pitt could be replaced by Addington without a party convulsion. In 1829, Wellington acted as if he were indispensable, although he expected the matter to be put to the proof : he was ready to resign, but he expected to resume office on his own terms once the King had discovered that no alternative set of Ministers could get his business done in the House of Commons. As it was, the King capitulated after a few anguished hours, during which he suffered pressure, within his intimate circle, from Lord and Lady Conyngham and Sir William Knighton; 'God knows what pain it costs me to write these words', he added to his message of consent.[9]

However, Wellington's victory precipitated the profound modification—if 'break-up' is thought to be too strong a phrase —of the Revolution Settlement; it was the beginning of the end of Protestant exclusiveness, toleration for Catholics unaccompanied by political rights, limited representation in the

[7] H. of C., 2 and 5 March 1810, cc. 7* sqq.
[8] J. Steven Watson, *The Reign of George III* (1960), p. 401.
[9] N. Gash, *Mr. Secretary Peel* (1961), p. 569.

House of Commons. Parliamentary reform was never part of Wellington's programme, but he hastened its coming because Catholic Emancipation dissolved his own party. The Government felt at once the chill winds of disapproval blowing from its back benches. It was beaten on Bills to remove Jewish disabilities and to amend the law on forgery, and it withdrew other Bills before they could be killed or mutilated. There was, as was customary, no great turnover of seats at the general election of 1830 (required, by statute, after the death of the King); but parliamentary reform had become an urgent issue which the House of Commons could no longer evade. Ministers were beaten on the civil list, and chose to resign, as a matter of tactics, on that issue rather than to risk defeat on the direct question of reform.

This was one of those rare occasions when a Ministry which retained the confidence of the King was driven to resign by a hostile House of Commons; the nearest precedent was in 1804, and before that in 1782, with the fall of Lord North. It cannot be said that the electorate pronounced against the Tories in 1830; the contests in the constituencies were, as usual, partial and confused. The Crown's servants never lost a general election to the unreformed House of Commons. Wellington fell from power because the coalition created by the younger Pitt and reassembled by Lord Liverpool had been corroded from within, above all by the Catholic issue. William IV might, reasonably enough, feel that the earth was rocking under his feet before the crown had been placed on his head. In previous times of popular disturbance, the grievances had been plain, the enemy identifiable and in sight. But now the demand was for an abstraction, and although it could be shown that 'reform' meant different, and often very definite, things in different places—corn laws in Manchester, currency in Birmingham, factories in Leeds—behind it all there was a menacing note of millennial enthusiasm. In the meantime, there were riots in cities, mob rule in Bristol and Nottingham, Captain Swing was at large in the southern counties, and the King was obliged, for his own safety, to cancel a visit to the Mansion House: this was the way in which worlds ended in Paris. Diagnosis was the same, by both Government and

Opposition: this was a very dangerous situation. The prognoses took the form of polar opposites: unless we give way, there will be revolution; if we give way, there will be revolution.

After Wellington's resignation, the King had no effective choice other than Lord Grey, and Grey accepted office on the understanding that the King would support him on reform. The King kept his word, in the long run. In his 'Memorandum of Events, 1830–1835', the King made little of Grey's request for a dissolution in 1831 (unusual though it was), merely remarking that, if he had not granted it, he would have compromised his own character 'as a Sovereign and a gentleman'.[10] However, his reaction explains why dissolutions were regarded as necessary evils, to be committed as near as was prudent to the end of the seven-year period specified in the Act of 1716. The country would, the King wrote,

> be thrown into convulsion from the Land's End to John O'Groat's house: miners, manufacturers, colliers, labourers, all who have recently formed unions for the furtherance of illegal purposes, would assemble at every point in support of a *popular* question, with the declared object of carrying the measure by intimidation.

In fact, the King was much less complaisant than his own account suggested; it required a formal Cabinet minute before he gave way. This was the first of several occasions on which he discovered that unsuccessful resistance to a Minister usually incurred a penalty. It was with a sound appreciation of the realities of political warfare that Lord Rosebery, before the result of the general election of 1892 was known, advised Queen Victoria to send for Gladstone at once, should the Liberals win. She would, as the experience of 1880 had shown, have to come to him in the end, since no Liberal could form a government without him and he would serve under no one else: the sooner, then, the better. If the Queen had to call on him as a last resort,

[10] RA 50498 sqq.

it would do harm to the prestige of the Sovereign, as it would elevate Mr Gladstone into a species of dictator whom the Queen was forced to accept. If, however, he was sent for at first he would no doubt accept office as Premier, but the Queen would no doubt be able to make some conditions with him.[11]

King William had an unfortunate propensity to fall into that form of error. In 1832, he placed himself in the very position which his brother had avoided in 1829: he preferred to accept his Ministers' resignations rather than create peers enough to give them a majority in the House of Lords, and found himself without a government as a result. The King sent for Wellington, who found the task of forming a Ministry to be impossible. Once Wellington had thrown up his commission, Grey's position was unassailable: he was the indispensable man. He used his victory with tact and moderation; he could afford to. On 18 May 1832, the restored Cabinet sent a formal minute to the King, advising the creation of 41 peers. Two days later, Sir Henry Taylor, the King's secretary, told Grey that he had spread the word among the Tories that the King's consent had been given; 'and I added that they, therefore, had before them the alternative of the Reform Bill with an addition to the Peerage, or a Reform Bill without it'.[12]

We are still a long way from Namier's sovereign (even if we will ever arrive there), merely receiving a designated Minister. Most wars are in defence of the past, real or imagined; the past is valuable partly because it is safe. Kitson Clark was not alone in pointing out 'how near to the political morals and methods of the eighteenth century was much that went on in the middle of the nineteenth'.[13] When Lord Grey retired in 1834, the King's immediate reaction was to try to put together a broad-bottomed administration, on the principles of Bolingbroke's *Patriot King*. He sent for Lord Melbourne, not as a prospective Prime Minister but as a Secretary of State, and required him to urge Wellington, Stanley and Peel to lay

[11] 3 LQV II, pp. 121–2.

[12] *Correspondence of Lord Grey with William IV*, p. 444.

[13] G. S. R. Kitson Clark, 'The electorate and the repeal of the Corn Laws', *TRHS* (1951), p. 111.

aside party feeling and to combine with members of the existing administration for the common good, so that the King's
government might be carried on 'without the embarrassment
constantly arising out of the collision of parties'. Events, the
King went on,

> have led him to feel very solicitous that means could be found
> to reconcile the jarring feelings and opinions of the most
> respectable, able and influential members of political parties
> in both Houses of Parliament, and in the Country, and to
> unite them in the support of the State, of the Constitution,
> and of the established institutions of the country, against
> those who seek, by innovation and agitation, to destroy all that
> exists, to disturb the peace of these Realms, to bring the
> various classes of society into fearful collision, and to produce
> a state of anarchy and confusion which shall render life and
> property alike insecure, and would be productive of advantage
> to those only who had been the instigators and abettors of
> such a state of things.[14]

Nor was he satisfied with perfunctory refusals; he wanted
answers in writing. Melbourne warned him that, however
desirable a union of parties might be, there was an insur-
mountable difference of principle between them, especially
over the Irish Church. However, he wrote as he had been
commanded to do, and received the refusals that he had
expected. Stanley sent a long reply, citing the decision to set
up a commission of inquiry into the Irish Church, and the
remission of tithes, as barriers of principle. Wellington and
Peel at first sent bare acknowledgments; when their reasoned
arguments were extracted, they were found to be essentially
similar to Stanley's; the convention of collective responsibility
was spreading to the Opposition. Without much enthusiasm,
the King turned at last to Melbourne. Four months later,
Melbourne was dismissed.

This remains a puzzling episode. The Ministry was divided
and quarrelsome, and some of them at least were not averse
to giving up office. The King would hardly have acted as he

[14] R. A. Melbourne Papers; the King to Melbourne, 9 July 1844.

did if he had not been conscious of the irresolution of his Prime Minister. One cannot, however, agree with the flat statement that 'the "dismissal" of Melbourne at his own suggestion was already an anachronism in constitutional practice'.[15] It is not clear why the final episode in a series should be regarded as chronologically out of place; there is no exponential jump between refusing to accept a Prime Minister's advice, knowing that his resignation must follow, and requiring a resignation *proprio motu*. Queen Victoria never abandoned the claim that she could dismiss individual Ministers, and she would probably have asked for Palmerston's resignation in 1851 if the Prime Minister had not done so first. In 1880, Gladstone regarded it as a serious possibility that the Queen might dismiss the entire Ministry, fresh from a general election though it was, if it persisted in reversing the policy of its predecessor over Kandahar; he was reminded, he said, of the pledge which George III had demanded from the Whigs not to stir the Roman Catholic question. When George V hinted to Asquith, in 1914, that he might dismiss the Ministry, Asquith did not question the King's right, but merely asked that, if it were to be done, it should be done quickly, in the interests of public business.

The occasion of the crisis was the death of the second Earl Spencer and the consequent elevation to the House of Lords of his heir, Lord Althorp, then leader of the House of Commons. Althorp was one of those men—Hartington was another—whose political indispensability depended neither upon oratory nor cleverness, but on the confidence of their fellows, given for their social position, their integrity and their capacity for seeing and saying the obvious. Writing of Althorp, Macaulay doubted 'whether any person has ever lived in England who, with no eloquence, no brilliant talents, no profound information, with nothing in short but plain good sense and an excellent heart, possessed so much influence in and out of Parliament'.[16] Littleton's diary gives a description of Althorp in action at a party meeting in 1832,

---

15 E. L. Woodward, *The Age of Reform* (2nd ed.), p. 101.
16 G. O. Trevelyan, *Life and Letters of Lord Macaulay* (1889 ed.), p. 175.

with his stout, honest face, and farmer-like figure, habited in ill-made black clothes, his trousers rucked up in a heap round his legs, one coat flap turned round and exposing his posterior, and the pocket of the other crammed full of papers, his hat held awkwardly in one hand and his large snuff box in the other, with which he kept playing the Devil's tattoo on his thigh—while he briefly and bluntly told his plain unsophisticated tale with his usual correct feeling and sound sense, and was warmly responded to by the whole party.[17]

The King chose to regard Althorp's departure from the House of Commons as a sufficient reason for withdrawing his confidence in the Ministry; he stood his ground on the contention that Althorp was indispensable because he could not be replaced to the King's satisfaction. His dialogue with Melbourne was concerned mostly with men, but below the surface there was profound disagreement on measures. In particular, the King disliked what he regarded as the hostility of the Ministry to the temporalities of the Irish Church, and he suspected that the commission of inquiry was a prelude to disendowment. Melbourne conceded the point that, as the King had not pledged himself with regard to the commission, he was therefore fully at liberty to refuse his assent to any measure based upon its report which might be presented to him in the future.

The King's own narrative of events states that, when he received Melbourne's request for an interview at Brighton, he 'had persuaded himself that he was coming to tender his resignation and had made up his mind to accept it'.[18] (Napoleon would have called this 'making pictures', a fantasy against which he was prone to warn his subordinates.) When the resignation was not proffered, the King asked for it instead, and whatever private feelings Melbourne might have had about his treatment were smothered beneath the almost fulsome respect which etiquette then required in formal communication with the Sovereign. Melbourne's manners had, after all, been formed under George III.

[17] A. Aspinall, *Three Early Nineteenth Century Diaries* (1952), pp. 205–6.
[18] RA 50506.

The King rejected at once Melbourne's proposal that Russell should lead the House of Commons, and when other names were suggested—those of Abercromby, Spring Rice and Hobhouse—the King objected to them too, adding for good measure his disapprobation of the 'injudicious and extravagant conduct of Lord Brougham'. Melbourne expressed confidence that government could be carried on, but the King was not to be persuaded, and he reminded Melbourne of his own previous agreement with Lord Grey's opinion that Althorp could not be spared from the House of Commons. The King's own impression, he recorded, formed

> partly by these previous circumstances and partly by his own views of the resources of the government in the House of Commons, was that they could not carry on the business satisfactorily and at any rate that, to carry it on, they must court and depend upon the support of those whose views, especially with respect to the Church, were at variance with the King's and must eventually, and probably soon after Parliament met, lead to a serious difference.

Wellington was sent for, declined in favour of Peel but, while Peel was being retrieved from his Roman holiday, was content to take possession of the government and hold it, like a frontier fortress, on Peel's behalf. Wellington appointed Lyndhurst as Lord Chancellor and took for himself, *pro tempore*, the offices of First Lord of the Treasury and Secretary of State for the Home Department. These three offices were all that were necessary for the transaction of essential business, at least while Parliament was not in session. In law, the Secretary of State was a fungible office, divided merely for convenience; Wellington, in addition to the cares of his nominal departments, was also technically responsible for the administration of foreign, colonial and military affairs. (Peel later quoted, as a precedent, the appointment of the Duke of Shrewsbury in 1714 as Lord High Treasurer, Lord Chamberlain, and Lord-Lieutenant of Ireland.)

Two questions were raised as soon as Peel's government met Parliament—the ascription of responsibility for the dismissal of Ministers, and the propriety of dissolving a Parliament that was barely two years old. The King was still hoping to appeal over the heads of those whom he had now come to regard as a faction to 'moderate men' both in the House of Commons and in the constituencies—to 'those who . . . felt, as His Majesty did, that it had become imperiously necessary to endeavour to stem the torrent of encroachment and to prevent useful and judicious reforms from being converted into engines of destruction'.[19] Far from promoting broad-bottomed unity, however, the King's actions had the effect of concentrating and defining the political parties. Professor Gash has suggested that the dismissal of Melbourne had three momentous consequences.

It gave Peel as Prime Minister the authority he needed to become party leader; it enabled him, as leader and head of government, to issue in the *Tamworth Manifesto* the first general exposition of Conservative principles; and it precipitated the General Election of 1835 which transformed a small divided Opposition into a substantial, united parliamentary party. If the growth of Conservatism was the product of many years, the birth of the Conservative Party can be assigned with unusual precision to the months of November–December 1834 . . . The stimulus to party unity and discipline administered by the events of November was not confined to one side. The shock of eviction brought Whigs, Radicals and Irish nationalists together, and their Lichfield House compact in February 1835 marks almost as clearly as the *Tamworth Manifesto* for their opponents the beginning of the Victorian Liberal Party.[20]

No one, this time, was disposed for lengthy wranglings over responsibility. Peel simply said: 'I claim all the responsibility which properly belongs to me as a public man; I am responsible for the duty which I have undertaken, and, if you please, I am, by my acceptance of office, responsible for the removal of the late Government.'[21] The House of Commons was content to leave it at that. Discussion of dissolution was more heated. Lord Melbourne threw at the Ministry those arguments,

[19] RA 50512.
[20] N. Gash in Lord Butler (ed.), *The Conservatives* (1977), p. 64.
[21] H. of C., 24 Feb. 1835, cc. 214–6.

intended to ricochet at their author, which the King had used in 1831—that general elections were invitations to public turmoil. 'What tends to agitation, and takes men from their public business, so much as a dissolution of Parliament?' True, he said, that there were precedents for premature dissolutions in 1784, 1807 and 1831, but they were 'bold, dangerous, desperate measures, all of them', only to be justified by 'success, constant success'.[22] Peel argued that a dissolution was a perfectly proper sequel to an extensive change of administration, and if dissolutions had been rare in the past it was because sudden extensive changes had been unusual. He, too, quoted Melbourne's precedents, with the addition of that of 1806, but in his own favour. But Peel was much less concerned with providing theoretical justification for an action that was unquestionably legal than with rebutting the contention, put forward by some Radical zealots, that he and his colleagues were morally debarred from taking office at all, because their previous opposition to the Reform Bill must be construed as a rejection of the reformed constitution. 'I have never,' he said, 'considered the Reform Bill to be a machine, the secret springs and working of which are only known to those by whom it has been constructed, or that its effect is to be the exclusion of any portion of the King's subjects from their Monarch's service.'[23] What Peel was anticipating here was an attempt to recreate the atmosphere of the years after 1714—a proscription of Tories on ideological grounds, exclusion on the grand scale not by a coercible monarch but within Parliament and in consequence of previous votes cast on a public measure.

> The rule of my conduct in office will be that which I have taken for my rule out of office, to make no sacrifice of public principle, but at the same time not to stand in fruitless opposition to the operation of changes in our institutions, the making of which I certainly deprecated, but which when made I was among the first to recognise as final and irrevocable.[24]

[22] H. of L., 24 Feb. 1835, c. 78.
[23] H. of C., 24 Feb. 1835, c. 227.
[24] Ibid., c. 230.

No more was heard of the argument that the opponents of Reform had disqualified themselves from office.

The general election of 1835 did not give the Conservatives a majority, but Peel nevertheless attempted to carry on. He appealed to the House of Commons that it should 'so far maintain the prerogative of the King as to give to the ministers of his choice, not an implicit confidence but a fair trial'.[25] If by this he meant that the hostile majority should lay aside its party convictions, he was no more successful than the King had been in 1834, when he had appealed to Peel, Wellington and Stanley to lay aside their own principles. There was no direct motion of no confidence, but the government was harassed by a sequence of minor but vexatious defeats. In the end, Peel was nagged into resignation by the House of Commons, but the reason he gave for surrendering office was not that he was in a minority, and thus had no title to govern, but that by retaining office without some certainty of carrying his measures he was weakening the executive power. There was, he said,

> great public evil in permitting the House of Commons to exhibit itself to the country free from any control on the part of the executive government, and usurping, in consequence of the absence of that control, many of the functions of that government.

This was a complaint that was frequently to be echoed by his successors.

Peel was asserting a Tory variant of the classical Whig doctrine that the essential function of the House of Commons was to control an executive which held office on sufferance. He was drawing upon an ancient and respectable theory: the maxim that 'the King's government must be carried on' did not merely mean that men should be ready to take office when called upon to do so, but that there existed in government itself an original power of initiation and execution, in which might be found an answer to the perennial question, 'Who or what is to represent the common good or public interest, as

25 Sir Robert Peel, *Memoirs* (1856–7), vol. II, p. 43.

compared with the more particular interests of the component parts?' That responsibility for defining the public interest had, in the past, been directly confided to the King; now, it had devolved upon the King's principal confidential servants. Peel was giving the House of Commons a repetition of arguments that had already been used by Wellington and were to be used again by Peel himself—that initiative was expected from political leaders and that they had a right to be sustained. There was a great deal more to Peel's argument than the mere assertion that resignation was to be preferred to encouraging in the House of Commons an appetite for meddling with matters of administration.

Peel's resignation made Melbourne the indispensable man once more; he used his opportunity with courteous firmness. The King had to take him back, and he was now able to insist on certain conditions: there were some matters that were to be 'precisely understood' before he would take office. The Ministry must have at its disposal the confidence and influence of the Crown, and full use of its powers. Among the marks of confidence that he demanded was the choice of members of the Royal Household. Melbourne had, he said, no wish to disturb the existing incumbents, provided that those with seats in Parliament supported the government, but future vacancies were not to be filled by men of adverse opinions. He wanted, too, the immediate creation of seven or eight peers. As to the composition of the Cabinet, he could not 'admit or acquiesce in any general or particular exclusions'. Furthermore, it must be understood that the government intended to execute any resolutions on the Irish Church passed by the House of Commons, and would expect to have the King's support in doing so.[26]

The King had lost, and he recognised that he must pay a price for his defeat. He conceded the point that, by summoning Melbourne, he had implicitly sanctioned proceedings upon the resolutions. But certain other possibilities, such as the appropriation of Crown livings in Ireland, put him in doubt as to whether he might not be asked to violate his coronation oath.

[26] RA 50522–37.

As a Ministry had yet to be formed, he had no one to advise him on this point; to relieve his mind, therefore, he would like the question referred to all fifteen of his judges. When Melbourne replied that he thought that such a proceeding would be inexpedient, the King asked to see Lyndhurst, who had been Peel's Lord Chancellor, and it was not until Lyndhurst had positively declined to give an answer that the King finally consented to the introduction of a Bill. He reminded Melbourne, however, that his assent would be needed when it had passed both Houses, and he implied that he would not regard it as a mere formality.[27]

However, the failure of his previous attempts did not deter the King from recurring to his scheme for a broad-bottomed administration. When rumours began to circulate, at the end of 1836, that Melbourne was contemplating retirement, the King wrote a memorandum as a guide to his future actions. The resignation of 'the Individual as the head of an Administration' entailed the dissolution of the government as a whole, and therefore the King was at liberty to exercise 'full prerogative' in the formation of its successor. Once again, he wanted both main parties to unite, and he proposed therefore, as soon as the opportunity offered, to appeal to four previous Prime Ministers—Wellington, Grey, Peel and Melbourne. (He did not, it seems, remember the existence of a fifth former Prime Minister, the Earl of Ripon who, as Viscount Goderich, had briefly held the office, a 'transient and embarrassed phantom' in Disraeli's phrase, after the death of Canning.) But before this possibility occurred, the King's own death and the succession of his niece brought a certain rejuvenation of Lord Melbourne, and enabled him to instruct the Queen in his own version of the theory of the constitution.

[27] Ibid., 50539–42.

3

Queen Victoria and Her Ministers

I had often heard it stated as the nature of the English constitution and the Royal Prerogatives, that the Sovereign could not interfere with the Government or the management of Parliament which are left to the sole control of the responsible Ministers, but that he was absolutely free in the choice of his Minister. Now I differed completely from that doctrine. I held the Sovereign to have an immense moral responsibility upon his shoulders with regard to his government and the duty to watch and control it . . . A sagacious Sovereign therefore would look forward and take his share in the preparatory arrangements of Party organisation even, when he could, in order to have those presented to his choice in times of emergency, who he had before recognised as eligible.

Prince Albert

Queen Victoria once reminded Lord Rosebery that she had inherited the constitution and intended to hand it down unimpaired to her successor. (She might have added that she had been on the throne for ten years before he was born.) William IV had asserted in 1835 that 'the confidence, the countenance, and the support of the Sovereign are indispensable to the existence and the maintenance of the Government, as long as the Constitution of the country is monarchial . . .'[1] This was a claim to the right to make or break a Ministry. The Queen probably subscribed to her uncle's doctrine in full throughout her life although, like him, she had to recognise that there was seldom any effective defence

[1] C. S. Parker, *Sir Robert Peel from his Private Papers* (1891–9), vol. II, p. 287.

against a determined 'storming of the closet'. Sometimes her language was curiously similar to William IV's. He wrote of the Whigs in 1835: 'They may become his Ministers, but never his *confidential* servants. He would receive all their advice with jealousy and suspicion.'[2] The Queen had much the same to say about Gladstone, nearly half a century later, although she too had to realise that royal favour alone could determine who was to be Prime Minister only in very rare circumstances. It was a lesson that took her a long time to learn. In 1894, after Gladstone's final resignation, the Queen wrote to Lord Salisbury what amounted to an apology for not turning out the government there and then.

> The Queen is most anxious that Lord Salisbury should *not* think she is wanting in openness towards him, or doubt that her wish to see him again at the head of affairs is as great as ever; but she feels that she could not act differently than she has done at the present time. It must be remembered that the present Government have still a majority in the House of Commons.[3]

The Queen showed every satisfaction with Lord Melbourne's administration when she inherited it in 1837. Indeed, Melbourne was more than Prime Minister: he was also mentor and older friend, appealing to that romantic streak which coexisted with the Queen's almost brutally business-like demeanour in her first days on the throne. He was *her* Minister, and she could not bear to part with him. The Bedchamber crisis of 1839 was much less a constitutional landmark than a contest of personalities. Peel, who had once more been offered the thankless task of forming a government that would be in a minority in the House of Commons, asked for some change among the ladies of the Queen's Bedchamber. It was not unusual for an incoming Prime Minister to ask for a gesture of confidence, and the reasonableness of Peel's request was demonstrated by the relationship of some of the ladies to the Ministers whom Peel was being asked to replace. They included

2 Ibid., vol. II, p. 289.
3 3 LQV, II, pp. 121–2.

Lady Normanby, wife of the Secretary of State for War and the Colonies whose conduct had been the occasion for Melbourne's defeat and resignation; two sisters of Lord Morpeth, the Chief Secretary for Ireland; the sister-in-law of Lord John Russell; and the daughters of the Lord Privy Seal and the Chancellor of the Exchequer. Moreover, some of them had been directly implicated in a nasty scandal that had begun with false accusations of pregnancy being made against Lady Flora Hastings, who had been a member of the Queen's Household. Many Tories had become convinced, with good reason, that the Queen had become an out-and-out Whig partisan; the case of Lady Flora became a party question, and some of Peel's followers wanted the removal of the ladies most deeply implicated. Melbourne admitted the importance of the issue; the Queen noted in her journal for 10 May 1839 that he had quoted the Duke of Richmond as saying that the treatment of Lady Flora had created a Tory prejudice against the ladies.[4]

The Queen was under emotional strain; she was tearful and petulant. She had escaped from maternal coercion only two years earlier, and she seemed to regard a change of government as the imposition upon her of political coercion. Thus she indulged herself with such phrases as 'the Queen of England will not submit to such trickery . . .' and 'the Queen felt that this was an attempt to see whether she could be led and managed like a child . . .'[5] In short, she was immature and over-excited. There was some misunderstanding about whether Peel required the sacrifice of all the ladies or only one or two of them. She sought, inevitably, Melbourne's advice, and the former Cabinet met and drafted a reply to Peel which she sent with the addition only of a single comma:

> The Queen, having considered the proposal made to her yesterday by Sir Robert Peel, to remove the Ladies of her Bedchamber, cannot consent to adopt a course which she conceives to be contrary to usage, and which is repugnant to her feelings.[6]

[4] RA C43/21.
[5] 1 LQV, I, pp. 162, 163.
[6] Ibid., p. 167.

It was an unedifying episode, but it set no precedents. Peel gave up the attempt to form a government and Melbourne returned. It is worth noting that no one considered that the possession of a parliamentary majority was a necessary condition of taking office. In theory, the House of Commons could still be considered as a non-partisan body; conventions had not yet been fully formed on the conduct and obligations of parties; and it was not preposterous to hope that a Minister designated by the Sovereign might be given a fair trial. The Queen had behaved with a rather frenetic immaturity. She wrote full and rather silly accounts of her meetings to Melbourne—how, for instance, 'she had never seen anyone look so frightened' as Peel (a description of which the accuracy may be doubted); and for some time afterwards a recurrent theme in her letters was that she could never appeal to Peel again. But, by the time that such an appeal became necessary, she had learned more sense. In 1839, she received more loyalty from the Opposition than her conduct deserved: two years later Melbourne told Anson that 'nothing but the forebearance of the Tories' had enabled him and his colleagues to support the Queen.[7] The difficulties were largely of Melbourne's making, and his advice was bad and potentially dangerous. By 1841, when Melbourne resigned for the last time, the Queen's marriage had provided her with alternative emotional dependence, and Peel's position, both in the party and the country, was strong enough not to need additional buttressing. Confidential communications were established with him (with Melbourne's knowledge) while the Whigs were still in office, through the intermediary of Anson, Prince Albert's secretary. The result of the general election of 1841 confirmed Peel's ascendancy. 'The year 1841 was the first time in British history that an Opposition, previously in a minority in the House of Commons, defeated the Government of the day and took office as the result of a victory at the polls.'[8] It was noted at the time that something new had happened; Croker thought that this was the first time in English history that the electorate had chosen a Prime Minister : 'Every Conservative candidate

[7] Ibid., p. 268.
[8] Gash, op. cit., pp. 72–3.

professed himself in plain words to be Sir Robert Peel's man, and on that ground was elected.'[9] Whatever constraint the Queen may have felt in the presence of her new Minister did not last long. Indeed, Peel was as reluctant to abandon the Queen in 1845 as Melbourne had been in 1839, and he then displayed no want of enthusiasm in accepting the 'poisoned chalice' that Russell handed back to him.

There were no constitutional difficulties when Russell succeeded Peel in 1846. There were no other serious claimants for office, and Peel did not ask for a dissolution, professing that it would be improper to seek to gain a purely party advantage. Russell's government, with considerable assistance from the Peelites, was able to maintain itself for nearly five years. This situation changed after Peel's death in 1850. Between Russell's abortive resignation in 1851, after a resolution on the franchise had been carried against him in a thinly attended division, and the formation of Palmerston's second Ministry in 1859, there were five administrations. One may note, as one watches the Queen and the Prince in their perennial search for government, how small were the ranks of the *ministeriabili*, let alone the *papabili*. Derby refused office (to Disraeli's disgust) in 1851 because he could not find enough Conservatives fit to be Ministers,[10] and he was to refuse again in 1855. The reluctance of a single colleague might be decisive, at least as an excuse; Russell gave as his reason for refusal in 1845 that Lord Grey would not serve if Palmerston went back to the Foreign Office.

By the 1850s, the Queen and the Prince had developed a close political partnership, based upon a constitutional theory that was rather more logically coherent than was warranted by English practice. They had no doubt at all that the choice of a Prime Minister was a prerogative power that belonged to the Queen alone, and could be exercised without advice. When Lord Derby resigned in December 1852, and volunteered the advice that the Queen should send for Lord Lansdowne to give her information on the state of parties, the Prince interrupted to say that 'constitutionally speaking, it did not rest

[9] Parker, op. cit., vol. II, p. 475.
[10] G. H. L. Le May, 'The Ministerial crisis of 1851', *History Today* (1951).

with him to give advice and become responsible for it . . .'[11]
The Queen and Prince decided to see Lords Lansdowne and
Aberdeen together; as it happened, Lansdowne had gout and
Aberdeen came alone. He was invited to form a Ministry, and
the Prince gave him a list of possible office-holders in which
Aberdeen purported to find 'valuable suggestions'. However,
the Queen was displeased when Aberdeen failed to consult her
during the formative phase of his negotiations, when it was
proposed that Lord John Russell should lead the House of
Commons, with a seat in the Cabinet but no other office.

> What the Queen complains of . . . is, that so important an
> innovation in the construction of the executive government
> should have been practically decided upon by an arrangement
> intended to meet personal wants under peculiar and accidental
> circumstances, leaving the Queen the embarrassing alternative
> only, either to forego the exercise of her own prerogative, or
> to damage by her own act the *formation* or *stability* of the new
> Government.[12]

The proposal was a novel one, but it had the support of the
Speaker, who thought that the task of leading the House of
Commons was so onerous that it should have attached to it an
office with no other duties.

Aberdeen's resignation in 1855 thrust the Queen and Prince
into yet another protracted round of negotiations. The convention was coming into being that if the Opposition had been
responsible for the fall of a government it had a moral right
to be invited to replace it and a moral duty to accept the
invitation. Thus the Queen's first reaction was to send for
Lord Derby. Nevertheless, he refused, and the Queen then
sent for Lord Lansdowne, not to form a government but to be
consulted on the present state of party warfare and to tell
her about current animosities and who would not serve with
whom. Lansdowne, who had first held office in the Ministry
of All the Talents, played in the Whig party that role of elder
statesman that had belonged to Wellington among the Tories.

[11] 1 LQV, II, p. 413.
[12] Ibid., p. 438.

The Queen then sent for Russell, to *consult* him (as she made very plain); he was sent away to talk to Lansdowne and Palmerston, and was told to report the result of his discussions through Lansdowne. It was only then that, at last, Russell was asked to form a Ministry, and the Queen added that it 'would give her particular satisfaction if Lord Palmerston could join in that formation'. If this codicil to the invitation was intended to remove any impression that Palmerston, as a result of the events of 1851, lay under some ban of exclusion it was, in his opinion, insufficient. He asked for, and was given, an audience as a demonstration that the Queen had no personal objection to him. Next, and at Russell's request, the Queen saw Lord Clarendon and tried unsuccessfully to persuade him to take the Foreign Office. Clarendon accused Russell of bad faith in seeking to break up the coalition by tripping up Aberdeen and driving out the Peelites as a prelude to putting himself at the head of a purely Whig administration; Clarendon would not, he said, 'forsake his former colleagues, step over their dead bodies to the man who had killed them'. Once again the Queen saw Lansdowne, and on his advice gave Russell a positive commission as a form of political therapy, to bring home to him what was clear to almost everyone else, that practically no one was willing to serve under him. The Queen reported Lord Lansdowne as having 'no idea that Lord John will succeed in his task, but thinks it a necessary course to go through, and most wholesome to Lord John to have his eyes opened to his own position, of which he verily believed he was not in the least aware'. In due course, Russell, by then presumably instructed and chastened, admitted his failure and returned his commission; only then, with all practical alternatives exhausted, did the Queen turn to Palmerston, who accepted with alacrity. The Prince wrote to encourage Aberdeen to join, if only as a bait to entice the Peelites back. Aberdeen declined: 'I can retire with perfect equanimity from the Government in consequence of the vote of the House of Commons; but to be stigmatized as the Head and tolerated as the subordinate member I cannot endure.'[13]

---

[13] 1 LQV, III, pp. 90–100.

When Palmerston fell in 1858, the Queen sent at once for Derby, who asked for time. 'Sending for' a politician, clearly enough, did not entail an invitation to form a Ministry. Derby said that he did not want an immediate invitation. 'After what had happened in 1851 and 1855, if the Queen made the offer he *must* accept it, for if he refused the Conservative party would be broken up for ever.' Derby thought that it was not always an advantage to be at the head of what might turn out to be a long queue. 'The person who was asked first by the Sovereign had always a great disadvantage; perhaps other combinations were possible, which, if found not to answer would make him more readily acceptable by the country.'[14] In the event, Derby formed a purely Conservative Ministry, which endured on sufferance until defeat and dissolution in 1859. On Derby's resignation, the Queen sent for Lord Granville as leader of the 'Liberal party' in the House of Lords; it was clear that she regarded him as no more than an adviser or intermediary, since she simultaneously told Russell and Palmerston that she did not wish to choose between them. This is not quite analogous to George IV's attempt to persuade the Cabinet to choose its own chairman; the Queen, more narrowly, was merely inviting two principal contenders to settle the matter between themselves. They did so, effectively, by saying each that he would take the second but not the third place. Russell said that he would serve under Granville only if he were given the leadership of the House of Commons, an office which Palmerston refused to concede to him. Forced to choose after all, the Queen turned to Palmerston, whereupon Russell claimed, and was given, the Foreign Office.

No agonising choices or extended negotiations were required of the Queen in the formation of the next five Ministries— those of 1865 (Russell), 1866 (Derby), February 1868 (Disraeli), December 1868 (Gladstone) and 1874 (Disraeli). Derby carried out some abortive negotiations with the Cave of Adullam in 1866, but these did not directly concern the Queen. The situation became more complicated after 1875, when Gladstone announced that he had retired from the leadership of the

---

[14] Ibid., p. 267.

Liberal Party. His decision was received with well-deserved scepticism. H. W. Lucy wrote, on 7 May 1875:

> Gladstone's retirement . . . is much such another withdrawal from the conduct of affairs as the captain of a ship effects when he turns in for the night. The first mate is left in charge . . . but on the slightest emergency the captain is to be called.[15]

By September 1876, Gladstone had convinced himself that the game was still afoot, and there was an open gap—indeed, a chasm—between the real and the nominal Liberal leadership. As early as September 1879, the Queen had begun to contemplate the disagreeable consequences of a possible Conservative defeat. Her point of contact with the Opposition was through her private secretary, Sir Henry Ponsonby, to whom she expressed in the most forthright terms sentiments which that tactful man softened before he transmitted them. 'I wish the *principal* people of the Opposition should *know* there are certain things which *I never can* consent to'—such as accepting either Gladstone or Lowe as a Minister again. By April 1880, she was threatening to express herself very plainly if the Opposition were to 'force themselves upon her'.[16] 'Storming the closet' might have seemed a thing of the past, but to the Queen it remained a reality. After the election, she applied in vain to Hartington and to Granville, but she had to accept Gladstone in the end. In the bitterness of immediate defeat, she wrote an hysterical and much-quoted letter to Ponsonby, which it is just as well that Gladstone never saw, insisting that, election promises or no, the Liberals should not alter the Conservatives' policies. She did not get her way. Beaconsfield, however, made things no easier for his successors by telling the Queen that the speech from the throne at the opening of Parliament was as much hers as her Ministers', and that opinions to the contrary were no more than parliamentary gossip.

In 1894, when Gladstone went at last after he had failed to carry his Cabinet with him, either on the reduction of the

[15] H. W. Lucy, *A Diary of Two Parliaments* (1885), p. 89.
[16] 2 LQV, III, pp. 47, 73.

naval estimates or on an attack upon the House of Lords, the Queen chose Lord Rosebery. If Gladstone had been asked for his advice, which he was not, he would have recommended Lord Spencer; he was hurt that the Queen did not wish for his opinion but, as Mr Roy Jenkins has pointed out, it was not reasonable that a Prime Minister who had been repudiated by his colleagues should choose his own successor. The Queen's choice of Rosebery, rather than Harcourt or Morley, was not directly challenged, although Harcourt continued to serve with the worst possible grace. In 1895, when Rosebery gratefully accepted the chance to unbind himself from Ixion's wheel, the Queen turned, with enthusiastic relief and without hesitation, to Lord Salisbury for the third time.

II

The Septennial Act of 1716 had fixed seven years as the maximum duration of a Parliament. The convention was quickly established that the normal duration should be about six years; it was thought prudent not to go on to the bitter end, partly because it would be highly inconvenient to hold an election in an untoward season of domestic or foreign crisis, and because Ministers needed to have an eye for the fixed points of the financial calendar and to ensure that they left adequate time for such annual events as the renewal of the Mutiny Act, without which it was illegal to keep a standing army in time of peace. Seven years was the statutory maximum, but there was nothing in law to prevent the King from dissolving parliaments at pleasure; moreover, in law, a demise of the Crown required that the existing parliament, no matter when it had been elected, should be dissolved within six months. The perennial question was whether dissolution was a prerogative of the Crown or of the King—whether the King was bound to accept the advice of his Ministers, or whether he could use his own discretion. It was a matter to be settled in each case, not by law or convention but by contingency. The question was not closed before the beginning of the Second World War, and there are those who believe that it is still open. Certainly, George V never considered a request for a dissolution as something to be granted automatically.

The practical limitation upon the King was that a refusal would probably be followed by the resignation of Ministers; but every nineteenth-century Prime Minister knew that he would have to argue his case, with the possibility that he might argue it unsuccessfully. Kings, no less than Foreign Secretaries, were reluctant to be bound by abstract or hypothetical principles of precaution. This was a general principle, which encompassed the particular. One of the maxims which William IV passed on to Queen Victoria for her guidance was: 'That the Sovereign should ever be cautious of *pledging* himself personally upon any point of public policy.'[17] Where he was not pledged, William believed that he retained his full freedom of action. In March 1831, the King was unwilling to grant at once the dissolution for which Grey had asked: an election would produce even more popular turmoil, and worse still, there was a danger that candidates might be required to pledge themselves 'to the support of measures of democratic and revolutionary tendency'. Grey's reply was in two parts. First (and here he hardly directed himself to the King's point), he said that Ministers had not excited the agitation for parliamentary reform but had found it in existence when they took office. Secondly, and more significantly, he argued that 'this Government is now without its natural support, the Parliament having been chosen by the late Ministers, and all the seats being now filled by their bitterest opponents'. Informal persuasion having failed, Grey sent the King a Cabinet minute, formally advising a dissolution. On the following day, the King accepted this advice as 'the lesser of two evils'. Plainly, he had pondered a refusal; but, as he reflected, a change of ministry would not dispel the demand for reform.[18]

Grey's complaint that Parliament had been 'chosen' by a previous administration raises the question of the direct and indirect influence of the Crown in elections. It seems that by the 1830s the direct influence was small, but the Crown still retained some means of favouring administrations in one or

[17] Ibid., p. 660.
[18] RA 50494–5.

two seats, which could be used for bringing in men who were urgently wanted in the House of Commons. Royal wishes counted at Windsor and Brighton. In 1832, under Grey, Windsor returned a Whig; in 1835, under Peel, a Tory; and in 1837, under Melbourne, a Whig again. In 1835, the influence of the Court was probably decisive for the election of Captain George Pechell, R.N., equerry to Queen Adelaide, at Brighton. Once in Parliament, Pechell began to behave as if he had got there on merit; he displayed froward independence and was warned, through Sir Herbert Taylor, that the King expected members of the Royal Household to vote with Ministers or to resign their posts.[19]

Before the Second Reform Act of 1867, Ministries normally went in or out of office rather in consequence of transactions at Court or in the House of Commons than as the result of general elections. The dissolution of 1835 was most unusual in not providing a majority for Ministers; it is this election, rather than that of 1841, which was the first at which a majority was returned 'smack against the Crown'. Considering the state of the Queen's temper in 1839, it is not clear what she would have said had Peel asked formally for a dissolution. When the matter was hinted at, her first reaction, predictably enough, was that she was against it, and Melbourne advised her, if the matter was raised again, 'not to give a promise that you will dissolve, nor to say positively that you will not'.[20] In 1841, Melbourne was against a dissolution, but his Cabinet voted for it and he felt that he must go along with the majority. Lord Brougham disagreed, and wrote to the Queen that the dissolution was 'wholly without justification, either from principle or from policy'[21]; he had the melancholy satisfaction of seeing his view justified by the result. Melbourne's opinions of 1841 were shared by Peel in 1846 :

I think no Ministers ought to advise the Sovereign to dissolve Parliament without feeling a moral conviction that Dissolution

---

[19] *Correspondence of Earl Grey with William IV* (1867), vol. I, pp. 158, 177–83, 225–31.
[20] 1 LQV, I, p. 159.
[21] Ibid., pp. 276, 281, 293.

will enable them to carry on the Government of the country . . . The Dissolution of the Whigs in 1841 was, I think, an unjustifiable act. Dissolution now, if the result is the same, would be equally so.

He said in Parliament that dissolution was not justifiable merely as a means of strengthening a party: it was 'a great instrument in the hands of the Crown; and it would have a tendency to blunt the instrument if it were employed without great necessity'.[22] The Queen echoed Peel's sentiments (and used some of his words) when she discouraged Russell from asking for a dissolution after Peel had resigned:

She considers the power of dissolving Parliament a most valuable and powerful instrument in the hands of the Crown, which ought not to be used except in extreme cases and with a certainty of success. To use this instrument and be defeated is a thing most lowering to the Crown and hurtful to the country. The Queen feels strongly that she made a mistake in allowing the Dissolution in 1841; the result has been a majority returned against her of nearly one hundred votes; but suppose the result to have been nearly an equality of votes between the two contending parties, the Queen would have thrown away her last remedy, and it would have been impossible for her to get any Government which could have carried on public business with a chance of success.[23]

The Queen did not look on parties as autonomous institutions competing for power but as means of carrying on her government. There was no hint that she thought that she should efface herself in the background of events, merely waiting to present the prize of office to whichever successful candidate emerged from the contest. The Queen disliked change; she did not like to see Ministries go, but in the middle years of her reign she identified herself with their successors, not merely as a patron but as an effective agent in the process of government. An unusual dissolution was, of course, to be distinguished from one made necessary by the effluxion of time, and her con-

[22] H. of C., 29 June 1846, c. 1043.
[23] 1 LQV, II, p. 91.

currence could be taken for granted when, for instance, Russell reported to her in March 1847 that his Cabinet favoured dissolution at the end of that session, 'conformable to the usage from the passing of the Septennial Act to 1830 . . .'[24]

In 1857, when Palmerston was threatened with a vote of censure on his Chinese policy, the Queen refused to give a contingent guarantee that she would agree to dissolve before the vote was actually taken; but the Prince wrote that the Queen felt herself physically unable to 'go through the anxiety of a Ministerial Crisis and the fruitless attempt to form a new Government out of the heterogeneous elements of which the present Opposition is composed, and would on that account prefer any other alternative . . .'[25] The general election of April 1857 was practically a plebiscite on Palmerston, an appeal by a Prime Minister over the heads of the House of Commons for the first time since the younger Pitt. It was successful; but the new House of Commons elected on a Palmerston ticket turned him out of office ten months later.

In May 1858, soon after he had taken office for the second time, Lord Derby tried to get from the Queen a contingent promise to dissolve, to head off a vote of censure on Lord Ellenborough's handling of Indian affairs, a matter which had already led to Ellenborough's resignation. The Queen at first refused; to Derby's mortification, she would go no further than to tell him that 'he might leave it quite undecided whether the Queen would grant a dissolution or not, and take the benefit of the doubt when talking to others upon the subject . . .' However, she modified her attitude after she had sent Sir Charles Phipps on her behalf to consult Lord Aberdeen, who coupled a rousing primary statement about the plenitude of royal power—'There was no doubt of the power and prerogative of the Sovereign to refuse a Dissolution—it was one of the very few acts which the Queen of England could do without responsible advice'—with a cautious warning about how that power should be used. It would, he said, be unconstitutional to hold a threat of dissolution over Parliament, with the object of influencing a decision to which it had not

[24] 1 LQV, II, p. 121.
[25] 1 LQV, III, p. 229.

yet come; but at the same time he assumed that if the Queen were given unequivocal advice about a dissolution she would accept it, because the alternative would be that 'the Queen would take upon herself the act of dismissing Lord Derby from office, instead of his resigning from being able no longer to carrying on the Government'. Hence, when Derby renewed his request on the following day, the Queen gave him the substance of the assurance for which he asked, with the proviso that he should keep it dark : she would not refuse a dissolution, she would tell him privately, 'and trusted that her honour would be safe in his hands as to the use which he made of the knowledge'. This was all that Derby needed; the motion of censure was withdrawn, and no mention of the Queen's part in the matter was made in public.[26]

The Queen made no objection when Derby chose dissolution rather than resignation in 1859. The dissolution of 1865 was routinely held at the end of the session beginning in Parliament's sixth year. In 1866, after the defeat of Russell's reform bill, the Queen at first refused to accept her Ministers' resignation; they insisted, giving as one reason that the lukewarmness of the country on reform, especially in the south, would make a dissolution inexpedient.

The Queen dealt sharply with Disraeli during the confused events that followed the passing of the Irish Church resolutions against Ministers at the beginning of the session of 1868. Here, and for the last time, the claim was made that a Prime Minister had a 'constitutional right' to ask for the dissolution of a Parliament elected while his political opponents were in office. Disraeli, by his own account, advised the Queen to dissolve Parliament but offered to resign instead, if that was what she preferred. Resignation then was not what she preferred, but she was not pleased at his next suggestion, that 'to feel the opinion of the House of Commons' would be the most convenient way of deciding when the dissolution should take place. She made it clear that she had no wish to see the House of Commons intruding upon either the executive power in general or her own prerogative in particular.[27]

[26] Ibid., pp. 283–9.
[27] 2 LQV, I, p. 528

In announcing his general intentions to the House of Commons, Disraeli made three important assertions : that it was solely for Ministers to decide whether a vote on a particular measure was to be regarded as expressing a want of confidence; that Parliament should not pronounce on important new questions which had not been placed before the electorate; and that a Prime Minister had a prescriptive right to ask for the dissolution of a Parliament elected under his opponents. He recalled that Lord Derby had taken office in 1866, although in a minority in a House of Commons 'which was elected under the auspices and at the appeal of his political opponents. It was therefore quite open to the Earl of Derby, in the spirit of the Constitution, to recommend Her Majesty to dissolve this Parliament . . .' Derby had chosen then to waive the right, but Disraeli was claiming to revive 'what was not strictly perhaps, though practically it had been held to be, the constitutional right of a Minister upon taking office, to advise the Crown to dissolve a Parliament elected under the influence of his political opponents'.[28] Indeed, experience since 1841 reinforced the belief that the Opposition could not expect to win a general election. Likewise venturing into the past, Gladstone protested in his turn against a 'penal dissolution'.

Disraeli created a constitutional precedent after the general election of 1868, when he chose to accept defeat at the hands of the constituencies instead of those of the new House of Commons, and resigned without meeting Parliament. This was a clear example of precedent crystallising about accident. Disraeli had no wish to consolidate the Liberal Party by presenting himself as a common target for its various elements. The party had disintegrated in the previous Parliament, it might do so again, and the chances of that happening would be better if it was not allowed to bind itself together in a vote of censure. In spite of its peculiar origin, the precedent was found to be convenient; it was followed by Gladstone in 1874 and by Disraeli (then Earl of Beaconsfield) in 1880. The Queen raised no objection in 1874; her relations with Gladstone were already hostile, and she was glad to be rid of him. Usage and

[28] H. of C., 4 May 1868, cc. 1695–6.

precedent, she told him, ought to give way to convenience. The convenience that she had in mind was her own, since she was shortly expecting her second son, the Duke of Edinburgh, back from St. Petersburg with his bride. However, she did not think that immediate resignation ought to become a general rule, 'because it might be a means for a Government, who had committed some grievous fault, to escape condemnation by Parliament, as the adverse party was seldom inclined to attack a fallen Government'.[29] But become a general rule it did, whenever the result of a general election was sufficiently clear to make the carrying of a vote of no confidence a certainty; its adoption may be taken as a measure of the development of party cohesion and solidarity. Gladstone resigned at once after the election of 1886. Salisbury chose to meet Parliament after the election of 1885, as Baldwin did after that of 1923; both were turned out almost at once. In 1929, in conditions roughly similar to those of 1923, Baldwin resigned at once: however obscure the result might be, he said, it showed that the electorate did not want him. The most spectacular recognition of reality behind formality was when Lloyd George resigned in 1922, not in consequence of votes either in Parliament or in the country but as a result of a meeting of the Conservative and Unionist Party at the Carlton Club.

In 1886, when her personal detestation of Gladstone was compounded by her profound disapproval of his Irish policy, the Queen considered whether she should refuse a dissolution to Gladstone, should he ask for one if his Home Rule Bill were defeated. She consulted Lord Salisbury, leader of the Opposition, who advised her not to refuse; if she did so, the fact would become public knowledge and would be damaging to the Queen herself. He wrote on 15 May, three weeks before the vote on second reading, that agreement to a request for dissolution

> is the natural and ordinary course; it will shield the Queen from any accusation of partisanship; it is likely to return a Parliament more opposed to Home Rule than the present;

[29] 2 LQV, II, pp. 316–8.

and it will adapt itself to the peculiar difficulties, as to the Queen's movements, which arise from the crisis coming at this particular date.

A week later, he added the reassuring information that 'a dissolution a little later, with a Unionist Government in office, will be less favourable than a dissolution now'.[30]

Namier's generalisation that the impartiality of the Crown was a function of the growth of party is flawed; it recognises that parties were changing, but it does not take sufficiently into account the Queen's stubborn reluctance to adapt her own attitude to the new conditions. In the years after 1832 there was a development, if not always a continuous one, in the cohesiveness of parties, in the theories which justified parties, the organisations which sustained them, and the customs, expectations and sanctions which bound them together in action. There was always a possibility, however, that the Queen might use the prerogative and risk the consequences. If she did not move from threat to action, it was not because she recognised the existence of new political forces, still less that she had modified her own code of constitutional conduct, but because she accepted warnings, in particular cases, that she might damage herself. The influence of her private secretaries was important; Sir Henry Ponsonby, in particular, was always conscious of how the monarchy might be damaged by party accusations of royal partisanship, especially if these were supported in the press. After her marriage, the Queen ceased to be a Whig partisan; but she became a Conservative partisan under Disraeli (though she did not need quite as much urging as legend suggests), and she retained that prejudice firmly for the rest of her life. She owed much to the reluctance of some politicians to see royal influence tilted too much and too openly in their direction. On 11 July 1893, she told the Duke of Argyll that, if Gladstone proposed to reintroduce his second Home Rule Bill in the House of Commons after its certain rejection by the House of Lords, she would insist upon a dissolution. Argyll told her that such an action would be

[30] 3 LQV, I, pp. 130–5.

unwise.[31] Salisbury cautioned her in a similar vein a month later, when commenting upon a suggestion from 'some leading Unionists' that the Queen should be asked, either by petition or by an address from the House of Lords, to dissolve Parliament over the heads of her Ministers. Salisbury said (in language that William IV might have found familiar) that this would be followed by the resignation of Ministers and the certain consequence that the Liberal Party would go to the country with a campaign hostile to royal pretensions.[32] On 25 October 1894, when the Cabinet was considering the framing of a resolution hostile to the House of Lords, she asked Salisbury whether she should warn the Prime Minister, Lord Rosebery, that 'she cannot let the Cabinet make such a proposal' and added: 'Is the Unionist party fit for a dissolution *now*?'[33] In November, she was thinking once more of a royal dissolution to forestall a campaign against the House of Lords, and sent her private secretary to consult Sir Henry James, in his capacity as Attorney-General of the Duchy of Cornwall. James sent a discouraging memorandum, to the effect that such an action would be self-defeating, by shifting the issue from that of the Commons against the Lords to that of the Queen against the Liberal Party, and that it was, anyway, unnecessary at that stage:

> No measure disapproved of by the House of Lords can be carried without the creation of some 500 Peers. If such a proposition were submitted to her Majesty, resort to a Dissolution would probably meet with popular approval.[34]

In short, the longer the Queen reigned the more tenacious she became in defence of what she regarded as her rights. Circumstances might have changed, but the Queen's pretensions and claims had not. She meant exactly what she said when, on 13 November 1894, she 'would ask Lord Rosebery and his Cabinet to bear in mind that 57 years ago the Con-

[31] 3 LQV, II, p. 279.
[32] Ibid., 297–9.
[33] Ibid., p. 431.
[34] Ibid., p. 434.

stitution was delivered into her keeping, and that, right or wrong, she has her views to the fulfilment of her trust'.[35]

III

For the last forty years of her reign, the Queen insisted on keeping, as closely as she could, to a rigid time-table of travel and residence. She disliked London, and she was always ready to move, as soon as business permitted and sometimes sooner, to Balmoral in Scotland or Osborne on the Isle of Wight. Her habits involved tedium and inconvenience for her Ministers, especially those required to be in residence with her when she was away from London; absence from the seat of government never meant that she waived her claims to admonish and to argue.

The sacred day of the Queen's calendar, which may conveniently be taken as the starting point of her annual round, was 14 December, the anniversary of the Prince's death; she liked to spend this day alone in the Blue Room at Windsor in which he died. This rite completed, she went as soon as she could to Osborne, where she generally stayed until the middle of February. She returned to Windsor for the opening of the parliamentary session, went to Osborne for Easter, then returned once more to Windsor, went to Balmoral in May, and returned to Windsor for June and part of July. As early as possible in July, she went back to Balmoral, and generally stayed there until the end of November, when she went back to Windsor. There were necessary alterations in this schedule, and there were state occasions in London that could not be avoided, but the Queen disliked most of them very much. In her widowhood, the habit of seclusion grew upon her. She performed ceremonial duties in public with distaste, but she was exceedingly reluctant to delegate any of them, for instance to the Prince of Wales. She constantly cited what she regarded as the poor state of her health as a reason why she should be absolved from what Bagehot called the dignified part of the constitution.

[35] Ibid., p. 435.

Gladstone, writing on what he considered to be the proper relationship between the Sovereign and Ministers, said:

> He is entitled, on all subjects coming before the Ministry, to knowledge and opportunities of discussion, unlimited save by the iron necessities of business. Though decisions must ultimately conform to the sense of those who are to be responsible for them, yet their business is to inform and persuade the Sovereign, not to overrule him.[36]

'Ultimately', when the Queen's prejudices were deeply engaged, could be a long way.

King William IV had drawn up for himself a list of maxims, which Sir Herbert Taylor put into a memorandum for the Queen after her accession:

> That the Sovereign should ever be cautious of *pledging* himself personally upon any subject of public policy.
> Should never agree to anything very material in *verbal* communication, but should require the written statement of it for consideration . . .
> That he should never declare that he is *resolved* not to do a thing, or not to agree to a measure, unless quite determined not to yield the point.
> That he should never make a promise unless *quite certain* that he will be able to perform it.
> That he should never break a promise.[37]

These were admirable as copy-book headings, but they would have served as well or better as maxims for a successful grocer. Changes of regime were important points of consolidation; Ministers were sometimes able to assert as rights against a new monarch claims that had been rejected as encroachments by his predecessor. J. M. Keynes ended *The General Theory of Employment, Interest and Money* with the reflection that ideas rather than vested interests were dangerous for good or evil, not at once but after a certain time, because few people were capable of modifying their ideas after about the age of two-

[36] W. E. Gladstone, *Gleanings of Past Years* (1879), vol. i, p. 232.
[37] RA 50494–5.

and-thirty. Few monarchs were able to modify the concepts of kingship that they brought with them to the throne. Queen Victoria did develop her ideas, from those implanted by Lord Melbourne to those worked out with Prince Albert. She was more exposed than most monarchs had been to constitutional theorists, even if the theories were sometimes rather strange. The Queen was scarcely upon the throne before her uncle by marriage, King Leopold of the Belgians, was recommending Baron Stockmar to her as a mentor: 'There is no branch of information in which he may not prove useful . . . a *living* dictionary of all matters scientific and politic that happened these thiry years.'[38] (Robert Louis Stevenson's great creation, Uncle Joseph Finsbury, might not have been dissatisfied with this as a reference.[39]) King Leopold never forgot that, but for the death of the Princess Charlotte, he would have been the husband of an English queen regnant, and he used this putative relationship with the realm of England as a justification for his constant advice to Queen Victoria, given as if to a fellow-member of a league in which an accretion of power to one was an accretion to all. He never ceased to insist that what was important was the exercise of power, not its mere title. 'All trades must be learned, and nowadays the trade of a constitutional sovereign, to do it well, is a very difficult one.'[40] It was a trade which, in England, was to be learned without a period of apprenticeship or a handbook of practice: even the most solemn ceremonies of the monarchy were sometimes a matter of hasty, even breathless, improvisation. Melbourne understood all this well enough:

> All the political part of the English Constitution is fully understood, and distinctly stated in Blackstone and many other books, but the Ministerial part, the work of conducting the executive government, has rested so much on practice, on usage, on understanding, that there is no particular publication to which reference can be made for the explanation and description of it. It is to be sought in debates, in protests, in letters, in memoirs, and wherever it can be picked up.[41]

[38] 1 LQV, I, pp. 81–2.
[39] See *The Wrong Box*, passim.
[40] 1 LQV, I, p. 105.
[41] Ibid., p. 358.

Prince Albert, with the enforced patience of Sisyphus, tried to impose some system upon this welter of contingencies. He never succeeded, because no logical system could be made to fit the changing complex of precedents, necessities, claims and concessions that faced an executive government that was perpetually the plexus of political dispute. Politicians might dine together in private, but they were often adversaries in public, and what was asserted by one would be denied by another. The Prince was always seeking to formulate a theory of the Court as an autonomous estate of the realm, the senior partner in the formulation of public policy and the choice of the best men to execute it.

> Nowhere does the Constitution demand an indifference on the part of the sovereign to the march of political events, and nowhere would such indifference be more condemned and justly despised than in England . . .
>
> Why are Princes alone to be denied the credit of having political opinions based upon an anxiety for the national interests and honour of their country and the welfare of mankind? Are they not more independently placed than any other politician in the State? Are their interests not most intimately bound up with those of their country? Is the sovereign not the natural guardian of the honour of his country, is he not *necessarily* a politician? Has he no duties to perform towards his country?[42]

The Prince was no more successful in persuading Ministers to accept his version of monarchical ideology than he was in codifying his own ambiguous position. He was clear enough about what he thought his part ought to be :

> As the natural head of her family, superintendent of her household, manager of her private affairs, sole *confidential* adviser in politics, and only assistant in her communications with the officers of the government, he is, besides the husband of the Queen, the tutor of the royal children, the private secretary of the sovereign, and her permanent minister.[43]

[42] Quoted in Brian Connell, *Regina v. Palmerston* (1962), p. 142.
[43] Roger Fulford, *The Prince Consort* (1949), p. 63.

It was the last of these capacities that no politician could ever concede to the Prince; he could never be the Queen's 'minister', Gladstone wrote, because his conduct was not controllable by Parliament. From this there followed the rejection of other aspirations to be more closely involved in politics : the Consort could not decently go into Cabinet to be out-argued and sometimes outvoted—'for in Cabinets, and even in the Cabinets reputed best, important questions have sometimes been found to admit of no other form of decision'.[44] The Prince could not be a 'minister' for the same reason that he could not be Commander-in-Chief—because he could not be dismissed. Resignation was a powerful weapon in the hands of Ministers because they might be supported either in the House of Commons or by the electorate, and the Crown could not afford to be seen to be defeated. It was doubtful whether the Queen ever appreciated how dangerous her own situation might become. It was legitimate, therefore, for Ministers to regard themselves as putting pressure on the Crown for its own protection. The Queen would, no doubt, have regarded as preposterous the suggestion that Gladstone was one of the most devoted royalists who ever served the House of Hanover, not least in his understanding that the preservation of the monarchy could not always be entrusted to its incumbent. He did not think that it could be preserved indefinitely. He wrote, in 1870 :

For our time as a Government, and my time as a politician, Royalty will do well enough in this country, because it has a large fund to draw upon, which was greatly augmented by good husbandry in the early and middle part of this reign, and which is not yet exhausted.

But the fund of credit is diminishing, and I do not see from whence it is to be replenished as matters now go . . . the outlook for ten, twenty, thirty, forty years hence is a very melancholy one.[45]

The most successful exertion of royal power during the Queen's reign was the dismissal of Lord Palmerston from the

---

[44] Gladstone, op. cit., pp. 37, 85.
[45] Quoted in Hanham, *The Nineteenth Century Constitution* (1969), p. 33.

Foreign Secretaryship in 1851; the episode demonstrates both the strength and the weakness of the Queen's position. In her salad days before her marriage, the Queen's relations with Palmerston had been cordial, and even girlishly gay; she asked for his advice on protocol, and was grateful to him when he gave it to her. But between Palmerston's departure from the Foreign Office in 1841 and his return to it in 1846, the Queen had changed and the tone and flavour of the Court were very different. The Court had become much more serious, more high-minded, more business-like, and much more disapproving of irregularities of all kinds; a sense of humour had gone out from it. Moreover, the Queen and the Prince now had their own network of foreign intelligence which, since it came directly from their blood relations, was nearly always different in emphasis, and sometimes more accurate, than that transmitted by British ambassadors and ministers abroad. In the eyes of the Court, Palmerston began to appear as a zealot—conservative, perhaps, at home, but a dangerous troubler of the waters abroad. The first extended arguments came over the affairs of Portugal; the Court's information came more quickly than that reaching the Foreign Office, and had a different bias. Palmerston found added to his ordinary labours those of conducting a formidable correspondence with the Court, requiring detailed explanations upon particular points. Bagehot, in his 'right to be consulted', never did justice to the Queen's pitilessness as a letter-writer; she did not demand a right to be 'kept in the picture' but to argue and be argued with. Her talents were buttressed by a memory of astonishing exactness. (Sir Henry Campbell-Bannerman told Ponsonby that once, when he was trying to persuade the Queen to withdraw an objection to some measure, she said: 'I remember Lord Melbourne using the same argument many years ago, but it was not true then and it is not true now.' Campbell-Bannerman said that he felt 'like a little boy talking to his grandmother'.[46]) And there was one priceless weapon of which the Queen could never be deprived: she could always waste her Ministers' time.

Palmerston found it tedious to be arguing on two fronts,

---

[46] Sir Frederick Ponsonby, *Recollections of Three Reigns* (1950), p. 12.

with foreign courts as well as his own. Very soon, he received a new complaint—that despatches were being sent before they had received the Queen's approval and had been amended to her satisfaction. Palmerston's exculpations were a descant upon two themes, pressure of business and the need for speed. The Queen thought that neither of these was a sufficient excuse. She and the Prince had a well-founded suspicion that Palmerston was concerned to present them—and sometimes his Cabinet colleagues as well—with *faits accomplis*, and that to this end he deliberately delayed his despatches until the post was about to leave.

There was another source of friction. Palmerston once told Russell that he was the sole decider of whom he would have in his house. He claimed a similar discretion in what he called his private correspondence, indicating that there was a distinction between the official views of Her Majesty's Government and such personal opinions as the Foreign Secretary might choose to express to British ministers abroad and foreign envoys at home. To this, it could reasonably be rejoined that the Foreign Secretary was not a private person. The protracted Portuguese affair was critical for future relations, because it imprinted at Court a chronic mistrust of Palmerston, so that his communications thereafter were subjected to microscopic and hostile scrutiny. The Queen frequently used the Prime Minister, and sometimes the full Cabinet, as a court of appeal against the Foreign Secretary. New differences arose, over policy towards Spain, Greece and the states of Italy, and these were overlaid by conflicting philosophies. Palmerston tended to regard the promotion of constitutional government abroad as a self-evident British interest; this often led him to countenance intrigue with opposition groups abroad; and this in turn produced friction with established governments, especially as opposition in an autocratic state was, almost by definition, clandestine. (Palmerston was not invariably consistent, and his liking for oppositions did not always include those that were French; he had, after all, come to manhood during the revolutionary wars.) The Court saw in Palmerston's diplomacy a danger both to monarchy and to European stability. On 29 August 1847, the Prince seemed to regard as well-founded the prevalent accusation against us that we are, for selfish purposes, trying to disseminate disorder and anarchy in all other States, in the name of liberty, which was the course the French Jacobins pursued . . .[47]

The Court did not mince its words. Palmerston was reported to the Prime Minister, for one of his draft despatches on Portugal, with the comment: 'The Queen thinks this almost a mockery of Lord John, the Cabinet, the country and herself which can really not go on so.'[48] Furthermore, Palmerston 'was not always straightforward in his conduct and kept back things which he did not like should be known'.[49] On 19 September 1848, she discussed Palmerston again with the Prime Minister and said that she could 'hardly go on with him'[50], and she wrote in her journal that a time might come when she 'could not put up with Palmerston any longer'.[51]

The Queen's expostulations achieved little immediately, because the Cabinet as a whole supported Palmerston's general policy, although there were some who were not happy with the tone of his language or the temper of some of his remonstrances. Apart from the general convention that a Foreign Secretary could expect a degree of immunity from day-to-day intervention by the Cabinet, Palmerston was not easy to 'group' or to isolate. His colleagues were reluctant to provoke a resignation that would certainly take him into opposition: at a time of party confusion and of friable majorities, the accretion of even one major politician to the Opposition might be enough to bring down a Ministry (as Palmerston had the satisfaction of demonstrating in 1852). Russell tried a well-thumbed manoeuvre in 1849, when he tried to persuade Palmerston to give up the Foreign Office to Lord Lansdowne and go to Ireland as Lord-Lieutenant; but Palmerston, who knew a poisoned chalice when he saw one, refused and Russell was not in a strong enough position to insist. But, surprisingly, Palmerston did not demur when Russell, at the Court's

---

[47] Connell, op. cit., p. 64.
[48] Ibid., p. 70.
[49] Ibid., p. 97.
[50] 1 LQV, II, p. 195.
[51] Connell, op. cit., p. 97.

insistence, gave an instruction that all Foreign Office drafts should go to the Queen for prior approval, merely pointing out that 28,000 despatches had been sent and received in the previous year.[52]

The Court's hostility became more intense in 1850. An incident, ten years old, was resurrected, when Palmerston had been extruded from the bedroom of one of the Queen's ladies-in-waiting. (Palmerston's explanation was to the effect that he had expected to find someone else there, and that if people changed their rooms without warning they must take the consequences.) But this, though it might be evidence of moral fickleness, was hardly cause for dismissal from office. ('I have known ten Prime Ministers,' Gladstone once said, 'and all but one of them were adulterers.') However, in his handling of the Don Pacifico affair, Palmerston got his colleagues into a scrape; although they decided that, on grounds of collective responsibility, they must stand or fall with him on that issue, Russell assured the Court that, once the crisis was over, he would 'no longer remain in office with Lord Palmerston as Foreign Secretary'.[53]

Russell was forced to eat his words. Palmerston might have got his colleagues into a scrape by his actions, but he got them out of it again by his oratory. The House of Lords had passed a resolution of censure which the Cabinet felt itself bound to counter in the House of Commons. J. A. Roebuck, a paradigm of the independent member, was put up to move a motion of general approbation; Roebuck was always a good indicator of the temper of the 'radical-conservative' wing of the Liberal coalition. The Government was opposed by a formidable battery—by Peel (in his last parliamentary speech), Disraeli, Gladstone, Bright, Cobden. The result was that Palmerston, after speaking 'from the dusk of one day to the dawn of the next', was vindicated by the votes of the House of Commons. With this triumph behind him, he was in no mood for a change of office. The Court was against him; the Prime Minister was willing to wound but afraid to strike; the Cabinet sometimes found him an uncomfortable colleague.

[52] 1 LQV, II, p. 221.
[53] Ibid., p. 243.

But while the Court objected both to the substance and the manner of his diplomacy, the Cabinet objected, if at all, only to the manner, to what Russell called 'the faults of carrying a good policy into effect by means too violent and abrupt and a demeanour which causes undefined alarm'.[54] The Queen, with grudging reluctance, was constrained to endure Palmerston still further, although she was 'personally convinced that Lord Palmerston at this moment is secretly planning an armed intervention in Schleswig . . .'[55] The Court, however, was able to extract one concession that was to be of importance later, a formal statement of the relations that ought to subsist between the Queen and the Foreign Secretary. The prototype of this statement had been drawn up by Baron Stockmar in March 1850; on 12 August, the Queen incorporated it in a letter to Russell:

> . . . she thinks it right, in order to *prevent any mistake* for the *future*, shortly to explain *what it is she expects from her Foreign Secretary*. She requires: (1) That he will distinctly state what he proposes in a given case, in order that the Queen may know as distinctly to *what* she has given her Royal sanction; (2) Having *once given* her sanction to a measure, that it not be arbitrarily altered or modified by the Minister; such an act she must consider as failing in sincerity towards the Crown, and justly to be visited by her Constitutional right of dismissing that Minister. She expects to be kept informed of what passes between him and the Foreign Ministers before important decisions are taken, based upon that intercourse; to receive the Foreign Despatches in good time, and to have the drafts for approval sent to her in sufficient time to make herself acquainted with their contents before they must be sent off. The Queen thinks it best that Lord John Russell should show this letter to Lord Palmerston.[56]

Palmerston accepted these conditions, but he did not let them affect his behaviour for long. But he weakened his position, in the matter of the reception of Kossuth, by setting

[54] Connell, op. cit., p. 120.
[55] Ibid., p. 122.
[56] 1 LQV, II, p. 264.

himself against Court, Prime Minister and Cabinet; he seemed to be trying to have it both ways. His first reaction to Russell's request not to receive Kossuth—that he would choose whom he would receive in his own house, as the Prime Minister would doubtless choose whom he would retain in his Cabinet —could not be squared with his public office or his obligation to his colleagues. Then, after he had apparently given way, it seemed that he had made his point after all, by having his words reported in the press after what was called a purely private gathering. Palmerston had allowed himself to appear as disingenuous. Thus he had already slighted and irritated his colleagues when he expressed his private approval, in advance of any Cabinet decision, of Louis Napoleon's *coup d'état* of 2 December 1851. Palmerston had, at last, isolated himself; and those who sang or recited doggerel about how 'small Lord John' had dismissed 'the people's darling' did not count where it mattered. Russell wrote to ask for Palmerston's resignation, having come to the 'painful conclusion . . . that the conduct of foreign affairs can no longer be left in your hands with advantage to the country'. Palmerston put up no effective resistance, either to Russell or in Parliament. This time, the 'floating vote' was not with him. The approval of an autocratic *coup*, however useful that might be in promoting stability and discouraging revolutionaries in France, did not commend itself to those Radicals who had voted for him in the Don Pacifico division. Indeed, Russell's disclosure to the House of Commons of the conditions which Palmerston had accepted had a double and decisive effect, alienating those who thought that it was ungentlemanly conduct to have broken an undertaking, and those who thought that no such undertaking should have been given. Russell's action, however, probably forestalled a serious constitutional crisis; if the Queen meant what she wrote in her journal for 20 December, she had made up her mind to put the 'constitutional right' of dismissal to the test :

It [*sc.* Palmerston's departure] is a great and unexpected mercy, for I really was on the point of declaring on my part that I could no longer retain Lord Palmerston which would have been a most disagreeable task, and not unattended with a small amount of danger, inasmuch as it would have put me too prominently forward.[57]

It is by no means easy to generalise about this episode. It is possible to argue that the Queen was attempting to put the Prince's doctrines into practice; it is even likely that Stockmar was seeking for ways of reviving the exercise of the prerogative. The monarch had always claimed special rights of consultation in foreign affairs; what made the contest so difficult to resolve was that the Queen was not complaining about Palmerston's manners as much as her Ministry's foreign policy. The critical sanction attached to her claim to influence, that of dismissal never became an issue; Palmerston had put himself in the wrong, by flouting his colleagues. His resignation, therefore, may also be interpreted as an example of the enforcement of collective responsibility. None the less, the Queen got what she wanted. As Palmerston's successor, the Cabinet preferred Lord Granville to the Court's wish for Lord Clarendon; the Court made a formal complaint, but did not press the matter.

The Queen protested against the Cabinet's taking upon itself the appointment of its own Members, which rested entirely with the Prime Minister and the Sovereign, under whose approval the former constructed his Government . . .[58]

'Collective responsibility' was approved by the Court when it was used to resist parliamentary encroachment, deplored when it appeared as an obstacle to the 'legitimate influence' of the Crown. On 10 October 1853, the Prince told Sir James Graham that he thought that Lord Aberdeen's anxiety to maintain Cabinet unity was harmful, by producing concessions that materially altered policy without achieving permanent agreement.

---

[57] Connell, op. cit., p. 134.
[58] 1 LQV, II, pp. 345–6.

Lord Aberdeen renounced one of the chief sources of strength in the Cabinet, by not making it apparent that he requires the sanction of the Crown to the course proposed by the Cabinet, and has to justify his advice by argument before it can be accepted, and that it does not suffice to come to a decision at the table of the Cabinet.[59]

This assumed that there was an alliance between the Prime Minister and the Court, with the rest of the Cabinet as a potential enemy of both. The Prince's complaint missed the point that collective responsibility could protect the Cabinet both against Parliament and the Queen. On the other hand, the Queen expected discipline in the ranks when it came to supporting a Cabinet decision of which she did approve.

The Queen hopes Lord Palmerston will make it quite clear to the subordinate Members of the Government that they cannot be allowed to vote against the Government proposal about the National Gallery tomorrow, as she hears that several fancy themselves at liberty to do.[60]

There were three areas in which the Queen was especially alert to any threats to her prerogative—foreign affairs, the Church and the Army. In foreign affairs, she and her Ministers often took a different view of where the national interest lay. Sometimes this was evident in public and led to criticism: during the Crimean War, a bizarre rumour spread that the Queen and Prince had been arrested for high treason, and credulous crowds gathered to watch for their arrival at the Tower of London. The Queen was supposed to have been pro-Prussian in 1870, because her daughter was the Crown Princess; but those who assumed that she was automatically on the side of those countries into whose ruling houses her children had married did not know her very well. There were times when she had very brisk passages of arms indeed with Ministers other than Lord Palmerston. Russell often attracted her wrath. He was not a tactful man.[61] The Queen did not

---

[59] Ibid., p. 455.
[60] 1 LQV, III, p. 186.
[61] J. Prest, *Lord John Russell*, passim.

relish, during the crisis of Italian unification, receiving from him an essay on Whig principles, including the reminder that 'all power held by Sovereigns may be forfeited by misconduct, and each nation is the judge of its own internal government'.[62] A month later, she reported Russell to Palmerston for insubordination, as she had in the past reported Palmerston to Russell. To one demand for an explanation, she had received the reply: 'Lord John Russell unfortunately does not partake of your Majesty's opinions in regard to Italy, and he is unwilling to obtrude on your Majesty unnecessary statements of his views.' Up with this she would not put, but she was relatively restrained when she wrote to Palmerston to remind him that ministers

> are responsible for the advice they gave her, but they are bound, fully, respectfully and openly to place before her the grounds and reasons upon which their advice may be founded, to enable her to judge whether she can give her assent to that advice or not. The Government must come to a standstill if the Minister meets a demand for an explanation with an answer like the following: 'I was asked by the Cabinet to give an answer, but as I do not agree with you, I think it useless to explain my views.'[63]

Beneath these exchanges there was a deep division of opinion between her and all her Ministries on the status of 'advice'. To her, this was not a term of art; it was counsel which she could accept or reject at pleasure tempered by prudence. As government became more 'popular', Ministers for their own survival had to interpret advice as a considered conclusion, which they might have to justify collectively to Parliament, and which the Queen therefore could not, in the last resort, be permitted to reject. On the whole, the forebearance of Ministers prevented the issue from ever coming to a head-on collision of principle; but there were repeated occasions when the prestige of the Court was at risk, when rumours spread that Queen and Ministers were at odds where

[62] 1 LQV, III, p. 383.
[63] Ibid., p. 388.

public sentiment was on their side. Thus, during the Schleswig–
Holstein crisis of 1864, when public sentiment was on the side
of the duchies, Palmerston warned her that she was reputed
to have taken up an unpopular pro-German attitude, and that
it was said that she had 'expressed personal opinions on the
affairs of Germany and Denmark which have embarrassed the
course of the Government'. She found it necessary to admonish
Russell : 'She must observe that she does not require to be
reminded of the honour of England, which touches her more
nearly than anyone else.'[64] The rumours were serious enough
for Lord Derby to take the rare course of referring publicly
to the belief that there was 'some unseen obstacle' in the path
of Ministers. The Queen always spoke her mind without
reserve in her private circle, and in this instance it seems that
General Grey and Sir Charles Phipps had been less than
discreet in repeating her remarks; Grey apologised to her for
not having been more guarded in his language.[65]

IV

No English sovereign endured with equanimity the erosion of
the prerogative, and where the Army was concerned the Queen
carried on, with particular intensity, the customary struggle
on two fronts—to preserve the executive's independence against
the House of Commons and her own against the Cabinet.
From first to last, the Queen interpreted literally the designation
'the armed forces of the Crown'. There is a more personal
tone in her correspondence about the Army than there is about
the Royal Navy. The clashes came when the Secretary of
State for War was at odds with the Commander-in-Chief.[66]
(The quarrel between the Frockcoats and the Brasshats during
the Great War was one of respectable antiquity.) Like the
Queen, Ministers had no wish to see Parliament prying into
the administration and day-to-day workings of the armed
forces; unlike her, they insisted that the last word must lie

with the Cabinet and not with the soldiers. This meant that, in the last resort, they would not resist a determined House of Commons. While he lived, the Queen found a certain ally in the Duke of Wellington; his suggestion that the Prince should become Commander-in-Chief was not concerned with military merit but with placing a royal obstacle in the path of parliamentary encroachment.

In April 1841, the Cabinet formally considered the conduct of Lord Cardigan, which had been particularly strange during the past year, in anticipation of a motion in the House of Commons praying the Queen to remove him from the command of the 11th Hussars. The opinion of the Prime Minister, Lord Melbourne, was that 'nothing is more to be apprehended and deprecated than such an interference of the House of Commons with the interior discipline and government of the Army'.[67] What he meant was that the decision must lie with the Cabinet. The Ministry was, however, in its last days, and Cardigan was saved by the influence of the Duke of Wellington, who was determined that no precedent should be set of civilian supervision of military discipline. (The Duke did not live to see the consequences of Cardigan's preservation on military operations in the Crimea.)

On the same grounds, the Queen did not want the report of the committee of inquiry into the conduct of the Crimean War to be tabled in Parliament. In a letter which she instructed Palmerston to read to the Cabinet, she said :

> It is quite evident that if matters are left so and military officers of the Queen's Army are to be judged as to the manner in which they have discharged their military duties before an enemy by a Committee of the House of Commons, the command of the Army is at once transferred from the Crown to that Assembly.[68]

This was the argument of the wedge, with a vengeance. The Queen was fighting a losing battle on the principle of political control, but she fought it with the greatest tenacity, giving up

[67] 1 LQV, I, p. 262.
[68] 1 LQV, III, p. 174.

positions only when they were hopelessly outflanked, and keeping open a sharp eye for any fallen outpost that might be recaptured. She found it distressing that the Government had surrendered a prerogative of the Crown in 1858, with the statutory provision that the newly-created Indian Army was not to be employed outside India without parliamentary sanction.[69]

Fortunately for her Ministers, the Queen's interest in the Army was not fortified by the same intimate knowledge that she claimed to possess on foreign affairs. She was concerned with the broad constitutional issue, and that could not be divorced from the personalities at the head of the War Office and the Horseguards. There was not much friction when the Duke of Wellington or Lord Hill was Commander-in-Chief, but the controversy became more heated after 1856, when the office was held by her cousin, the Duke of Cambridge. The Queen persisted in regarding the rights and duties of the Commander-in-Chief as settled; what mattered to her, therefore, was who was to be Secretary of State for War. When General Peel resigned in 1867 and Disraeli told her that Lord Derby was considering appointing Lord Grosvenor to succeed him at the War Office,

> Her Majesty did not seem to think, that young men of no official experience, and of no shining abilities, were fitted for such offices as Secretary for War. Her Majesty said in her present state of health she really had neither inclination nor energy sufficient to educate boys for such offices as War and Admiralty.[70]

The office went to Sir John Pakington.

From 1856 until 1895, the Duke of Cambridge conducted a delaying action against the changes which reformers urged upon him. He was astute at appealing to his vested rights, and he found the Queen to be an ardent ally, although her support was always tempered by consideration for her own position. She was not convinced of the wisdom of Cardwell's reforms,

[69] Ibid., p. 294.
[70] 2 LQV, I, p. 397.

although she did consent to the issue of a royal warrant abolishing the purchase of commissions, as a means of avoiding the obstruction of the House of Lords. Her dislike of the substance of the change was mollified by the form in which it was made; that exercise of the prerogative was a defeat for Whig principles, by whomever they were expressed. (Russell, who liked to think that the principles of Charles James Fox remained incarnate in his own person, never quite forgave Gladstone for that recourse to the prerogative.) She could not approve but could not prevent the formal subordination of the Commander-in-Chief to the Secretary of State in the Army Regulation Bill of 1871; indeed, at the Ministry's insistence she put pressure on the Duke of Cambridge to speak in the House of Lords to the effect that the Bill ought to pass. She also warned him that loose talk about the reforms and their authors by him, his staff or his family would be damaging to his office and thus to the Crown.[71]

However, the passage of the Bill did not extinguish the Duke's pretensions. When Childers became Secretary of State for War, in Gladstone's second administration in 1880, the Duke wrote to him :

> The command of the Army rests with the Commander-in-Chief, as representing the Sovereign; the Secretary of State is the high political official who controls all army matters and represents the departments, for which he is fully responsible to Parliament. But he certainly does not command the army . . . the Commander-in-Chief cannot be merged in the Secretary of State, under present conditions, and my position must have an individuality, which it is essential and necessary to maintain . . .[72]

No Secretary of State, with the possible but unlikely exception of Wellington in 1834, would have claimed to command the Army; but the Duke's definition of his own position was one that no Ministry of the time could accept. Childers was firm : 'To say that the Secretary of State has no controlling power

[71] 2 LQV, II, pp. 141–7, 150–1.
[72] Hamer, op. cit., pp. 38–9.

in such matters, when he is responsible to Parliament for any improper exercise of the Queen's prerogative . . . is manifestly absurd.'[73] Childers won his point, but the Queen did not forgive him and successfully refused to have him back at the War Office when Gladstone formed his third administration in 1886.[74]

The Queen claimed a voice in the choice of soldiers for high command. In 1879, Lord Beaconsfield had difficulty in persuading her to agree to the appointment of Sir Garnet Wolseley as High Commissioner and Commander-in-Chief in South-East Africa; she objected partly because she thought that to give the double office to Wolseley would amount to condemnation of Sir Bartle Frere and Lord Chelmsford, both of whom would be superseded, and partly because the Duke of Cambridge preferred Lord Napier of Magdala to Wolseley.[75] It took Lord Beaconsfield some time to get his own way, but he managed it in the end by adroitness, tact and by steering the argument away from the issue of principle. He wrote to Lady Chesterfield, on 28 May 1879 : 'We have had a terrible time of it : six Cabinets in eight days. I believe it never happened before. However, Sir Garnet Wolseley goes to S. Africa, and goes tomorrow night, tho', between ourselves, the Horse Guards are furious, the Princes all raging, and every mediocrity as jealous as if we had prevented him from conquering the world.'[76] In one of those letters in which he claimed to write to the Queen 'with that complete and unlimited confidence which, he trusts, has always distinguished the remarks he has the honor of submitting to his Sovereign', Beaconsfield added the reassuring comment : 'It is quite true that Wolseley is an egoist and a braggart. So was Nelson.'[77] Later, the Queen found in Wolseley a useful stick with which to beat Gladstone. She urged Gladstone's Cabinet to give him a free hand in Egypt (and told Ponsonby to tell Wolseley that she had done so), encouraged Lady Wolseley to egg on her

[73] Ibid.
[74] 3 LQV, I, p. 38.
[75] W. F. Monypenny and G. E. Buckle, *Life of Disraeli* (ed. of 1929), vol. II, p. 1302.
[76] Ibid., p. 1305.
[77] Ibid., p. 1307.

husband to use high words with the Government and threaten to resign, and allowed Wolseley himself, without rebuke, to write her a letter which contained general abuse of the Prime Minister :

> It is very disheartening to the soldiers of this army to find that Mr Gladstone and all his colleagues have completely ignored all the toil they endured without a murmur on the river, all the fatiguing marches under a burning sun in the desert, and all the severe fighting they have had. It is very ungracious on Mr Gladstone's part, seeing that it is his fault that all these trials have been endured in vain, and all our dead comrades killed to no purpose. He might have said a few cheering words to these soldiers : they would have cost him nothing, and even from him, unpopular as he is in the army, they would have been valued. However, if the Queen is satisfied with the conduct of her troops, I don't think our men care very much what Mr Gladstone may think of them : *they* certainly don't think much of *him*.[78]

In 1890, the Queen thought the report of the Hartington Commission to be 'really abominable', talked about her constitutional duty to 'hand down . . . her crown unimpaired', insisted that she would not permit the Commander-in-Chief to be reduced to a mere cypher, and claimed that 'one of the greatest prerogatives of the Sovereign is the *direct communication*, with an immovable and non-political officer of high rank, *about the Army*'.[79] The Duke of Cambridge's command was prolonged until 1895 ; then, the Queen herself wrote to him, at Ministers' request, to say that the end was inevitable. She was emphatic, however, that her action should not be construed as prejudging the future claims of her son the Duke of Connaught.[80]

Conflict between the Secretary of State and the Commander-in-Chief did not end with the retirement of the Duke of Cambridge ; Wolseley, who succeeded him, could be quite as vexatious to civilians, in his own way. The Queen maintained her claims until her death. On 19 December 1899, after the decision had been taken to send Lord Roberts to South Africa to supersede Sir Redvers Buller in the chief command, Balfour wrote to Lord Salisbury:

> When I arrived at Windsor yesterday, I found Bigge full of grievances as to the recent treatment of the Queen by her Ministers. According to him, she complained
> (1) that no account of the Defence Committee's proceedings had been sent to her on Saturday;
> (2) that she had not been consulted before the telegram ordering Buller to relieve Ladysmith was sent;
> (3) that Roberts had been appointed without giving her an opportunity of expressing an opinion; and
> (4) that the Commander-in-Chief had not been consulted with regard to this important military decision.
> I told Bigge as regards (1) that Roberts was really asked to command in South Africa not on Saturday but on Sunday afternoon . . .
> As regards (2) I said that this represented a theory of constitutional government which I could not accept. The Queen's advisers *must* be permitted to issue important military orders without her previous sanction.
> As regards (3) I had absolutely no excuse to offer . . .
> As regards (4) I told him that it was impossible to consult the Commander-in-Chief upon such an appointment, as his well-known jealousy of Roberts made his advice on such a subject perfectly worthless.[81]

One of the last political actions of the Queen's life was to attempt, unsuccessfully, to persuade the Cabinet to withdraw its undertaking to set up a commission of inquiry into the conduct of the war in South Africa, as soon as it was over. She had not forgotten the inquiry into the Crimean War.

v

The Queen took Church patronage very seriously, and as her Prime Ministers did the same disagreements between them were especially lively. These matters were unusually com-

[81] Blanche Dugdale, *Arthur James Balfour* (1939), vol. I, p. 224.

plicated, and there were pitfalls of all kinds to trap the unwary in an age when religion was probably more important than economics as a source of political division. Not only were there doctrinal discords within the Church of England but there was also the question (especially when Liberal Governments were in power) of how Nonconformists would react to a particular Anglican appointment. Moreover, ecclesiastical preferment was generally regarded as a barometer from which the general intentions of a Ministry might be read; and the actions of ecclesiastical persons of all ranks could easily become politically embarrassing.

> Tract XC, Hampden, Gorham, Papal Aggression, St. Barnabas, Manning, Denison, St. George's-in-the-East, *Essays and Reviews*, Colenso, Mackonochie, Penzance, Green, King— each name rang like a tocsin arousing men to defend the right and attack the wrong, and every Prime Minister was aware that he had it in his power to add to the list.[82]

The Queen had her own views: in matters of doctrine, she was for sturdy moderation. She had her own sources of information, and the Deans of Windsor were, in matters of church, the analogues of her private secretaries in matters of state. Palmerston always insisted upon the primacy of the Queen's official over her non-official advisers; he was of a Low Church persuasion, and appointments when he was Prime Minister often took the form of contests between candidates favoured by the Dean of Windsor and those favoured by Lord Shaftesbury. In 1864, the Queen objected to Palmerston's recommendation of Dr Jeune as Bishop of Peterborough, on the ground that he had only recently been appointed as Dean of Lincoln. Palmerston replied:

> All that the first Minister of the Crown can do is to pick out for ecclesiastical dignities men whom he has reason to believe fit for the posts to be filled, without at all undertaking that other persons, if they had the duty of advising your Majesty, might not in the crowd find others who might in many

---

[82] D. W. R. Bahlman, 'The Queen, Mr Gladstone and Church patronage', 3 *Victorian Studies* (1930), p. 351.

respects be equally fit; but the responsibility of advising your Majesty must rest with somebody, and it happens to rest with the First Lord of the Treasury.[83]

Plainly, he did not regard 'advice' as equivalent to 'helpful suggestion'. In July 1864, he did comply with the Queen's request to have more than one name submitted to her for appointment to the united cures of Canon of Westminster and Rector of St. Margaret's, but added that 'this in some degree implies a reference of a recommendation by one of your Majesty's responsible advisers to your Majesty's irresponsible advisers in such matters . . .' The Queen would not concede that the Prime Minister had a monopoly; he could, she replied, 'never pretend that the Sovereign has not the right, as everyone else has, to ask anyone she chooses about anyone who is recommended for an appointment to her'.[84]

Whether a Prime Minister prevailed over the Queen depended largely on how much time and energy he was prepared to expend in the contest and what he thought the opportunity-cost of that particular victory might be when, as was usually the case, there was a variety of other matters in dispute at the same time. Even those Prime Ministers whom the Queen liked and trusted seldom found their recommendations accepted without argument. The Queen took seriously her title of 'supreme head' of the Church, and it was prudent of Gladstone to resist the temptation to explain to her that the view which she took of her position was legally and doctrinally erroneous. In general, she wanted no Puseyites, no persons inclined to Romishness, no zealots. She was never forgetful of her position in the Established Church of Scotland, and she tended to think rather meanly of bishops as a class.

On the death of Archbishop Langley, the Queen had her way in preferring Bishop Tait of London (who, incidentally, happened to be a Liberal) to Disraeli's choice of Bishop Ellicott of Gloucester; she had asked Dean Wellesley, of Windsor, what he thought, and Wellesley was against Ellicott. To the dismay of her Prime Ministers, the Queen was often quite uncon-

[83] 2 LQV, I, pp. 177–9.
[84] Ibid., pp. 286–7.

cerned with the political nuances of her own preferences. Disraeli commented, when in 1875 she sent him a list of clerics whom she was prepared to approve in advance for vacancies as they occurred, that there would be a 'disruption of the Cabinet' if some of them were preferred. Even a Prime Minister as favoured as Disraeli was made aware of some of the limitations and tribulations of his office when he set out on a long journey around the Queen's objections to his efforts to find suitable promotion, as an act of *pietas*, for the Reverend Sydney Turner, founder of reformatories and son of Sharon Turner, historian and friend of the late Isaac D'Israeli. It took a great deal of time, pleading and correspondence before Turner was safely lodged as Dean of Ripon.

The Queen always regarded the deanship of Windsor as an office for which her own preference ought to be unchallenged. When Wellesley died in 1882, she appointed Henry Connor, vicar of Newport in the Isle of Wight; she told Gladstone that she did not wish to receive advice. Within a year Connor was dead, and the Queen then acted very swiftly indeed in asking Archbishop Benson whether he thought that Boyd Carpenter or Randall Davidson would be fitter as a successor. Benson favoured Davidson. Gladstone would have preferred someone older (Davidson was 35) but, as he wrote rather wearily to Ponsonby:

> I should have submitted my scruple on the score of age to her Majesty, had I not been estopped by the heavy artillery she was pleased to bring into the field, which reduced my little point to dust and ashes.[85]

The loss of Wellesley was potentially serious; he had the standing and the age to act as an intermediary and sometimes as a buffer between Queen and Prime Minister. Sometimes, too, she said things to Wellesley that she wanted other people to hear. In 1874, the Queen wanted legislation against ritualism, and she got it in Archbishop Tait's Public Worship Regulation Bill, which started as a private member's Bill in the House of Lords, and was then practically taken over by the Cabinet,

[85] 2 LQV, III, p. 421.

somewhat to its embarrassment. Dean Wellesley told the Archbishop that the Queen had written to him that 'if my faithful Commons had not supported me, I should have been fain to give up my heavy crown to some of my Italian cousins —the representatives of the Stuarts'.[86]

Such remarks need not be taken too seriously; the Queen occasionally used emotional blackmail as a weapon. In fact, she was able to disagree with most of her Prime Ministers without acerbity. She was successful in opposing Salisbury's choice for the see of Oxford in 1888. 'She is greatly opposed to Canon Liddon being made a Bishop, but Bishop [of] Oxford he must never be. He might ruin and taint all the young men as Pusey and others did before him . . .'[87] But Salisbury could stand firm when he thought the matter important enough. In 1890, he would not have Randall Davidson when the Queen wanted him as Bishop of Winchester; it would, he said in effect, look like a job. The Queen asked the Archbishop of Canterbury to intervene, but Davidson became Bishop of Rochester instead of Winchester. The Queen gave way to Rosebery, who wanted Percival as Bishop of Hereford, after an opening broadside that she would 'on no account appoint a Disestablisher'.[88] She had the satisfaction of being right about her warning that Percival would not be able to live in peace with the Anglican community in his diocese.

These encounters were unmalicious, with one massive exception—the Queen's behaviour towards Gladstone. At least one student of their relationship has concluded that, after 1880, the Queen tried to nag Gladstone into retirement.[89] In 1881, after the death of Dean Stanley of Westminster, she telegraphed to him a string of names in a tone peremptory enough to provoke him to write: 'Does she think the two positions of Sovereign and Minister are to be inverted?'[89] The substance of the objections which she made to Gladstone's proposal was no different from those which she made to his predecessors, but there is a rasping note of hostility in her communications

[86] Bahlman, op. cit., p. 362.
[87] 3 LQV, I, p. 427.
[88] 3 LQV, II, p. 468.
[89] Bahlman, op. cit.

with Gladstone. She wrote directly to him as seldom as she could; the fact that much of her correspondence with him was indirect meant that she could say things which common courtesy would otherwise have prevented. As always, however, she could win only when Gladstone chose not to insist. Their most hostile collision, in Church matters, came after the death of Archbishop Tait in 1882. For his successor, Gladstone wanted Bishop Benson of Winchester, aged 53; the Queen objected that he was too young. The Queen wanted Bishop Browne of Winchester, aged 71; Gladstone objected that he was too old. (The Queen purported to find this objection strange, since he was two years younger than the Prime Minister.) This fight coincided with another over Gladstone's wish to put into the Cabinet Sir Charles Dilke and the 15th Earl of Derby, one of whom the Queen detested as a republican and the other as a renegade. It seemed at times that relations between Queen and Prime Minister would explode into a public quarrel, and there was one occasion when Gladstone lost his temper, when he inferred from one of Ponsonby's letters that she was blatantly taking unofficial advice. But Gladstone had his way on all three appointments, at the cost of a great deal of unpleasantness. As Bahlman put it, the Queen was adding another to Bagehot's trinity of rights—the right to harass.

VI

What real power did the Queen have? She was, in a literal sense, a conservative. She disliked change very much, but she understood that its recognition, from time to time, was an act of necessity. She began her reign as an impulsive and immature Whig, and made herself unpopular with Tories as a result. Then, for twenty years, the predominating influence in her life was her husband. This was the period when the Court tried to behave in accordance with a theory of constitutional monarchy that contained both innovations and anachronisms. After the Prince's death, she went into seclusion, and often galled her Ministers by claiming special privileges on grounds of sex or health as excuses for not carrying out her ceremonial duties. In the 39 years of her reign after Prince Albert died, she opened Parliament in person only seven times.

At the end of her life, she was a Conservative partisan, but not because she had been corrupted by Disraeli. He certainly made use of her influence. She allowed him to cast her as the Faery. At the end, two lonely and bereaved people found a strange consolation in each other. But to argue that Disraeli bewitched her and that she became, as it were, an honorary member of the Primrose League in his memory, is to stretch the facts. Certainly, she mourned Disraeli; she regularly recorded the anniversary of his death in her journal, along with her other anniversaries of bereavement. But, underlying her affection for Disraeli was a deep agreement with the nature and purpose of government for which he claimed to stand. But agreement in principle did not entail agreement in detail, and Disraeli had his difficulties with her, like every other Prime Minister. It did not need Disraeli to turn her against Gladstone: she had found that relationship grating ever since 1871, when she quarrelled with him simultaneously over two issues—the insistence that she should stay at Windsor until the end of the parliamentary session, and that the Prince of Wales should be given something constructive to do. Bagehot, in the first paragraph of his chapter on the monarchy, had referred to 'a retired widow and an unemployed youth'; there was criticism that the Queen hoarded payment made to her on the Civil List—that she did not give value for public money; there was a brief flurry of republican sentiment. Gladstone had the best interests of the monarchy at heart in his unwelcome advice; that was what made him insufferable. The Queen would not be patronised.

She never adapted herself to the growth of parties as part of the working constitution. The general election of 1841 was the last in which the Queen attempted to exert influence; that was the end of a long process which had started with the Rockingham Ministry and been carried on under Lord Liverpool. This was made explicit, in relation to the borough of Windsor, in 1845. On 11 October, Peel wrote:

. . . the Queen does not wish to interfere in Elections and there is no separating in this matter the Court from the Sovereign.

The Prince tells me that the interference that did take place during the last administration was contrary to the express wishes of the Queen and himself. Non-Interference must therefore be the Rule—and I cannot authorise any acts or any declarations at variance with that principle. I cannot promise (to take the case specified by Col. Reid) 'that all the persons belonging to the Royal Establishments who have votes, shall be *required* to support Col. Reid'.

Neither can I sanction 'an authorised intimation to the Royal Tradesmen that Col. Reid has the best wishes of the Court'.

Such things would be wholly at variance with that principle to which Her Majesty wishes to adhere, not with reference merely to this Election but to all Elections at Windsor . . .[90]

She thought of herself, after 1841, as giving her confidence in terms of 'measures not men' and of promoting 'national' policies; but men could not be separated from measures as parties came to stand for different things. She never understood that men might find themselves committed to public programmes, especially when she disapproved of their content. She came to detest both Gladstone and his policy, but she found that policy no less distasteful when it was put forward by Rosebery, whom she chose and found personally agreeable.

The choice of Rosebery was open to her because no party had, by the 1890s, constructed a mechanism for the choice of its own leader. Since 1834, when Lord Grey retired, only one other Prime Minister in office had retired from politics, Lord Derby in 1868, and circumstances then pointed clearly to Disraeli as his successor. When Gladstone adjourned his leadership of the Liberals in 1875, the party chose, or accepted, Lord Hartington as leader in the Commons and Lord Granville in the Lords; the Queen communicated mostly with Granville. When Lord Beaconsfield died in 1881, the Conservatives likewise adopted dual leadership—Northcote in the Commons, Salisbury in the Lords. The Queen originally told Northcote

[90] N. Gash, *Politics in the Age of Peel* (1953), pp. 382–3.

that she would regard him as leader, for the purpose of communication; by 1885, when it came to a choice of Prime Minister, Northcote's standing had been diminished in the House of Commons, and circumstances pointed to Salisbury. When Gladstone resigned in 1894, he left no obvious successor, and the Queen could have pleaded, in equity, that there was a good reason why she should not ask for his advice. A politician of our own times has commented:

> No doubt her motive was rooted in prejudice : she wanted no more advice from Gladstone. But she was on strong ground. When a Prime Minister is forced out by his colleagues because, although they venerate his past, they no longer trust his judgment, it is hardly reasonable that he should be allowed to nominate his successor.[91]

Gladstone would have liked Lord Spencer, who was hardly an obvious choice. Radicals on the back benches would have liked Harcourt, but his Cabinet colleagues knew just how exasperating he could be, and the Queen was working with the grain of politics when she sent for Rosebery. She was exercising a casting vote rather than expressing a purely personal preference. She had made her soundings; but it is worth noting that her private secretary thought it necessary to remind her that parliamentary majorities had acquired rights. Ponsonby wrote to her, on 28 February 1894 :

> The general belief was that your Majesty would send for Lord Rosebery as the easiest solution of the difficulty and that the Liberals would press him to accept the offer if made.
>
> But Sir William Harcourt has said that he would not serve under Rosebery, and this may make some trouble.
>
> Lord Salisbury could not accept without a dissolution and the Duke of Devonshire must also have a change in the Representation.[92]

[91] Roy Jenkins, 'From Gladstone to Asquith', *History Today* (1964), p. 447.
[92] RA A69/77.

Rosebery accepted with typical reluctance. He did not, he said, want the *damnosa hereditas*: he would be dependent on the leader of the House of Commons while

> shut up in an enemy's prison . . . a Liberal Peer, as Prime Minister, is in a wholly false position. He cannot control the House of Commons, or his representative there, he can only watch them from the Strangers' Gallery.[93]

Nor could he control the House of Lords. A Conservative Prime Minister in the Lords was not in a position of similar weakness; none the less, Lord Derby had his difficulties over snap decisions on policy with Disraeli, and it was not mere nepotism when Salisbury chose Balfour, his trusted nephew, as leader of the House of Commons.

The Queen was invariably defeated when she was opposed by a united Cabinet. It is significant that Gladstone, the Prime Minister with whom her relations were worst, reintroduced the practice of sending formal Cabinet Minutes to the Queen. When the Cabinet was not united, there was a chance that the Queen could exploit the division to her own advantage. Depending upon the issue and her relations with the Prime Minister, she could be either a helpful auxiliary or an abrasive adversary. Disraeli was nearly always able to enlist her as an auxiliary. During the protracted arguments over the Second Reform Bill, he indicated that he would like her to whip some of his colleagues back into line: it might 'be necessary that the personal authority of your Majesty should be invoked and that the thunder of Olympus should sound!'[94] That thunder sounded from time to time during his second Ministry. For instance, she wrote to him on 16 July 1877: 'The Queen . . . must say—and she does not care if he repeats it—that she is *shocked* and *bitterly* disappointed at the conduct of the Chancellor, the Duke of Richmond and others!'[95] Gladstone thought it 'abominable' when he heard that certain Ministers had been summoned by the Queen for a 'wigging' because of

[93] RA Add. A/12/2137.
[94] 2 LQV, I, p. 414.
[95] RA B52/8.

their opinions. It was probably this use of the royal influence that he had in mind when he wrote, in 1878, of a Prime Minister's duties :

> He reports to the Sovereign its [*sc.* the Cabinet's] proceedings, and he also has many audiences of the august occupant of the Throne. He is bound, in these reports and audiences, not to counterwork the Cabinet; not to divide it; not to undermine the position of any of his colleagues in the Royal favour. If he departs in any degree from strict adherence to these rules, and uses his great opportunities to increase his own influence, or pursue aims not shared by his colleagues, then unless he is prepared to advise their dismissal, he not only departs from rule, but commits an act of treachery and baseness. As the Cabinet stands between the Sovereign and the Parliament, and is bound to be loyal to both, so he stands between his colleagues and the Sovereign, and is bound to be loyal to both . . .[96]

The Queen always wanted to know the individual opinions of Ministers, and she was remarkably successful in finding out what they were. She was by no means dependent only upon the Prime Minister's letter for her knowledge of what went on in the Cabinet; and even when Gladstone made a point of never revealing to her the details of Cabinet debates, Lord Granville, for one, often supplied her with extended accounts.

Until 1880, when she clearly regarded the Liberals' election victory as the triumph of a wanton attack upon 'national' policies, she identified herself with all her governments, once they were in office. She did not wish them to resign; she had no wish to see the House of Commons grow in power and pretension as the maker and unmaker of Her Majesty's Government. Thus she strongly urged Russell to carry on after Ministers had been beaten on Dunkellin's amendment to the Reform Bill of 1866, which she regarded as a defeat on a detail rather than a principle. Her advice was often shrewd, and she had excellent intuition of how the middle orders of her subjects were likely to react. One example may stand for many, when she would have no truckling to the cholera in 1854 :

[96] Gladstone, op. cit., pp. 242–4.

The Queen must repeat what she has frequently done, that she strongly objects to these *special* prayers which *are*, in fact, *not* a sign of gratitude or confidence in the Almighty—for if this is the course to be pursued we *ought* to have one for every *illness,* and certainly in '37 the influenza was notoriously more *fatal* than the cholera had ever been, and *yet no one* would have thought of having a prayer against *that.* . . . What is the use of the prayers in the Liturgy, which were no doubt composed when we were subject to other equally fatal diseases, if a new one is always to be framed specially for the cholera?[97]

The Government would have spared itself embarrassment in 1871, had it heeded the Queen's warning about how unpopular Lowe's tax on matches would be.[98]

She never regarded herself as, in Stockmar's phrase, 'a mandarin figure which has to nod its head in assent or shake it in denial as its Minister pleases'. She had learnt her doctrines before the consolidation of parties threw up leaders who could maintain themselves without recourse to royal influence, and before the expectation became general that the electoral pendulum would swing more or less regularly. She never, therefore, reconciled herself to being deprived of a government which she liked and confronted instead with politicians chosen elsewhere and with a programme of measures that she found obnoxious but unavoidable. It was in those circumstances that she deployed in full her formidable talents for remonstrance and delay. Joseph Chamberlain was a perceptive observer of her tactics:

. . . she writes to the Prime Minister about everything she does not like, which when he is a Liberal means almost everything that he says or does . . . She insists that administrative acts should not be done without delay, for the purpose of consulting with regard to them persons whose opinions she knows will be unfavourable . . . it would be difficult to maintain that with her immense experience the Queen is not

[97] 1 LQV, III, p. 40.
[98] 2 LQV, II, p. 131.

justified in asking for time in order that men of distinction should not be consulted upon various acts.[99]

In her widowhood, the Queen was a lonely woman with an unrequited capacity for affection; she wanted to be spoilt. In 1868, Dean Wellesley warned Gladstone that 'everything depends upon your manner of approaching the Queen. Her nervous susceptibility has much increased since you had to do with her before, and you cannot show too much regard, gentleness, I might even say, tenderness, towards her.' Gladstone tried, but tenderness did not come easily to him in politics. After 1880, she seldom wrote to Gladstone except on formal and official business; it was a measure of the change that the development of party had brought about that a Ministry could exist so easily when deprived of royal favour. She could not exclude individuals, although she was usually able to insist that those whom she particularly disliked were not given offices that brought them into personal contact with her. Once, at least, Gladstone wondered whether he could remain, after the Queen sent him a public telegram of rebuke after the death of Gordon. Her secretary covered up for her although, as she told him, 'she had deliberately sent it *en clair* so that everyone should know what she thought of him'.[100] She could not keep Dilke out of the Cabinet, but she did insist on his sending her what amounted to a written recantation of his republicanism.[101] She disapproved most heartily of the attitudes of Bright and (in his younger days) Joseph Chamberlain, and was prone to badger colleagues of theirs whom she trusted, such as Hartington, to oppose them. She once told Forster that 'she *cannot* and *will not* be the Queen of a *democratic monarchy*'.[102] She could not stop Gladstone from giving office to Lord Derby (Disraeli's former Foreign Secretary), who she thought was wet and weak, but she warned him that he would 'introduce a most disagreeable and irresolute, timid Minister into his Cabinet', and added that Lord Derby 'cannot expect a cordial reception'.[103]

[99] J. Chamberlain, *A Political Memoir.*
[100] Ponsonby, op. cit., p. 43.
[101] 2 LQV, III, p. 24.
[102] Ibid., p. 166.
[103] Ibid., pp. 378, 380.

She could be exceedingly tiresome about decorations. She wanted to give the Garter to Lord Lansdowne, in 1894, in spite of the opposition of the Ministry. She told Gladstone that this was not a Cabinet matter, since the Queen was the fountain of honour. He replied: 'It is true indeed, as your Majesty observes, that the Sovereign is the fountain of honour; but it is also true that the Sovereign is the fountain of law.'[104] But Lansdowne was marked down for the next vacant Garter.

At the very beginning of Lord Rosebery's administration, she objected to the mention of Welsh and Scottish disestablishment in the Speech from the Throne, and was unimpressed when Rosebery said that the Government had put these matters on its election programme. She tried to reassert a principle from the days of George III, in resistance to resolutions against the House of Lords being moved in the House of Commons without her previous sanction. She consulted Lord Salisbury, leader of the Opposition, who told her that a Prime Minister 'has no constitutional right to announce a totally new policy without first ascertaining your Majesty's pleasure on the subject, and if he is unable to convince your Majesty, it is his duty to tender his resignation'. Rosebery outflanked this contention; he would never, he said, have dreamed of proposing a constitutional resolution in the House of Commons before submitting it, after Cabinet consideration, to the Queen but he did not think that royal approval was necessary before the question was canvassed before a popular audience.[105] The Queen might not recognise herself as a democratic monarch, but democracy kept breaking through.

In 1879, the Queen's name was introduced into a debate on the prerogative in the House of Commons, but in so cautious a manner that it was not clear whether the target was the Queen herself, one or more of her Ministers, or the absence of collective responsibility within the Cabinet and its replacement by a 'government of departments'. Rumours had been circulating that the Queen had conducted a private correspondence, on matters of policy, with the Viceroy of India, that she had written a letter of sympathy to Lady

[104] 3 LQV, I, p. 350.
[105] 3 LQV, II, pp. 433, 440.

Chelmsford, whose husband was blamed for the disaster to a British force at Isandhlwana, and written a letter of encouragement to Sir Bartle Frere, who had been censured by the Cabinet for provoking war with the Zulus. L. L. Dillwyn, member for Swansea, proposed a motion that the 'mode and limits of the action of the prerogative should be more strictly observed'; but he safeguarded himself from an accusation that he was directly attacking the Queen by alleging that ministerial power was being augmented under power of the supposed personal interposition of the Queen. In some sense, this was a revival of the spirit of Dunning's motion: Dillwyn complained that the House of Commons had not been consulted on the purchase of the Khedive of Egypt's shares in the Suez Canal, on the movement of Indian troops to Malta, on the policy that led to an Afghan war, on the Anglo-Turkish treaty, and on the annexation of the Transvaal. He wished, he said, 'to do what he could to stop the progress of the system of departmental government. He wished to see the advice of the Cabinet given to the Crown, and not the advice of a single Minister.'[106] Leonard Courtney, his seconder, argued that Ministers had 'protruded the name and authority of the Queen, so as to obtain undue power through the respect due to her name, and because they had initiated and pursued great lines of policy in comparative independence of one another, thus minimising the collective judgment, the collective authority, and the collective responsibility of the Cabinet, and also minimising the control of the House'. He quoted from one of Disraeli's early works, *A Vindication of the English Constitution*, as evidence that the Prime Minister was concerned to twist the constitution in a monarchical direction. But he did make a significant point when he asked what security there was for the abuse of the prerogative when a party majority in the House of Commons was prepared to support Ministers in unusual actions; he cited Gladstone's ending of purchase in the Army by royal warrant when he found that he could not do so through Parliament.

The Government had no difficulty in repelling this attack, the more so since it drew no support from any leading figure

---

[106] H. of C., 13 May 1879, cc. 242 sqq.

in the Opposition. Gladstone occupied several columns of Hansard in denying any intention of giving his vote either one way or the other. Lord Robert Montagu, in a speech pregnant with antiquarian curiosities, gave his opinion that every Cabinet had been illegal, and every Cabinet member had violated the constitution, because the third section of the Act of Settlement was still in force, which required advice to the monarch to be signed by members of the Privy Council; his speech was punctuated by repeated attempts to count out the House. Lord Hartington made it clear that he gave no credence to theories that a revival of 'personal government' was in train.[107]

Hartington was quite right. It is impossible to answer the question about the extent of the Queen's power, precisely because it could not be isolated. The Queen was built into the process of government; she formed part of the necessary friction of administration. It is possible that Cabinets were deterred from doing certain things because they knew that the Queen would not agree to them; but it is impossible to prove the point. The fact is that she was there, and Ministers had to learn to live with her. She, for her part, had to live with them.

[107] Ibid., cc. 254, 260.

4

Cabinet and Prime Minister

> This subject, like the procreation of eels, is slippery and mysterious.
>
> Sir Claud Schuster

In 1851, a Committee of the House of Commons proposed that some precedence should be given to Cabinet Ministers at the opening and prorogation of Parliament; the House rejected this, on the ground that the Cabinet was unknown to the constitution.[1] In 1854, Homersham Cox was 'glad to say, that the words Minister, Prime Minister, Cabinet, and the synonymous word Administration, are all foreign to our language and our law'.[2] The Cabinet existed, of course, but there was a disposition to smother its reality under the legal fiction that its members were no more than Privy Counsellors who happened to be charged with departmental duties. It was not until the last year of the century that the word appeared for the first time on the order paper of the House of Commons, when G. C. T. Bartley (a critic of what had come to be called the 'Hotel Cecil') moved an amendment to the Address, on 10 December 1900, expressing 'regret at the advice given to your Majesty by the Prime Minister in recommending the appointment of so many of his own family to offices in the Cabinet and Government'. This formalism is, happily, no longer a characteristic of constitutional history, but its long existence should be borne in mind; it was a measure of Bagehot's originality that, when he tried to come at the living

---

[1] Sidney Low, *The Governance of England* (1904; rev. ed., 1914), p. 28.
[2] Homersham Cox, *The British Commonwealth* (1854), p. 111n.

reality behind the paper description, he devoted the first chapter of *The English Constitution* to the Cabinet.

That chapter, like the rest of the book, still makes attractive reading; it is a period piece, full of luminous generalisations, by a great political journalist who was writing of English government in the last days of the age of Palmerston, and contrasting it with the presidential system of the United States. Bagehot knew, only too well, that his political world was passing away even while he described it.

All through the period between 1832 and 1865, the pre-'32 statesmen—if I may so call them—Lord Derby, Lord Russell, Lord Palmerston, retained great power. Lord Palmerston to the last retained great prohibitive power. Though in some ways always young, he had not a particle of sympathy with the younger generation; he brought forward no young men; he obstructed all that young men wished. In consequence, at his death a new generation all at once started into life; the pre-'32 all at once died out. Most of the new politicians were men who might well have been Lord Palmerston's grandchildren. He came into Parliament in 1806, they entered it after 1856. Such an enormous change in the workers necessarily caused a great change in the kind of work attempted and the way in which it was done. What we call the 'spirit' of politics is most surely changed by a change of generation in the men than by any other change whatever. Even if there had been no Reform Act, this single cause would have effected grave alterations.[3]

It is, then, with these qualifications of his own making that we may examine Bagehot's interpretation of the working of the 'efficient parts' of the constitution; his point of view would clearly have been recognised at the time as that of a 'liberal-conservative'. He began by denying the existence either of a separation between the legislative, executive and judicial powers, or of a balanced union of monarchial, aristocratic and democratic elements.

The efficient secret of the English Constitution may be described as the close union, the nearly complete fusion, of

[3] Introduction to the Second Edition, op. cit., p. 269.

the executive and legislative powers. No doubt, by the traditional theory, as it exists in all the books, the goodness of our constitution consists in the entire separation of the legislative and executive authorities, but in truth its merit consists in their singular approximation. The connecting link is *the Cabinet* . . . A Cabinet is a combining committee—a *hyphen* which joins, a *buckle* which fastens, the legislative part of the State to the executive part of the State. In its origin it belongs to the one, in its functions it belongs to the other.[4]

Bagehot came to the House of Commons only in his fourth chapter, after the Monarchy and the House of Lords. Its most important functions were first to choose and then to maintain the Ministers. 'It does not, it is true, choose them directly; but it is nearly omnipotent in choosing them indirectly.' He was well aware that the House of Commons was not a neutral or dispassionate assembly : it 'lives in a state of perpetual potential choice; at any moment it can choose a ruler and dismiss a ruler. And therefore party is inherent in it, is bone of its bone, and breath of its breath.'[5] But in his period, party feeling was not automatically productive of disciplined servility. The outlines of two parties could be clearly seen, but only the outlines; for each of them had fringes of independent members—those men who, in the cant of the day, could not be depended upon. It was they who were, *par excellence*, the unmakers of Ministries. 'Six parliaments were elected between 1841 and 1868; and in all six of them the House of Commons had brought down at least one administration, and sometimes two, before its dissolution.'[6] Bagehot was concerned that party might make for weakness in the maintenance of the Queen's Government : he was speaking prescriptively when he asserted that 'the principle of Parliament is obedience to leaders. Change your leader if you will, take another if you will, but obey No. 1 while you serve No. 1, and obey No. 2 when you have gone over to No. 2.'[7] Bagehot was dead before parties had developed into instruments through which the House of Commons could

[4] Ibid., pp. 64, 68.
[5] Ibid., p. 158.
[6] Robert Blake, *The Office of Prime Minister* (1975), p. 36.
[7] Bagehot, op. cit., p. 158.

be controlled and the electorate manipulated.

The House of Commons could remove Ministries by its votes, but it could not stipulate by whom they were to be replaced, and its control over what they could do when in office was limited and indirect. By its own standing order, it would not consider any Bill or motion for the expenditure of public money, unless recommended by the Crown; this was a self-imposed restraint, but a restraint none the less. Ministers were as jealous as the Queen about infringement of the pre-rogative. But they were constantly in mind of the 'law of anticipated reactions'—about what the House of Commons would do about their proposals. Often, they were made aware of likely attitudes well in advance; the secrecy of Cabinet proceedings, then as later, was largely a myth. Some Cabinet Ministers deliberately used the press; many more of them gossiped to their friends. Wellington's disclosures to Mrs Arbuthnot, as recorded in her diaries, are now a prime source for the student. Considering what he wrote to Miss Venetia Stanley, Asquith was on poor ground when he complained 'that Cabinet Govt. was impossible if *The Times* was to be able to give a shorthand report of all our proceedings and proposals as it had done yesterday.'[8] The catalogue of Cabinet 'leaks', attributable and unattributable, is endless. Most men in the inner circle of politics did not find it difficult to discover what was going on. Disraeli published in *The Press* of 24 December 1853 a parody that was remarkably accurate in substance :

Lord Aberdeen moved that it was very disagreeable weather. Carried Nem. Con. (with an addition by Mr Gladstone that we ought to be very thankful to Providence that we had any weather at all) . . . Lord Aberdeen moved, Sir James Graham seconded, and it was carried by seven to four (Sir Charles Wood, by mistake, voting both ways) that a message be sent to Lord Palmerston offering to surrender everything if he would, by returning to office, save the Coalition Ministry from its inevitable doom.[9]

[8] Edward David (ed.), *Inside Asquith's Cabinet. From the Diaries of Charles Hobhouse* (1977), p. 150.
[9] Kingsley Martin, *The Triumph of Lord Palmerston* (1924; rev. ed., 1963), p. 150.

Well might Lord Granville describe Aberdeen's Cabinet as 'very leaky'![10] Fashionable London heard very quickly about the allegedly drunken meeting at Pembroke Lodge at which it was resolved to send an expedition to the Crimea. Lord John Russell tried to explain that the effective decision had been taken much earlier:

. . . I gave a Cabinet dinner at Pembroke Lodge, and as the members of the Cabinet, with the exception of the Chancellor, had been present at the previous deliberation, they cared little for criticizing after dinner the exact form of the sentences in which the number of the troops and the disposition of the fleet were minutely specified.

It is no doubt true that several members of the Cabinet went to sleep during this discussion. It is what they had often done before when the style of a dispatch or the phrases of a bill to be introduced into Parliament were discussed after dinner . . . The fact was that the expedition to the Crimea had occupied the anxious thoughts of the members of the Cabinet for several months and the dinner at Pembroke Lodge at a round table in a small room seemed better adapted for rest than for new exertions from the critical faculty.[11]

A memorandum by Prince Albert on Lord John Russell's first Ministry gave a picture of disorganisation, disarray and lack of morale. 'The curious part of all this is that they cannot keep a secret, and speak of all their differences.'[12] Lord Randolph Churchill in 1886, as Chancellor of the Exchequer, wrote to Joseph Chamberlain who was neither a member of the Cabinet nor of the Conservative Party:

Please let me beg of you to keep all the budget schemes I broached to you very secret. Only one other person outside the Government has an inkling of them, and any premature publicity or announcements or comments in the Press would destroy me . . .[13]

[10] Sir A. West, *Recollections, 1832–1886*, p. 391.
[11] Sir Spencer Walpole, *Life of Lord John Russell* (1889), vol. II, p. 223.
[12] 1 LQV, II, p. 102.
[13] Robert Rhodes James, *Lord Randolph Churchill* (1959, 1969), p. 285.

Maitland wrote that the solidarity of the Cabinet was evident by the reign of George III, and could be analysed into three principles: '(1) political unanimity, (2) common responsibility to parliament, (3) submission to a common head.'[14] In 1889, John Morley analysed cabinet government in his own times in terms similar to Maitland's but with an additional reference to the electorate. Morley's work appeared as a digression in his biography of Sir Robert Walpole; it had considerable influence, then and later, partly because it was thought to have the approval of Gladstone.

> The principal features of our system of Cabinet government to-day are four. The first is the doctrine of collective responsibility . . . The second mark is that the Cabinet is answerable immediately to the majority of the House of Commons, and ultimately to the electors whose will creates that majority . . . Third, the Cabinet is, except under uncommon, peculiar, and transitory circumstances, selected exclusively from one party . . . Fourth, the Prime Minister is the keystone of the Cabinet arch.[15]

Had the Act of Settlement of 1701 not been amended before it became effective with the accession of George I, it would have been impossible for collective responsibility to have been legally asserted. The Act required all matters relating to the governance of the realm to be considered in the Privy Council, and that all resolutions should be signed by those Privy Counsellors 'as shall advise and consent to the same'. The intention was clear enough: first, there should be no more cabals; secondly, there should be struck from the hands of the official servants of the new dynasty one of their weapons of self-defence. Collective responsibility is as old as the first round-robin or cry of 'No victimisation!' (Benjamin Franklin had the root of the matter in him when he is supposed to have said, at the signing of the American Declaration of Independence: 'We must all hang together, or, most assuredly, we shall all hang separately.')

[14] F. W. Maitland, *The Constitutional History of England* (1908), p. 395.
[15] John Morley, *Walpole* (1889; 1922), pp. 154, 156, 157.

As it happened, George I did not make a practice of attending Cabinet meetings. He was not especially interested in the minute intricacies of English politics; what he wanted was advice, and he did not trouble himself overmuch with the deliberations that preceded it. His habitual absence was the necessary condition of the Cabinet's acquiring the dual characteristics that were to be of its essence: it was both a gathering of heads of the departments of state, and simultaneously a steering committee of the party which could obtain the support of a majority in the House of Commons. This statement needs qualification. The House of Commons in the eighteenth century was not polarised between parties; the works of Sir Lewis Namier are a standing warning to those who venture upon glib generalisation. But the functions of Minister and party manager (however 'party' may be defined) were intertwined; majorities had somehow to be contrived—by avoiding unpopular policies, by appeals to loyalty, by the distribution of rewards and punishments, by the arts of *amicitia*. The accident that Ministers met alone enabled them to weave together their functions as officers of state and as party men, and to agree upon what they would say to the King or to Parliament.

Richard Pares offered a reconstruction of the way in which Ministers habitually transacted their business with the King.[16] The King normally received his Ministers, one by one, in his Closet. The initiative in discussion lay with him, and they were usually required to confine themselves to the business of their own departments. It was a sign that the office of Prime Minister (if not the name) was beginning to take shape when a particular Minister could claim, as a matter of course, to range more freely over the affairs of governance; a general defence of a Ministry's policy, in either House, required more than a succession of specialists' statements. The King's separation of Ministers, and the confining of each to his own departmental business, could be counteracted by Ministers' agreeing beforehand to take the same line of argument or to tell the same tale. Language to be used in the Closet could be

---

[16] Richard Pares, *George III and the Politicians* (1953), pp. 148–9.

concerted in Cabinet or, for that matter, in country houses. Pares quoted an instance when Lord Temple, at Stowe, promised the Duke of Bedford, then at Woburn, to give the same answers as Lord Rockingham, who was in London, if the King should send for him. The world of high politics was small and cohesive.

It was important to show a 'united front to the King, because Ministers needed his assent to their measures. It was also important to show a united front when justifying those measures to Parliament: confidence might be refused if Ministers spoke at cross purposes in public. That is what Melbourne had in mind when he insisted on Cabinet unanimity on an occasion that has become famous. After the meeting which agreed upon a fixed duty on corn, he put his back to the door and asked: 'What are we to say? Is it to make out corn dearer, or cheaper, or to make the price steady? I don't care which, but we had better all be in the same story.'

There are several versions of Melbourne's words, but the point is clear enough: the semblance of unanimity might be as important as its reality. Cabinet secrecy might be a necessary condition of collective responsibility; both were rooted in considerations of prudence. L. S. Amery ignored this point: 'The essence of our Cabinet system is the collective responsibility of its members . . . The secrecy of Cabinet proceedings, originally based on the Privy Counsellor's oath and antecedent to collective responsibility, is in any case the natural correlative of that collective responsibility.'[17] It is certainly a correlative, if one regards both as means of self-protection, but it is doubtful whether any oath was a necessary ingredient. There was at least one occasion when Charles James Fox found it hard to say whether the Cabinet meeting which he had attended was concerned with state or party. Secrecy might be important enough where Parliament and the outside world were concerned, but it could have nothing to do with the business that Ministers had with the King, from which the 'doctrine' of collective responsibility owed part of its origins. The word 'doctrine', one may think, was often used optatively, to

[17] L. S. Amery, *Thoughts on the Constitution* (1947), p. 70.

reinforce a practice that was fitful rather than continuous. There were occasions when Ministers took collective action to bend the King to their will—the joint resignation of 1746 was a spectacular example—but they were rather the ultimate medicine of the constitution than its daily bread. King and Ministers were not in a condition of perpetual strife. By the reign of George III, Ministers had established the custom of putting united advice on general questions, sometimes in writing in the form of a Cabinet minute; but no member of the Cabinet questioned, even by implication, the King's right to ask for individual opinions. In 1825, for instance, George IV asked for separate answers in writing to his questions about the Ministry's South American policy. He received a collective minute, to the effect that separate answers were unnecessary because all Ministers were in agreement, but there was no suggestion that he had no right to ask. It was Gladstone who was an innovator, in his refusal to give details of different opinions and the names of the Ministers who held them, in his Cabinet letters to the Queen. On 15 April 1885, the Queen wrote to Sir Henry Ponsonby:

With respect to Mr Gladstone, the Queen does feel that she is always kept in the dark.

In Lord Melbourne's time she knew *everything* that *passed* in the Cabinet and the different views that were entertained by the different Ministers, and there was no concealment. Sir Robert Peel, who was completely *master* of his Cabinet (and the Prime Minister *ought* to be) was after the first strangeness for her [who] hardly knew him, also very open. Lord Russell less communicative but still far more so than Mr Gladstone and Lord Palmerston too. They mentioned the names of the Ministers and their views. Lord Palmerston again kept his Cabinet in great order. Lord Derby was also entirely master of his Cabinet. Lord Aberdeen was most confidential and open and kind. Lord Beaconsfield was like Lord Melbourne. He told the Queen everything (he often did not see her for months) and said: 'I wish you to know everything so that you may be able to judge.' Mr Gladstone never once told her the different views of his colleagues. She is kept completely in the dark—and when they have quarrelled over it and decide amongst themselves he comes and tries to *force* this on her.[18]

Gladstone's secretiveness was an act of policy; he did not wish to give the Queen greater scope than she already had to exploit the divisions in a discordant Ministry. Prince Albert, indeed, would have liked a revival of Cabinet minutes, though he did not seem to appreciate that this was a term of art; plainly, what he wanted was a report of the discussion. 'I have always felt it to be a source of great weakness for the Sovereign not to be allowed to follow the arguments which may have decided the Cabinet in coming to a conclusion upon the advice which they may have to give.'

This was consistent with the Prince's view of the political role of the Court, but no Ministry was prepared to accept that in its entirety. No case comes easily to mind when the Queen was able to resist the combined will of her Ministers, but there were many occasions on which she appealed to the Cabinet as a whole, usually against a subordinate Minister but sometimes against the Prime Minister as well. Morley thought that this might be a means of reducing the Prime Minister's pre-eminence :

> . . . it is well understood that the sovereign has the right to demand the opinion of the Cabinet as a court of appeal against the Prime Minister or any other minister . . . This is clearly a political power left to the Crown, and if there chanced to be a strong Cabinet, the use of such a power might result in a considerable reduction of the Prime Minister's normal authority, and its transfer to the general body of his colleagues.[19]

Could collective responsibility be regarded as a doctrine? Certainly not, if the word is to be taken in a metaphysical sense. But a doctrine might also be defined as a principle established by past decisions. Roughly speaking, collective

---

[18] A. Ponsonby, *Sir H. Ponsonby, His Life from His Letters,* p. 193, quoted in W. C. Costin and J. Steven Watson, *The Law and Working of the Constitution: Documents 1660–1914* (1952), vol. II, pp. 438–9.
[19] Morley, *Walpole,* p. 159.

responsibility fell into some such category; public men regarded it much as they regarded marital fidelity—a general rule but not an invariable custom. Collective responsibility was a maxim of prudence rather than a binding obligation. The usages of the Cabinet were grounded, in the last resort, upon a recognition that certain types of conduct were inimical to the proper conduct of business or plainly 'ungentlemanly'. Without a certain degree of loyalty among colleagues, collective action would hardly be possible. It was no less important that confidences should be kept in public than in private life. Most politicians justified collective responsibility and confidentiality on empirical grounds. Thus, in 1834, Lord Melbourne objected to William IV's granting of permission to Lord John Russell to disclose what had taken place in Cabinet in 1831 and 1832. Russell was engaged in a tiresome dispute with Lord Durham about which of them might more appropriately be described as 'father of the Great Reform Bill'; there was no danger to the security of the state here, since the episode was a matter of history. Melbourne argued that secrecy was one of the conditions that were necessary if Cabinets were to debate frankly and thereafter continue in cohesion, if not in amity. He would emphasise, he wrote to the King, the consequences of publicity,

> how extremely inconvenient this course is likely to prove, how much crimination, recrimination and general altercation it is likely to produce, and how entirely subversive it is of all the principles upon which the government of this country has hitherto been conducted . . . The publicity of debates in Parliament established of late years is, I believe, on the whole advantageous. At the same time, it must be admitted that there are inconveniences, and particularly that it prevents that fearlessness and sincerity which would otherwise take place. If the arguments of the Cabinet are no longer to be protected by an impenetrable veil of secrecy, there will be no place left in the public councils for the free investigation of truth and the unshackled exercise of the understanding.[20]

[20] *Lord Melbourne's Papers* (ed. Sanders), quoted in Costin and Watson, vol. II, p. 381.

Lord Salisbury argued in much the same way a generation later; absence of secrecy would make for inefficient debating.

> A Cabinet discussion was not the occasion for the deliverance of considered judgments but an opportunity for the pursuit of practical conclusions. It could only be made completely effective for this purpose if the flow of suggestions which accompanied it attained the freedom and fulness which belong to private conversations—members must feel themselves untrammelled by any consideration of consistency with the past or self-justification in the future. The convention which forebade any note being taken of what was said— futile as a safeguard for secrecy—was invaluable as a guarantee for this irresponsible licence in discussion. Lord Salisbury would have extended it in principle to the record preserved in each man's memory. The first rule of Cabinet conduct, he used to declare, was that no member should ever 'Hansardise' another —ever compare his present contribution to the common fund of counsel with a previously expressed opinion.[21]

Salisbury preferred Cabinet meetings to be held in the Foreign Office, where members sat dispersed about the room in armchairs; to sit around a table, as at 10 Downing Street, tended to encourage prolixity.

An example of conduct that was not acceptable was that of the 15th Earl of Derby, Foreign Secretary in Disraeli's second administration. He was a man of wobbling disposition, whose wayward and almost contumacious claims to independence at last ended with his resignation; thereafter, he dissociated himself in public from actions which the Cabinet had taken while he was still a member. Salisbury twice rebuked him, and one of these is often quoted as the definitive statement of the 'doctrine' of collective responsibility.

> Now . . . am I not defending a great constitutional principle, when I say that, for all that passes in Cabinet, each member of it who does not resign is absolutely and irretrievably responsible, and that he has no right afterwards to say that he agreed in

[21] Lady Gwendolen Cecil, *Life of Robert, Marquess of Salisbury* (1921–32), vol. II, p. 223.

one case to a compromise, while in another he was persuaded by one of his colleagues? Consider the inconvenience which will arise if such a great constitutional law is not respected.[22]

Salisbury, like Melbourne before him, was talking about the practical conduct of business. But the departure from the canons of decent behaviour by a former colleague might be a good enough reason to waive the conventions of secrecy in order to repudiate his repudiations. Salisbury wrote to his nephew, Arthur Balfour, who was not then in office:

> Is it not time to dissipate the absurd assumption that the present Cabinet is responsible for all that Derby said or did or left undone? Of course we cannot, in view of the constitutional fiction, repudiate the responsibility ourselves; but no such hindrance need affect others.

Balfour took the hint and, as he recalled in his autobiography, 'possibly some notice of my efforts may have appeared in the local newspapers'.[23]

The point was that the Queen's Government was an entity, and it was self-evident that members of it, junior and senior, should not embarrass one another. What Ministers said or did in public affected one another. Obligations ran two ways: a Cabinet member had a right to expect that his colleagues would defend him, and they in turn had a right to expect that he would not drag them into scrapes. By accepting office, an individual surrendered part of his independence, and consideration for his colleagues was a condition of receiving power; he could not have it both ways. Thus Palmerston, as Prime Minister, could take towards Gladstone, as Chancellor of the Exchequer, an attitude similar to that taken by other Prime Ministers to Palmerston himself, when he was in subordinate office:

> . . . a Member of the Government when he takes office necessarily divests himself of that perfect Freedom of individual action which belongs to a private and independent Member

[22] H. of L., 8 April 1878, c. 833.
[23] A. J. Balfour, *Chapters of Autobiography* (1930), p. 131. Salisbury's letter is dated 18 March 1880.

of Parliament, and the Reason is this, that what a Member of the Government does or says upon public Matters must to a certain degree commit his colleagues, and the Body to which they belong if they by their silence appear to acquiesce; and if any of them follow his Example and express as publicly, opposite opinions, which in particular cases they might feel obliged to do. Differences of opinion between Members of the same Government are unnecessarily brought out into Prominence and the Strength of the Government is thereby impaired.[24]

There were times when a Minister's behaviour was so wayward that his colleagues felt little disposition to defend him —Brougham after 1832 and Palmerston in 1851 provided examples. But those occasions were rare, and individual resignations rarer still; usually, the sinner was sustained for the sake of the Ministry. Lord John Russell's letter on free trade, in 1841, was a case in point. This was

> much objected to in the Cabinet, in which there was a warm debate upon it, threatening to break up the Government, when Lord Melbourne put an end to discussion by saying : 'Well, Gentlemen, there is no doubt that John Russell's letter is a d——d letter; but he has written it and we must go through with it.'[25]

Professor S. E. Finer, in an exhaustive examination of attacks upon Ministers in Parliament, and their consequences, has found only seven instances between 1855 and 1914 when members of the Cabinet were constrained to resign.[26] In 1855, Lord John Russell returned from Vienna with a draft treaty, the terms of which leaked out and provoked a hostile motion in the House of Commons. The critical action seems to have been a revolt by junior Ministers—under-secretaries—who threatened to hand in their own resignations unless Russell went. In 1858, Lord Ellenborough published a despatch to

[24] P. Guedalla (ed.), *The Palmerston Papers: Gladstone and Palmer* (1928), p. 288.

[25] 2 LQV, I, p. 563.

[26] S. E. Finer, 'The individual responsibility of Ministers', *Public Administration,* 1956.

the Governor-General of India, without consulting his colleagues, and resigned after they had disowned him; it was on this occasion that Lord Derby was able, circumspectly, to threaten a dissolution in order to ward off a hostile motion in the House of Commons. Lord Westbury, the Lord Chancellor, resigned after charges of personal corruption had been brought against him in 1865. In 1867, Spencer Walpole, the Home Secretary, resigned after criticism of his handling of the popular disturbances in Hyde Park. In 1894, A. J. Mundella, President of the Board of Trade, resigned after the collapse of a trading company in which he had a personal interest. In 1905, George Wyndham accepted responsibility for negotiations undertaken, only partly with his knowledge, by his permanent under-secretary for Ireland. In 1914, Colonel J. E. B. Seely, Secretary of State for War, resigned after his colleagues had repudiated some additions which he had made, without consulting them, to a Cabinet statement after the Curragh incident.

It is very difficult to deduce from these incidents anything resembling a rule. Circumstances determined cases, and what happened to a Minister depended upon the toughness of his own personality, the attitude taken by the Prime Minister, the state of feeling among the back-benchers of his own party, and public reaction in the constituencies; if a Minister resigned, a by-election would follow (unless he were replaced by a peer). There was a scandal in 1873, when it was discovered that the Chancellor of the Exchequer, the Postmaster-General and the First Commissioner of Works had used money in the post office savings banks for capital expenditure without the consent of Parliament; none of them offered to resign and Gladstone, as Prime Minister, did not feel that he could force them out. He wrote to the Queen:

> There probably have been times when the three gentlemen who in their several positions have been chiefly to blame would have been summarily dismissed from your Majesty's service. But on none of them could any ill-intent be charged. Two of them had, among whatever errors of judgment, done much and marked good service to the state : and two of them were past 60 years of age. Mr Gladstone could not under the

circumstances resort to so severe a course without injustice and harshness, which your Majesty would be the last to approve. The last embarrassment has been this : that all three have shown a tenacity of attachment to office certainly greater than is usual. And unfortunately the willingness of each person to quit or retain office, and still more their active desire, form a very great element in cases of this kind apart from the question how far the retention of it, or its abandonment, may on other grounds be desirable.[27]

Eventually, Lowe, Chancellor of the Exchequer, was shuffled into the Home Office; Ayrton, First Commissioner of Works, was persuaded . to become Judge-Advocate-General; and Monsell, Postmaster-General, retired from office on condition that he was elevated to the House of Lords—'punished with a peerage', as the quip went.

As groups and factions within the House of Commons solidified into party coalitions, so the quality of representativeness became increasingly important in the composition of a Cabinet, and the diversity of personalities which this entailed added a new dimension to the Prime Minister's difficulty of working a team. Sir William Molesworth was brought in by Lord Aberdeen in 1852 to attract support from Radicals of the Manchester School. Gladstone said that he took Bright into the Cabinet in 1868 because 'he touched the political world at its meridian—Birmingham'.[28] For the same reason, his colleagues would be anxious to keep a representative man, once he had been admitted; his resignation might forfeit that support which was the reason for his acquisition. As the electorate became larger and better organised, Prime Ministers had increasingly to look for support outside the House of Commons. Joseph Chamberlain and Lord Randolph Churchill drew their strength from the constituencies, and each took an independent line in Cabinet.

But collective responsibility might also be a device for muzzling a man of distinctive opinions. Charles Villiers told the editor of *The Times* that Bright's acceptance of office had

---

[27] P. Guedalla (ed.), *The Queen and Mr Gladstone* (1930), vol. I, p. 424.
[28] Add. MSS 44543, f. 7.

disqualified him from political agitation, and Lord Granville told Gladstone that he had heard Villiers 'abusing Bright, taking for his text that which perhaps may meet your approval. "If a man takes the shilling he is bound to serve" '[29]—a deadly thrust, considering that Bright was a Quaker. John Burns's radicalism ended when he entered the Cabinet in 1905.

From time to time, Cabinets agreed that certain topics should be treated as 'open questions' where collective responsibility did not apply and each man might speak and vote as he pleased. Catholic Emancipation was 'open' between 1812 and 1829; it is doubtful whether, otherwise, any Ministry at all could have been formed. But, as Canning wrote to Lord Lansdowne in 1827 :

> The inconvenience (now unavoidable) of having *one* open question in the Cabinet, makes it all the more necessary to agree that there should be no other. All the existing members of the Cabinet are united in opposing the question of Parliamentary Reform, and could not acquiesce in its being brought forward or supported by any member of the Cabinet.[30]

Women's suffrage was an open question in 1884 and again between 1906 and 1914, and tariff reform between 1903 and 1905. Macaulay argued that open questions were the rule, and that there was nothing novel in the treatment of Catholic claims by Lord Liverpool and his successors :

> Within the memory of many persons living, the general rule was this, that all questions whatever were open questions in a Cabinet, except those which came under two classes—namely, first, measures brought forward by the Government as a Government, which all the members of it were, of course, expected to support; and, second, motions brought forward with the purpose, express or implied, of [censuring] the Government, or any department of it, which all the members were, of course, expected to oppose.[31]

[29] Agatha Ramm (ed.), *The Political Correspondence of Mr Gladstone and Lord Granville.*

[30] A. Aspinall (ed.), *The Formation of Canning's Ministry* (1937), quoted in Costin and Watson, op. cit., vol. II, p. 371.

[31] H. of C., 18 June 1839, c. 464.

There were two particular difficulties in the way of enforcing the collective responsibility of the Cabinet: there was no effective sanction, and there was no record of proceedings to which to refer. It was very difficult to enforce discipline upon a politician of the first rank. In 1832, indeed, Sir Henry Parnell, Secretary at War, was dismissed after a Cabinet decision for failing to vote in a division on what amounted to a vote of confidence. But this, although it fits Macaulay's definition of a 'closed question', was an isolated incident and Parnell was a subordinate figure. There was only one occasion, in Queen Victoria's reign, when a major politician was dismissed, and no one was anxious to see the episode of Lord Palmerston repeated. In 1884, for instance, Joseph Chamberlain, who was in the Cabinet, and two junior Ministers who were not, abstained in a division on the franchise Bill. Gladstone, in a memorandum for the Cabinet, stated 'the elementary rule, necessary for the cohesion and character of Administrations, that on certain questions, and notably on questions vital to their existence, their members should vote together. In the event of their not doing so, their intention to quit the Government is presumed, and in all ordinary cases ought to take effect.' But he added the qualification that this was not an ordinary case, because the situation of the Ministry was too precarious 'for the minds of men at such a juncture to be disturbed' and he therefore proposed that the erring three 'will do us the favour to retain their respective offices'.[32] Apart from the technical reason that resignations might put seats at hazard in by-elections, it was sound politics not to let a powerful man go into opposition, especially while the House of Commons still contained many unanchored members. Palmerston demonstrated this with his 'tit-for tat' in 1852 when, a few weeks after his own dismissal, he successfully moved an amendment to a militia Bill which brought down Russell's government. Gladstone made this explicit to the Queen when declining to ask Lowe for his resignation in 1873; he wrote that he 'naturally is not willing, first to abandon an eminent colleague at the moment of his

[32] Cabinet Papers. Cab. 37/12/31. Quoted in H. J. Hanham (ed.), *The Nineteenth Century Constitution* (1969), p. 88.

distress, and at the same time to present the Opposition with a most powerful instrument of attack upon himself at a difficult moment'.[33] In 1884, Gladstone could not bring himself to dismiss Lord Carlingford, although he badly wanted his place for Lord Rosebery.

Gladstone once said that the next most serious thing to admitting a new man to the Cabinet was to leave out someone who had once been a member.[34] It was tacitly understood that a Minister, once appointed, had a prescriptive right to that office or a superior one, and that claims could be carried over from one administration to another, with a gap of years between them. The idea that it was proper to ask a veteran to stand aside, so that younger men might be brought forward, developed only when parties became strong enough to generate needs and claims of their own.

'The position of most men in Parliament,' wrote Bagehot, 'forbids their being invited to the Cabinet; the position of a few men ensures their being invited.'[35] Palmerston consulted his Cabinet colleagues before making new appointments to their number; in 1882, Gladstone denied that the Cabinet had any right to be consulted:

> I can affirm with confidence that the notion of a title in the Cabinet to be consulted on the succession of a Cabinet office is absurd. It is a title which Cabinet Ministers do not possess. During thirty-eight years since I first entered the Cabinet, I have never known more than a friendly announcement before publicity, and very partial consultation perhaps with one or two, especially the leaders in the second House.[36]

But there was no clear understanding, throughout the nineteenth century, that the power to appoint entailed the power to dismiss. Salisbury felt that he could not get rid of Matthews, in spite of his failure as Home Secretary. 'There is no instance of dismissal; and it would require some open

[33] 2 LQV, II, p. 274.
[34] Low, op. cit., p. 168.
[35] Bagehot, *English Constitution*, p. 67.
[36] John Morley, *The Life of William Ewart Gladstone* (1903), vol. III, p. 101n.

and palpable error to justify it.'[37] It was not clear how free a hand to reconstruct the Ministry could be assumed by a new Prime Minister taking over a continuing administration. Between 1832 and 1914, changes of this kind occurred six times, after the resignations of Grey in 1834, Derby in 1868, Gladstone in 1894, Salisbury in 1902 and Campbell-Bannerman in 1908, and after the death of Palmerston in 1865. In 1868, Disraeli had difficulty in ridding himself of Lord Chelmsford, who had held the Lord Chancellorship in 1858–9 and again from 1866, and had to fall back upon a previous arrangement which Derby had made with Chelmsford, to retire in favour of Lord Cairns. The controversy became public, because Chelmsford told the press about his grievances; but Disraeli carried his point.

> Accordingly, Chelmsford retired in dudgeon; and society and the clubs were entertained by stories of his bitter jokes and of Disraeli's pungent retort. It was said that the ex-Chancellor talked of premature elevation making some people *dizzy*, and that he distinguished the old and new Administrations as the 'Derby' and the 'Hoax'; while the new Prime Minister was declared to have curtly summed up his former colleague in the biting words, 'Useless in council, feeble in debate, and— a jester'.[38]

There was a touch of duplicity in the manner in which Balfour rid himself of unwanted colleagues in 1903. In 1908, Asquith (who was later to demonstrate that he could be a very good butcher indeed) asked for Lord Tweedmouth's resignation from the Admiralty, but it was thought in some quarters that Asquith had been guilty of ungentlemanly conduct and that 'even a housemaid got better warning'.

Harcourt, whom Gladstone consulted in the matter of Lord Carlingford in 1884, gave a logical answer :

> . . . I confess I have never doubted that Cabinet offices were held *durante bene placato* of the Prime Minister . . . in the ordinary working of a Cabinet I have always supposed that the Prime Minister has the same authority to modify it as he

[37] 3 LQV, I, p. 646.
[38] W. F. Monypenny and G. E. Buckle, *The Life of Benjamin Disraeli* (1910–20); 2 vol. ed., 1923), vol. II, p. 329.

has to construct it . . . The interests at stake are far too serious
to admit of the doctrine of fixity of tenure.

That this must be so is obvious because the first Minister
can always say to any other member of the Administration,
'if you don't go I will.' But it is incredible that things should
ever be pushed to such a point as that.[39]

But the life of politics is based not on logic but experience.
Harcourt can hardly have meant that a Prime Minister should
break up his government and take it out of office rather than
permit a single colleague to keep his place; that would have
been throwing the baby out with the bathwater. He seemed
to have been thinking of a technical resignation, followed at
once by an offer to form a new Ministry, which would give
the Prime Minister *tabula rasa* on which he could write the
names of all his former colleagues but one. This has not yet
happened in England, but there is a precedent from one of
the Dominions. In 1912, General Botha, Prime Minister of the
Union of South Africa, asked in vain for the resignation of
General Hertzog. Botha himself then resigned, was invited
forthwith by the Governor-General to form a new government,
and did so with Hertzog left out. In 1877, Lord Beaconsfield
seemed to have had some manoeuvre such as that in mind.
He wrote to the Queen, on 17 December :

> He thought he expressed an usual, and constitutional, practice
> when he found half his Cabinet at that moment arrayed
> against him, in saying that if not supported, he should feel
> it his duty to resign to Your Majesty the trust which Your
> Majesty had, so graciously, bestowed on him. But that would
> not prevent Your Majesty, if Your Majesty graciously saw fit,
> to entrust to him the formation of a new Ministry—and,
> certainly, in that case, he would do his utmost to form one.[40]

This ultimatum brought the mutineers to heel, and on 18
December Lord Derby, the principal recalcitrant, produced a
modus vivendi. But Disraeli's weapon was not one for all

---

[39] A. G. Gardiner, *The Life of Sir William Harcourt* (1923), vol. I, pp.
508–9.
[40] RA B64/16.

seasons; it is tempting to speculate on how the Queen might have acted if Gladstone had presented her with such an opportunity.

II

It was once fashionable for Englishmen to point out, with a certain pride at yet another anomaly, that the Prime Minister, like the Cabinet, was unknown to the constitution. 'Nowhere in the wide world,' wrote Gladstone, 'does so great a substance cast so small a shadow; nowhere is there a man who has so much power with so little to show for it in the way of formal title or prerogative.'[41] Before the Ministers of the Crown Act of 1937, the Prime Minister had neither salary nor statutory duties. It was usual for him to take the office of First Lord of the Treasury, which did entitle him to a salary (and the occupancy of No 10, Downing Street); but in law, as Gladstone remarked, this meant that he was 'no more than the first named of five persons, by whom jointly the powers of the Lord Treasurership are taken to be exercised; he is not their master, or otherwise than by mere priority their head: and he has no special position or prerogative under the formal constitution of his office. He has no official rank except that of Privy Councillor. Eight members of the Cabinet, including five Secretaries of State, take precedence of him.' In two of his three Ministries, Lord Salisbury did not take the office of First Lord, preferring to be Foreign Secretary and then Lord Privy Seal. A Royal Proclamation in December 1904 gave the Prime Minister a place in the order of precedence, immediately after the Archbishop of York.

No one questioned the reality behind the fiction—that the Prime Ministership was the greatest political prize in the land. 'Yes,' said Disraeli in 1868, 'I have climbed to the top of the greasy pole.'[42] Morley described the office as one 'of exceptional and peculiar authority'.[43] It was a later generation, and

---

[41] W. E. Gladstone, *Gleanings of Past Years* (1879), vol. I, p. 244.
[42] Monypenny and Buckle, op. cit., p. 334.
[43] Morley, *Walpole*, p. 157.

not his own, that was confused by Morley's additional comment, that the Prime Minister, in his Cabinet, was *primus inter pares* : the stress was upon primacy and not upon parity. The office was largely what its holder chose to make of it, and a resolute Prime Minister could either absorb himself in administration or exercise a more remote control; Gladstone chose the first of these roles, Salisbury the second. Peel was probably the last Prime Minister who took it upon himself to supervise the work of all departments, and to concern himself with what all his Cabinet colleagues were doing. He described his concept of his duties to Gladstone in 1846 :

> There is the whole correspondence with the Queen, several times a day, and all requiring to be in my own hand, and to be carefully done; the whole correspondence with peers and members of parliament, in my own hand, as well as other persons of consequence; the sitting seven or eight hours a day to listen in the House of Commons. Then I must, of course, have my mind in the principal subjects connected with the various departments . . . and all the reading connected with them . . . Then there is the difficulty that you have in conducting such questions on account of your colleague whom they concern.[44]

Peel took direct charge of some of his budgets. Gladstone took the Chancellorship of the Exchequer from 1880 until the end of 1882. It was unfortunate, perhaps, that he took Peel for his model; times had changed, and Gladstone's preoccupation with particular cares meant that his Cabinet sometimes lacked the direction of a mastering mind. In his obituary of Gladstone, in the *Review of Reviews*, James Stansfeld said that he was strongest in the country, less strong in the House of Commons, and weakest in Cabinet. Lord Granville told him, in 1886 : 'I think you too often counted noses in your last Cabinet.' What Granville had in mind may perhaps be deduced from Gladstone's own description of the dispute in 1883 over the removal of the Duke of Wellington's statue from Hyde Park Corner : 'A vote took place, and three times over he took

[44] Morley, *Gladstone*, vol. I, p. 297.

down the names. He was against removal, but was unable to have his own way over the majority.'[45] (If this was, as Gladstone said, the severest fight that he had ever known in any Cabinet, it was a remarkable example of Parkinson's Law that the heat engendered in discussion is in inverse proportion to the importance of the subject discussed.)

Whatever he did, a Prime Minister could not escape criticism from his colleagues, although one may doubt whether it was often made to him face to face. Gladstone was thought to be too involved with business, Disraeli to be too detached from it. Salisbury said of Disraeli, after he had fallen from power :

As the head of a Cabinet his fault was want of firmness. The chiefs of Departments got their way too much. The Cabinet as a whole got it too little, and this necessarily followed from having at the head of affairs a statesman whose only final political principle was that the Party must on no account be broken up, and who shrank therefore from exercising coercion on any of his colleagues. Thus it became possible that the Transvaal should be annexed—not indeed against the wish of the Cabinet, but actually without its knowledge. Lord Carnarvon wished to do it. Lord Beaconsfield was persuaded that it was an excellent thing to do, and it was done.

Again—Bartle Frere should have been recalled as soon as the news of his ultimatum [*sc.* to the Zulus] reached England. We should then have escaped in appearance, as well as in reality, the responsibility of the Zulu War. So thought the majority of the Cabinet, so thought Dizzy himself. But the Queen was strongly opposed to it; and Hicks Beach was strongly opposed to it; and the Prime Minister was unable to resist his Sovereign and the Colonial Secretary together. Again, it was decided in Cabinet that the invasion of Afghanistan should take place only through one Pass. Lytton objected. Because Lytton did, Hardy did. Because Hardy did, Dizzy did : for was not Hardy the head of the India Office? And so the plans were altered.[46]

[45] Ibid., vol. III, p. 4.
[46] Arthur James, first Earl Balfour, *Chapters of Autobiography* (1930), pp. 113–24.

Most of Salisbury's criticisms focused on those 'outposts of Empire' that were extraordinarily difficult to control from London. Salisbury himself allowed his Colonial Secretary a wide latitude in dealing with the Transvaal and was in the habit of referring to the Boer War as 'Joe's war'. As to keeping the party from breaking up, Salisbury was twenty-five years younger than Disraeli, and had not the same cause to remember the years which the Conservatives spent in the wilderness after 1846.

The success or failure of a Ministry, whether in legislation or administration, depended largely upon the Prime Minister. He might or might not be adept at managing his Cabinet, but that was a task that no one else could do for him. The Cabinet was co-ordinated by the Prime Minister or it was not co-ordinated at all. A single department might be admirably conducted even if the Cabinet became a beargarden, but no subordinate Minister could extend his authority across those administrative frontiers where conflict might bring deadlock. The failure of Gladstone's second Ministry, from 1880 to 1885, lay in his own inability to give directions or insist upon decisions.[47]

A Prime Minister was always besieged by claims for office. One advantage of the convention that Ministers who had sat in one Cabinet had acquired vested rights was that it lightened the burden of making a choice that might leave a Prime Minister with several enemies and one ingrate. In 1852, Disraeli said : 'England does not love coalitions', and this has been repeated as a slogan ever since. Parties have seldom been willing to give England a chance of expressing a preference, and it might be more accurate to say that Prime Ministers do not love coalitions because they multiply claims to office while diminishing the share of them that can be given to any particular faction. In 1852, Lord Aberdeen had about a dozen posts to fill; Lord Derby told the Queen that if Aberdeen were to satisfy all those who demanded office he would have to include at least 32 people in his Cabinet.[48]

[47] Agatha Ramm, Introduction to *The Political Correspondence of Mr Gladstone and Lord Granville, 1876–1886* (1962), vol. I, passim.
[48] Low, op. cit., p. 168

Coalitions apart, each **Prime** Minister had to consider the various groups and sub-divisions within his own party, when making up his Cabinet. That is one reason why Cabinets increased in size—from 13 members in 1858 to 20 in 1900. The Cabinet grew proportionately faster than the whole 'parliamentary executive' of both senior and junior Ministers, which numbered 66 in 1868, went up to 70 in 1887, dropped to 61 in 1901, and had gone up again to 66 in 1910.[49]

A Prime Minister might find the task of Ministry-making distasteful, but he was in a very strong position. Once he had the King's commission to form a government in his hand in 1905, Campbell-Bannerman was able to make short work of the 'Relugas compact' by which Asquith, Grey and Haldane had hoped to extort concessions from him by refusing to take office unless he went to the House of Lords; they entered the Ministry, and Campbell-Bannerman stayed in the House of Commons. J. A. Spender's description of the atmosphere surrounding the formation of that Ministry remains of general significance :

It is customary to laugh at politicians in the throes of office-seeking, but men of other professions may ask themselves what they would feel and how they would conduct themselves if at a given moment their entire career were at stake on the will or whim, as it might seem, of an inscrutable power which can neither be approached nor pleaded with, and whose decision when given is blasting and irretrievable. To be obliged to keep a perfect dignity and reticence when others may be intriguing, to spend miserable hours waiting for a summons which may never come, to be fearful of going out lest it may come in your absence or of returning home to find it not there, to see the days passing and offices filled and yourself forgotten, to be conscious that a large audience is watching your discomfiture—this is the fate of even distinguished men, let alone the scores of others who at this moment are feeling for their footing on the first rung of the ladder. Who shall cast stones if a Prime Minister's letter-bag at such times reveals some of the secrets of human nature?

One man is taking an untimely holiday at Cairo, and sends a forlorn telegram to say that a cabled word will bring him home by the next boat. Alas for him, he is not indispensable, and there are a dozen candidates on the spot for the place that he desires. Another rashly attaches conditions to his acceptance of the offer made to him, and to his dismay the Prime Minister answers blandly regretting that he should have 'declined' . . . The wives, meantime, are not negligible. Some of them boldly break through the rules which are binding on husbands and sons, and even rush the inner sanctum where the Prime Minister sits guarded by his secretaries. All the time the Press must be at the door, seeking intelligent anticipations of facts officially withheld.[50]

Such might be the miseries of party victory!

The development of the idea that Cabinets ought to be a representative cross-section of the back benches may be measured by the protests made when that expectation was frustrated. Gladstone's Cabinets were never accurate reflections of the changing composition of his party. He balanced a Radical preponderance among followers by a Whig preponderance among leaders, and had no prejudice against lords. In 1880, a Cabinet of fourteen contained six peers and the eldest son of a duke, and even in 1892, after most of the Whigs had left him, there were five peers in a Cabinet of seventeen. In 1892, Harcourt complained to Gladstone about inequitable distribution:

. . . more than half of what are considered the places of greatest emolument and dignity are assigned to the Peers . . . I feel that besides all the tremendous difficulties which you have to face and the powerful opposition you will encounter, you will add the greatest of all discouragements, that of a dissatisfied party.[51]

It depended very much upon the Prime Minister how formal the conduct of business would be, and which departmental

[50] J. A. Spender, *The Life of the Right Hon. Sir Henry Campbell-Bannerman, G.C.B.* (n.d.), vol. II, pp. 201–2.
[51] Gardiner, op. cit., vol. II, pp. 182–3.

Ministers might be left to their own devices. Gladstone is said to have been careful to prepare agenda for meetings, although the fragments among his papers suggest that these were rudimentary enough. Lord Carlingford's diary for 1885—admittedly when the Ministry was moving acrimoniously towards its close—suggests that discussion hopped from topic to topic, without form or conclusion.[52] One is not surprised that misunderstandings occurred. In 1882, Hartington's private secretary wrote to Gladstone's private secretary:

> Harcourt and Chamberlain have both been here this morning and *at* my Chief about yesterday's Cabinet proceedings. They cannot agree about what occurred. There must have been some decision, as Bright's resignation shows. My Chief has told me to ask you what the devil *was* decided, for he is damned if he knows. Will you ask Mr G. in more conventional and less pungent terms?[53]

There was an even more significant episode in 1902–3, which precipitated the disintegration of Balfour's government. Chamberlain left for South Africa in the belief that the Cabinet had decided, before he went, to retain a duty upon imported corn: in his budget for 1903, Ritchie, the Chancellor of the Exchequer, insisted that the duty should be remitted. After his return, and resignation, Chamberlain wrote to the Duke of Devonshire:

> What did I ask of you before I went to South Africa? That you should retain the shilling corn duty and give a drawback to Canada. I thought you had all, except Ritchie, accepted this policy. While I was slaving my life out you threw it over as of no importance, and it is to this indifference to a great policy, which you had accepted, that you owe the present situation.

Devonshire's reply was revealing in its conciliatoriness.

> . . . I think that we must go back to the Cabinets immediately before and after your visit to South Africa, the proceedings

---

[52] A. B. Cooke and J. R. Vincent (eds.), *Lord Carlingford's Journal* (1971), passim.

[53] Lord Hankey, *Diplomacy by Conference* (1947), pp. 66–7.

at which are still extremely obscure to me. As you know, I am rather deaf, and I am afraid sometimes inattentive. I certainly failed altogether to understand that at the first of these a decision was even provisionally taken of such importance as that to which you refer, and it must have been taken after very little discussion . . .[54]

III

Some of the qualities or accidents that commonly brought men into the Cabinet have been considered. There is one attribute that has not been mentioned—that of the demagogue, appealing directly to the masses. That was a practice neither cultivated nor approved by men of Palmerston's generation; to appeal to great popular audiences from the public platform was to step outside the established conventions. Peel, when he was consciously drawing together the broken fibres of conservatism after 1835, occasionally made important political speeches outside Parliament, but to carefully chosen audiences —to the merchants and bankers of the City of London, to civic dignitaries at a subscription dinner in Glasgow after his election as Rector of the University in 1837.[55] Bright, of course, habitually drew great audiences—but he was an 'agitator'. It was a sign that the Reform Act of 1867 required new methods to appeal to new electors when Disraeli delivered two great public speeches in 1872, at the Free Trade Hall in Manchester and at the Crystal Palace in London. Both occasions were carefully planned in advance. Disraeli was concerned to put beyond doubt his own leadership of the party, which had been at risk since the Liberal victory of 1868, by demonstrations of his own powers to the new Conservative associations that were being created in the constituencies. The first politician of prime ministerial capacity to use the platform regularly was Gladstone in the 1860s; it was he, more than anyone else, who created the conception of the party leader as demagogue, and his

---

[54] Bernard Holland, *The Life of Spencer Compton, Eighth Duke of Devonshire* (1911), vol. II, pp. 356–7.
[55] Gash, *The Conservatives*, pp. 70–1.

example was followed by Joseph Chamberlain, Lord Randolph Churchill, Lord Salisbury, Lloyd George and Winston Churchill. Pitt had described the Prime Minister as carrying the chief weight in the counsels of Ministers and the chief place in the confidence of the Crown; after 1867, it was also necessary to hold a conspicuous place in the eye of the electorate.

Writing in 1947, G. M. Young said that to be an acceptable Prime Minister 'a man should be at once a popular figure, a party figure and a parliamentary figure' and he qualified this by saying that a standing in Parliament was the most important of the three qualifications.[56] To be successful in Parliament, continuously over a long period, was the indispensable condition for the highest positions. It might be true that, more and more, it was the electorate which decided which party should provide the Ministry, but Parliament never lost its power to break the reputation of Ministers.

[56] G. M. Young, 'Government' in *The Character of England,* edited by Sir Ernest Barker (1947).

5

The House of Lords and the 'Doctrine of the Mandate'

It is commonly said that the House of Lords is a conservative body which acts as a drag on hasty legislation, and holds back until the nation shows clearly that it has made up its mind. This is undoubtedly true, and if it were the whole truth the limited authority retained by the House would provoke no strong resentment in any quarter; but it is only a part of the truth. The word 'conservative' has two distinct meanings in England, according as it is spelled with a small or a capital C.

A. Lawrence Lowell, 1908

The House of Lords recovered its confidence remarkably quickly after its public humiliation in 1832. For the next fifty years, the two Houses lived together in general harmony, quarrelling rather about privilege than about policy. The great crisis of Reform was an aberration in their habitual relationship, not a parting of the ways. In 1814, Lord Liverpool had opposed a lavish creation of peers because he believed that it would withdraw 'the natural landed aristocracy of the country' from the House of Commons.[1] That aristocracy remained there in large numbers for a long time to come; in 1865, it was calculated that a quarter of the members of the House of Commons were connected with 31 great families.[2] The Great Reform Bill might alter the content and tone of measures coming before the House of Commons, but it made no substantial difference to its composition. Whatever advanced

[1] Quoted in H. J. Hanham, *The Nineteenth Century Constitution* (1969), p. 176.
[2] Low, op. cit., p. 183n.

Radicals might think, either of the behaviour of the House of Lords or of the hereditary principle in the abstract, the peers stood in greater danger from the mob in 1832 than they did from the House of Commons. Lord Grey had asked for a creation of peers to break down obstruction to a particular measure and not to destroy the powers of the House in which he sat; and if the Lords had not given way he would have been ready to fall in with the King's wishes that the new creations should change the estate of the peerage as little as possible. Family trees were scrutinised in search of eldest sons and collateral heirs of childless noblemen who were thought to be well-disposed to the Bill, and it was understood that these sources should be exhausted before there were any creations that would entail a permanent addition to the peerage.

Thus, in addition to the sentiments of the King, the House of Lords was protected by two complementary attitudes—the reluctance of the Whigs to impair an estate of the realm, and the reluctance of the Tory leaders to provoke another outburst of popular resentment. There were conservatives on both sides in both Houses. A sign that matters were returning to normal was given on 3 June 1833, when the Duke of Wellington carried a motion, by 79 to 69, on the affairs of Spain, which amounted to a vote of censure on the Ministry's foreign policy. No one expected Ministers to take very much notice of a vote which condemned a general disposition in policy, and had no effect upon legislation. Macaulay, however, was premature in his forecast:

Nobody seems to care one straw for what the Peers may say about any public matter. A Resolution of the Court of Common Counsel, or of a meeting at Freemasons' Hall, has often made a greater sensation than this declaration of a branch of the Legislature against the Executive Government. The institution of the Peerage is evidently dying a natural death.[3]

[3] G. O. Trevelyan, *The Life and Letters of Lord Macaulay* (1889 ed.), p. 216.

The Tory peers were greatly influenced by the attitude of the Duke of Wellington. He was convinced that, whatever the House of Lords might think of the merits of particular measures, it ought never to put itself into lonely opposition against the Crown and the House of Commons, especially when the public mind was deeply stirred. There was more, however, both to Wellington's authority and his attitude to government than is contained in Lord Clarendon's quip about the terms in which he would recommend the passing of the Catholic Relief Bill in 1829: 'Oh, it will be easy enough. He'll say: "My lords! Attention! Right about face! March!" '[4] He regarded himself as standing in a personal relationship to the Crown—paid and rewarded, and therefore retained—but he led the House of Lords as much by his arguments as by his example. In July 1833, when the Irish Church Bill came up to the Lords, Wellington attacked it in debate, and then summoned his followers to a meeting at Apsley House, where he told them why he thought that the Bill must pass. In August 1834, the Lords rejected the Irish Tithes Bill, but this was a measure to which the deep aversion of many peers was known to be shared by the King. Wellington's consistent conviction was that it was better to consent to a bad Bill than to run a serious risk of civil disturbance. This was the principle upon which he urged the Lords to pass Catholic Emancipation, Reform and the repeal of the Corn Laws. On the last of these measures, he is supposed to have told a protectionist peer who expressed a bad opinion of it: 'Bad opinion of the Bill, my lord! You can't have a worse opinion of it than I have, but it was recommended from the throne; it was passed by the Commons by a large majority, and we must all vote for it. The Queen's Government must be supported.'[5] He gave a bleak warning to the House of Lords of the consequences of rejecting the Bill. Their lordships could do so once, but did they really believe that would end the matter? The Bill would assuredly come back to them, and would they take the risk of rejecting it a second time? The greater wisdom was to pass it at once, although this might

[4] Ibid., p. 115n.
[5] Quoted in 132 *Quarterly Review* (April 1872), p. 239.

seem to be against their immediate interests. This might, on a narrow view, seem tantamount to saying that the Lords could only keep their powers if they did not use them; but the argument could be developed beyond the trivial point. The House of Lords, it ran, was the ultimate guardian of the constitution. It must therefore preserve its powers intact against the day when it might have to spend them upon some great occasion.

During the half-century that followed the Reform Act, the Liberals were in power for most of the time, and created the greater number of peers—198 between 1830 and 1885, against 70 created under Conservatives—but they remained a perpetual minority in the House of Lords. Many peers who were created as Liberals did not remain so, but found a certain gravitational pull drawing them towards the Conservatives. Those who remained Liberals did not show excessive zeal in supporting their party, and Liberal governments sometimes found it difficult to get their business done in the House of Lords. In 1835, when the Lords numbered about 430, Lord Hatherton calculated that the total available to the Whigs was only 87; many of those were not in London, and most of those who were displayed no appetite for regular attendance:

> But the unintelligible thing to me, who am used to the whipping-in of the House of Commons, is the squeamishness that exists about asking Peers to stay in town and attend the Committees. Who shall make such a request to such august personages as the Dukes of Devonshire and Sutherland?[6]

It was to remedy both this mischief and the Lords' insulation from opinions in the constituencies that induced Lord John Russell to suggest, in 1836, that there should be a creation of peers, to the number of eight or twelve, whenever a Whig Ministry was thwarted by the House of Lords.[7] The suggestion came to nothing: it was by no means established that the royal fountain of honour would play automatically at a Ministry's

[6] A. Aspinall, 'Extracts from Lord Hatherton's diary', 17 *Parliamentary Affairs*, p. 253.
[7] Sir Spencer Walpole, *Life of Lord John Russell* (1889), vol. II, p. 267.

request. Peel had asked for six new peerages, when he took office in 1835, as a sign of the King's confidence; after Peel's resignation, Melbourne asked for eight, but was able to obtain only enough to counter-balance Peel's creations.

The usage was quickly established, after 1832, that a Ministry would not resign only because of proceedings in the House of Lords. Melbourne said explicitly that he would remain in office for as long as he retained the confidence of the Crown and the House of Commons. But it was still felt necessary, from time to time, to meet adverse votes in the Lords by countervailing resolutions in the Commons. Melbourne took this course in 1839, after the Lords had expressed no confidence in his Irish policy; he told the Queen that if the question were lost in the House of Commons, or carried only by a small majority, the Ministry must resign.[8] In the event, the majority of 318 to 296 was considered to be sufficient. Lord John Russell took a similar course in 1850, after the Lords' disapproval of Lord Palmerston's actions over the claims of Don Pacifico. These resolutions were an oblique but mildly effective form of opposition, in that time had to be found to rebut them in the House of Commons, where there was always pressure upon business.

By mid-century, then, it seemed that the House of Lords had settled down to play what Bagehot described as a dignified, rather than an efficient, role in the workings of government. Its powers remained in being, but it showed no disposition to use them imprudently. Bagehot thought that its condition was an indication of political tranquillity in the country :

In fact the House of Lords, as a House, is not a bulwark that will keep out revolution, but an index that revolution is unlikely. Resting as it does upon old deference, and inveterate homage, it shows that the spasm of new forces, the outbreak of new agencies, which we call revolution, is for the time simply impossible. So long as many old leaves linger on the November trees, you know that there has been little frost and no wind; just so while the House of Lords retains much

[8] 1 LQV, III, p. 402.

power, you may know that there is no desperate discontent
in the country, no wild agency likely to cause a great
demolition.[9]

In 1860, the House of Lords revived an ancient power when
it rejected Gladstone's Bill to repeal the paper duties, one of
the 'taxes on knowledge' that were a perpetual grievance to
Radicals. This was a challenge to the spirit, if not the form, of
the Commons' resolutions of 1671 and 1678, which asserted
that the Lords ought not to alter money Bills. The Lords had
never explicitly admitted the claims of the Commons, but they
had in fact submitted to them. The right of the Lords to
reject a money Bill remained, on the tacit assumption that it
would not be exercised. The rejection of 1860 did not provoke
a major constitutional crisis, because the Cabinet was divided
on the merits of Gladstone's proposal. Lord Palmerston, the
Prime Minister, was personally hostile to the repeal of the
paper duties: he told the Queen that, notwithstanding the
constitutional impropriety of its rejection, 'the opinion of the
great majority of the public is that the Lords have done a right
and useful thing'.[10] The House of Commons passed three
resolutions, reasserting that grants of aid and supply were the
sole concern of the Commons 'as to the matter, manner,
measure, and time'; though the House of Lords had rejected
money Bills in the past, 'the exercise of that power has not
been frequent and is regarded by this House with peculiar
jealousy'.[11] Further than that, Palmerston would not go. There
was, he said, no means of taking from the Lords their right
to reject Bills of any kind, except by an Act to which they
had assented or by revolution; he did not believe that the
Lords had taken the first step towards constitutional aggression.
Indeed, the Lords had been given their opportunity by the
Ministry's mismanagement of the time-table of the House of
Commons. Two controversial measures had been taken in
tandem—the repeal of the paper duties and Russell's reform
Bill—, debate had lingered on towards the tail of the session,

[9] Bagehot, *English Constitution,* pp. 132–3.
[10] 1 LQV, III, p. 511.
[11] H. of C., 5 July 1860, c. 1384.

when members began to drift away from London, and the majority for the repeal in the House had finally sunk to nine. An impartial observer, Palmerston said, might reasonably conclude that opinion on this measure was changing, and that the House of Commons should be given an opportunity of reconsidering its decision.[12]

But Gladstone had his way in the end. In 1861, he circumvented both the House of Lords and his opponents in the Cabinet by combining all the taxation measures for the year in a single Customs and Internal Finances Bill, thus confronting the Lords with the choice between accepting the budget as a whole and taking the ultimate step of refusing to grant supplies to the Crown. The Prime Minister accepted both expedients—the single consolidated Bill, and the repeal of the paper duties contained within it—with small enthusiasm; he appeared to lose his temper in Cabinet, and shocked Gladstone by declaring that he did not propose to regard the Bill as a 'Cabinet question' in the House of Commons.[13] But it passed both Houses, and the precedent of the omnibus Finance Bill became established at once. That was how Harcourt's highly controversial budget of 1894, which altered the system of assessing death duties upon land, passed the House of Lords; that, too, was displeasing to the Prime Minister. There were some who argued that the House of Commons, in both these years, had revived the old and obnoxious device of 'tacking'—adding extraneous matters to a money Bill, so that the Lords could not amend it. Opponents on the other side retorted that, if this were so, the Lords had only themselves to blame, by reviving powers that had become obsolete. That case was easier to make in 1894 than in 1861. By Harcourt's time, the House of Lords had greatly inflated its pretensions by adopting a new theory of the mandate. This went much further than the argument sometimes used (notably by Lord Stanley in debate on the repeal of the Corn Laws) that the Lords had a duty to protect the nation from its representatives; it was a claim to interpret what the nation really wanted. The occasion was an accident; a precedent

[12] Ibid., p. 1392–4.
[13] Morley, *Gladstone*, II, p. 32.

rapidly crystallised about it; and from the precedent a doctrine
was developed that owed much to a single ingenious mind,
that of Lord Salisbury.

The accident occurred in 1868, when Disraeli was Prime
Minister at the head of a party in a minority in the House of
Commons. Gladstone had erupted out of one of his bouts of
recuperation in Italy, had reunited the vagrant Liberal
factions, and had carried against the Ministry resolutions
declaring an intention of disestablishing the Irish Church.
Disraeli, after some havering, decided to remain in office and
to ask for a dissolution later in the year. The two decisions
were linked together, at least in the subtleties of Disraeli's
intentions. Not only did he refuse to treat the vote on the Irish
Church resolutions as one of confidence, but he denied the
moral competence of that House of Commons to deal with
disestablishment at all, since it was a matter that 'had never
been hinted at on the hustings when this Parliament was
elected'. Furthermore his Ministry, although in a technical
minority on this issue, had in the past been 'morally supported
by a majority', and he expressed 'a profound conviction that
the opinion of the nation does not agree upon this subject
with the vote of the House of Commons'.[14] Gladstone, after
objecting to a 'penal dissolution', produced some generalised
arguments that could be taken to point in the same direction.
Following a well-worn track, he said that there were two
conditions—and by implication only two—to be fulfilled
before a defeated Ministry had a right to ask for an appeal
to the electorate—an adequate cause of public policy and a
rational prospect that the result would lead to a reversal of a
vote by the House of Commons. But, he added, a rational
prospect would always be in the eye of any Prime Minister,
if he chose to put it there.[15]

At Disraeli's initiative, then, the general election of 1868
was deemed to be fought on the issue of the Irish Church:
both parties had stated their policies in the House of Commons,
and it was now for the constituencies to choose between them.
There is of necessity an element of fiction in ascribing to the

[14] H. of C., 4 May, 1868, c. 1702.
[15] Ibid., c. 1712.

result of a general election a single answer to any question, and the fiction was compounded when many seats, for local reasons, were uncontested—212 of them in 1868.[16] But when the returns were in, one thing at least was clear : 'the age of equipoise' was over. The Liberals had a majority of 112. The grant of power was emphatic.

The Conservative Party in both Houses accepted the verdict : the fate of the Irish Church had been settled, in principle at least. The Queen felt sufficiently alarmed, at the possibility that the House of Lords might resist, to send a warning to Lord Derby. She disliked the measure, she said, 'but after the Dissolution last autumn, and the large majorities with which the Bill had been passed in the House of Commons, for the House of Lords to throw it out, and thus place itself in collision with the House of Commons, would be most dangerous if not *disastrous*.'[17] She added the practical advice that, if the Lords did not oppose the Bill on second reading they would still be in a strong position to make amendments in committee.

It was left to Salisbury to elaborate what might have been regarded merely as yet another exercise of prudence, upon Wellingtonian principles, into a doctrine that might have been approved by Jean-Jacques Rousseau. He enunciated a general theory of the role of the House of Lords—or, as a cynic might have said, of the House of Lords when Liberal governments were in office. It was not the function of the Lords to be no more than an echo of the Commons. 'The object of the existence of a second House of Parliament is to supply the omissions and correct the defects which arise in the proceedings of the first.' But constitutional fictions must be distinguished from facts. 'In ninety-nine cases out of a hundred the House of Commons is theoretically the representative of the nation, but is so only in theory. The constitutional theory has no corresponding basis in fact, because in ninety-nine cases out of a hundred the nation, as a whole, takes no interest in our politics.' In those indifferent cases, he would make no differ-

[16] Trevor Lloyd, 'Uncontested seats in British General Elections, 1852–1910', 8 *Historical Journal* (1965).
[17] 2 LQV, I, p. 604.

ence whatever between the prerogatives of either House. But there remained the hundredth case, when

> the nation must be called into council and must decide the policy of the Government. It may be that the House of Commons in determining the opinion of the nation is wrong; and if there are grounds for entertaining that belief . . . it is the duty of this House to insist that the nation should be consulted, and that one House without the support of the nation shall not be allowed to domineer over the other. We must decide whether the House of Commons does or does not represent the full, the deliberate, the sustained convictions of the body of the nation.

But when it was clear that the House of Commons and the nation were at one, then 'the vocation of this House has passed away'. Such a situation obtained at that moment: 'the nation has decided against Protestant ascendancy in Ireland, and . . . [the House of Lords] would not be doing its duty if it opposed itself further against the will of the nation.'[18]

Contained in Salisbury's speech, there was a doctrine that was explosive in its implications for representative government. It would have been very difficult for a Liberal politician to have quarrelled with Salisbury in 1869, since his doctrine, as he then applied it, was in the Liberal interest. For much the same reasons, it would have been difficult for a Jeffersonian Democrat to have quarrelled with Chief Justice Marshall's decision in the case of *Marbury* v. *Madison* in 1803. But just as Marshall was asserting the right of the Federal Supreme Court to judge between the Congress and the Constitution of the United States of America, so Lord Salisbury was asserting the right of the House of Lords to judge between the House of Commons and the 'nation'.

Salisbury was going significantly further than either Wellington or Disraeli. Later, as leader of the Conservative Party in the House of Lords, he was to put his theory into action and establish a pattern of behaviour that led eventually

[18] H. of L., 17 June 1869, cc. 83 sqq.

to the rejection of the budget of 1909. Wellington had warned the House of Lords against unwise resistance when the Crown and the majority in the House of Commons were in accord. Disraeli had appealed from the House of Commons to the electorate, and had resigned as soon as the electorate's decision had been given, without waiting to be defeated in Parliament. Salisbury was claiming for the House of Lords a general right to challenge the representativeness of the majority in the House of Commons. That challenge, although made by an hereditary and therefore unrepresentative body, would be issued in the name of the nation. If the majority of the House of Commons was so certain that it had the electorate behind it, he was saying, what was wrong in asking it to put the matter to the proof? Dilke, in 1881, pointed out that Salisbury's doctrine contained a double standard of judgment when he said that, pushed to its logical conclusion, it meant 'annual Parliaments when we are in office, and septennial Parliaments when they are in office'.

Salisbury knew exactly what he was doing, as he made clear in a letter to Lord Carnarvon on 20 February 1872:

> The plan which I prefer is frankly to acknowledge that the nation is Master, though the House of Commons is not, and to yield our own opinion only when the judgment of the nation has been challenged at the polls and decidedly expressed. This Doctrine, it seems to me, has the advantage of being: (1) Theoretically sound, (2) popular, (3) safe against agitation, and (4) so rarely applicable as practically to place little fetter upon our independence.[19]

Put this way, and coupled with Salisbury's general views on popular apathy and the irrelevance of parliamentary politics to the ordinary citizens, this was a doctrine not of balance but resistance. This became clear after 1880, when Salisbury had convinced himself that Gladstone was leading the nation in a direction in which it did not wish to go.

The House of Lords asserted itself as soon as the Liberals

[19] Lady Gwendolen Cecil, *Life of Robert, Marquess of Salisbury* (1921–32), vol. II, p. 25.

took office in 1880. At the end of the first session of that Parliament, *The Spectator* commented that Lord Beaconsfield towered above Her Majesty's Government:

> He has a complete veto on all legislation. He says that this Bill is to be thrown out, that emasculated, and another rendered meaningless, and it is done. He dislikes the Compensation for Disturbance Bill, and it is dead. He says he will not oppose the Hares and Rabbits Bill, and it is safe. He is the Jove of the situation. The constituencies of the nation are nothing before the man whom they have just formally condemned.[20]

Salisbury succeeded to the leadership in the Lords on Beaconsfield's death in 1881. In the following year, he tried to reject the Irish Arrears Bill, with the avowed object of forcing a dissolution. The Queen warned him that if he provoked a constitutional crisis it might have unfortunate consequences for institutions of many kinds, but he was not to be deterred. He replied that his conviction and that of the Conservative leaders in the House of Commons was 'that in the interests of the Crown and nation, as well as in that of the Conservative Party, a dissolution would have been welcome'.[21] He failed to push the matter to a conclusion because he could not get enough Conservative peers to follow him; some of them did not think that an election would favour their party.

Lord Rosebery said that Lord Salisbury was 'a little impetuous in the exercise of the weapon committed to his charge. He never likes to keep it in its sheath. He is always trying its temper—if he is not hacking about and dealing destruction and death with it, he is always flourishing it and threatening with it. He is like a King of Hungary on his coronation, who rides to an eminence and brandishes his sword to the four corners of the globe.'[22] This is not an unfair description of Salisbury's behaviour in 1884, when the House of Lords did bring on a constitutional crisis by rejecting the

[20] Quoted in Emily Alleyn, *Lords Versus Commons* (1931), p. 92.
[21] 2 LQV, III, pp. 327–9.
[22] Lord Rosebery, *The Reform of the House of Lords. Three Speeches* (1910), pp. 45–6.

first of the Liberals' franchise Bills. Salisbury would have liked a dissolution upon the existing register; what he did not want was a dissolution with a new register and the old constituencies. The Lords were given a plausible reason for rejecting the franchise Bill by Gladstone's insistence on postponing redistribution. Relations between the party leaderships had deteriorated to the point where Conservatives were not willing to accept Liberal assurances that redistribution would be forthcoming in the next session.

Gladstone would not admit that the House of Lords had any right to demand a dissolution. He wrote to the Queen:

> Mr Gladstone will not trouble your Majesty with details, beyond observing that in no period of our history, known to him, has the House of Commons been dissolved at the call of the House of Lords, given through an adverse vote; that in his opinion the establishment of such a principle would place the House of Commons in a position of inferiority, as a Legislative Chamber, to the House of Lords; and that an attempt to establish it would certainly end in organic changes, detrimental to the dignity and authority of the House of Lords.[23]

It was the implied threat in the last sentence that troubled the Queen. She tried to mediate in this franchise controversy, as she had tried to mediate in 1866. 'The great object,' she wrote to the Duke of Richmond, 'must be to maintain the important position of the House of Lords unimpaired.'[24] The calculation of remote consequences did not often obtrude upon Lord Salisbury's devout and habitual fatalism: a man made the decision that seemed best at the moment and, thereafter, what would be would be. He had always believed that there were things stronger than House of Commons majorities, and he was unimpressed by mass meetings, especially when they were organised by his opponents. 'A Minister,' he told Ponsonby, 'always commands a majority in the House of Commons, and he can always get up demonstrations.'[25]

[23] 2 LQV, III, pp. 517–18.
[24] Ibid., p. 546.
[25] Ibid., p. 552.

Gladstone had no wish, then, for a fight to the death with the House of Lords, and the issue was settled by an arrangement made by leaders of both parties, and presented to Parliament as a *fait accompli*. (The final stages of the Redistribution Bill were passed under Salisbury's government in 1885.) Labouchere got no support from Gladstone when, on 21 November 1884, he proposed a resolution in the House of Commons asking for 'such alterations in the relations of the two Houses of Parliament' as would make it impossible for the Conservative Party 'to alter, defeat, or delay legislation, although recommended by the responsible advisers of the Crown'. Labouchere was in lighthearted mood :

> If there were a House of 500 shoemakers of Northampton and the Conservatives when in power had to submit everything to these excellent Radicals, honourable Gentlemen would say the system was monstrous. The present system, in his view as a Liberal, was *mutatis mutandis* equally monstrous.[26]

Gladstone came out with a modified defence of heredity; it was a better principle of selection than some others, such as wealth. Moreover, if the House of Lords were abolished peers would be found in the House of Commons in numbers disproportionately higher than their numbers in the country.[27]

The resistance of the House of Lords in 1884 brought a very important reward indeed to the Conservative Party—a share in the redistribution. Previously, one of the prizes for carrying a reform Bill was that the successful Ministers had in their own hands the consequent reshaping of the constituencies. In this instance, redistribution was the work of a conclave—Gladstone, Hartington and Dilke from the Liberals, Salisbury and Northcote from the Conservatives—and the final result was principally the work of Salisbury and Dilke.

Furthermore, converts were being made to the 'doctrine of the mandate' outside the ranks of the Conservatives. In 1886, Lord Hartington used language similar to Disraeli's in 1868 in opposing Gladstone's first Home Rule Bill. He knew, he

---

[26] H. of C., 21 Nov. 1884, c. 141.
[27] Ibid., c. 161.

said, that there was no such thing as a 'principle of the mandate' in the English constitution, but none the less there were certain moral limits that should not be transgressed, and one of them was that the House of Commons should not 'initiate legislation, especially upon its first meeting, of which the constituencies were not informed . . . and as to which, if they had been so informed, there is, at all events, the very greatest doubt as to what their decision might be'.[28] By 1893, when he opposed Gladstone's second Home Rule Bill, the Duke of Devonshire (as Hartington became in 1891) had accepted the full Salisbury doctrine in its most emphatic and tendentious form. On great questions touching the fundamental institutions of the state, he said, it was the business of a second chamber 'to prevent changes of that character being made without the absolute certainty that they are in accordance with the will of the majority of the people'. As for Home Rule, 'we have no knowledge and we can have none' of what the electorate wanted. He compared Home Rule in 1893 with Irish Disestablishment in 1869, when legislation 'was only proposed . . . after it had formed the single issue submitted to the country at a general election, and after the verdict of the country had been given in the most unmistakable terms'. The existing situation was very different :

> . . . no human being can tell on what question the majority which put the present Government in power was returned. No doubt some electors voted for Home Rule, but it is quite certain that a larger number voted for disestablishment, or local option, or for parish councils, or for changes in the incidence of taxation in towns, or for changes in the labour laws . . . I deny that the House of Commons received any mandate upon Home Rule at all at the last election.[29]

The Duke of Devonshire was echoing Salisbury, not only in the substance but in the details of his argument. In November 1892, Salisbury had written in *The National Review*, after the general election :

---

[28] H. of C., 9 April 1886, c. 1244.
[29] H. of L., 8 Sep. 1893, cc. 27–31.

What policy the electors intended by their votes to promote is a question which must probably be answered in a different manner in different localities. No reasonable person doubts that a large number of the Radical members have been elected on account of their views on other subjects than Home Rule. It is notorious that the Welsh voted for Radical candidates, not for their love of Home Rule, but for their aversion towards the Welsh Church. The crofters of the Scottish Highlands and the peasants of Norfolk were full of agrarian projects and aspirations; but they gave little heed to Ireland. In Wiltshire and Oxfordshire the labourers, misled by a falsehood of magnificent audacity, voted to prevent the Tories from imposing duties upon corn. The mining constituencies voted for the Eight Hours Bill; the Leicester people voted against vaccination; the Dockyard constituencies were fired with indignation against some obscure Admiralty wrongs . . .[30]

In all this, there were formidable denials and claims. There was a denial both of the sovereignty of Parliament and of the Crown's prerogative right (as exercised by Ministers) to propose such measures as were considered expedient. It is significant that it was at this time that the adoption of the referendum began to be seriously discussed in England.

Almost as soon as the Liberals had taken office in 1892, Salisbury warned the Queen that the House of Lords would use its powers against them.

The object of their [*sc.* the Lords'] existence is to be a check on hasty legislation, and the action of a check is necessarily displeasing to the person checked. Of course this would not justify them in setting themselves against the clear and deliberate judgment of the country; but this mistake they have never committed.[31]

The claim that the House of Lords had never gone against the popular will was breathtaking in its audacity, but on Salisbury's principles it could not be disproved, except by a referendum (and even then with reservations) or (with similar

---

[30] Quoted in S. Maccoby, *English Radicalism, 1886–1914* (1953), p. 132.
[31] 3 LQV, II, pp. 129–30.

reservations) by annual elections, each of them limited to a single issue. Having rejected the Home Rule Bill of 1893, by 419 votes to 41, the Lords went on to reject or mutilate the rest of the proposed legislation. It was useless for Liberal spokesmen to plead that their measures were based on the programme put together at the Liberal conference at Newcastle in 1891, and that therefore the electorate had known all about them when it voted in 1892. The sheer abundance of the Newcastle Programme detracted from the moral authority that could be claimed for any single item within it. At Newcastle, the faddists and crotchet-mongers of the Liberal Party had been allowed to gratify their whimsical fancies: planks in the platform had been distributed like cutlasses in *The Wind in the Willows*—'There's one for Rat, and there's one for Mole, and there's one for Badger.' The galling thing was that Salisbury seemed to be right: there was no great public outcry as the Lords did their destructive work. When, at last, Gladstone was ready to lead a crusade against them—to dissolve and go to the country—his Cabinet would not follow him. In his last speech from the front bench, Gladstone said that the differences between the two Houses had become intolerable, and that a decision in favour of one or other of them would be given by a higher authority than either of them, by the nation itself.[32] It was an authority to which the Liberals were markedly unwilling to appeal. Local option on the sale of alcoholic drink, Welsh disestablishment, metropolitan reform—it was hard to think of any of these as a suitable issue for a grand confrontation on sovereignty within the constitution. Salisbury was able to inflate his doctrine, and to tease the Liberals with arithmetical might-have-beens. The Lords did not reject Harcourt's budget of 1894, in spite of what they thought about his new death duties, but Salisbury used the occasion to reiterate his now familiar distinction between the legal and the moral authority of the House of Commons. He paid the usual encomium to the irresistibility of the national will. However, he added, the Finance Bill had passed the Commons with a majority of only 14; therefore,

[32] H. of C., 1 March 1894, c. 1150.

if eight votes had gone the other way on that division, it would have been rejected. His researches had revealed to him eight constituencies with majorities so small that if 150 votes had gone the other way at the last election, all of them would have been lost to the Liberals.

> I repeat that the legal authority is good if it is exercised by a single vote, but the moral authority of the House of Commons depends on the popular strength which it represents, and which lies behind it. This particular measure undoubtedly has been passed by moral authority of the very weakest kind—150 householders and lodgers, not better men than 150 Peers.[33]

Salisbury had transformed the House of Lords into a decisive factor in government, and at the same time had popularised a distinctively Conservative theory of the constitution: the national will was supreme, and the Conservative Party represented it. The House of Lords was the instrument that ensured that the national will should be respected. By 1884, the *Quarterly Review*, an excellent reflector of conservative opinion, was writing as if Salisbury's gospel had become the conventional wisdom. 'Rejection by [the House of Lords] means, as is well-known and understood, simply a reference to the people.'[34] 'Lord Salisbury *challenged* an appeal to the people, he did not claim it; and the distinction involves a very substantial difference . . . The constitutional right of the House of Lords is, not to demand a dissolution, but to abide by its own judgment till a general election shall have decided the issue.'[35] Moreover, the House of Lords did not find itself menaced by a dangerous outburst of popular wrath. A shrewd American observer went to the heart of the matter. In 1908, Lowell, the President of Harvard University, wrote: 'Now the very accentuation of party has made it easier for the peers to resist a Liberal ministry, because in doing so they are evidently opposing, not the people as a whole, but only a

---

[33] H. of L., 10 July 1894, c. 1225.
[34] *Quarterly Review,* July 1884, p. 232.
[35] Ibid., October 1884, pp. 579–60.

part of the people, and a part that is a majority by a very small fraction.'[36]

The Liberals, then, laboured under a permanent handicap, even in elections. 'The workingmen have been told that although the Conservatives promise them less, they are better able to fulfil their promises than the Liberals who cannot control the House of Lords.'[37] The erosion of Liberal confidence may be seen in the admission—never made before 1867—that slender majorities in the House of Commons were not enough. After the general election of 1892, Morley confessed in private that Gladstone's composite majority of 40 was too small for him to pass a Home Rule Bill that had any chance of passing the Lords. In the franchise debates in 1884, Duncan McLaren, a Liberal back-bencher, pressed to a division his amendment to abolish faggot-voters, although he knew that the House of Commons would not accept it, because the Bill as a whole would have a better chance of passing the Lords 'if it was found that a large number of persons were anxious to make it stronger and more drastic'.[38] The Lords could turn such arguments to their own advantage by asserting that 'moderate' Liberals had voted for certain Bills in the confidence that their more drastic clauses would, to their own secret satisfaction, be rejected or amended in the other House. In the face of all this, the Liberals seemed unable to agree upon any strategy more aggressive than sending up item after item of the Newcastle Programme for slaughter, in the hope that sooner or later the electorate would become righteously enraged: this ritual was called 'filling up the cup' or, more realistically, 'ploughing the sands'.

II

During the nineteenth century the House of Lords retained its powers intact; it made only one important change in its

---

[36] A. Lawrence Lowell, *The Government of England* (1908; 1912), vol. I, p. 409.
[37] Ibid., p. 411.
[38] H. of C., 26 May 1884, c. 1407.

procedure, the ending of voting by proxy in 1868; and it experienced only minor changes in its composition—the admission of 28 Irish representative peers and four bishops in 1801, the disappearance of the Irish bishops in 1869, and the admission in 1876 of two judges (later increased to four) as Lords of Appeal in Ordinary. The law lords were originally admitted until their retirement; in 1887, they became peers for life. They were there to strengthen the House of Lords in its judicial capacity as the final court of appeal.

The admission of the law lords to life peerages was done gradually and on grounds of utility. In 1856, the doctrine of the balanced constitution was invoked to prevent the admission of non-hereditary lords temporal. The Queen was in favour of life peers, to improve the judicial quality of the House without ennobling men too poor to keep up an estate. (It had already been suggested that life peerages might be appropriate rewards for victorious generals.) In 1851, the Queen agreed to the offer of a barony without remainder to Dr Lushington, a judge of the Court of Admiralty; he refused.[39] In 1855, she encouraged Lord Palmerston to recommend someone else. The choice fell upon Sir James Parke, and it was carefully made: he had more than fifteen years' service on the bench, and was therefore entitled to a pension, he was over seventy and he had no son. He was created Baron Wensleydale, without remainder, in 1856. The House of Lords refused to let him take his seat as a life peer. Lord Lyndhurst led the insurgents, and his argument distinguished between the right of the Sovereign to create a peer and the right of the House of Lords to determine its own membership; usages, in short, should not be changed and the basis of the constitution was static convention:

> . . . long-considered usage is the basis and principle of our laws and our constitution . . . the constitution consists of three estates—of King, Lords and Commons—united in the State, but each independent of the other, and producing harmonious action by the balance of their powers . . .

[39] 1 LQV, II, p. 284.

The Sovereign may by his prerogative, if he thinks proper, create a hundred Peers, with descendible qualities, in the course of a day. That would be . . . strictly legal, but everybody must feel and everybody must know that such an exercise of the undoubted prerogative of the Crown would be a flagrant violation of the principles of the constitution. In the same manner, the Sovereign might place the Great Seal . . . in the hands of a person, a layman, wholly unacquainted with the laws of the country. That, also, would be a flagrant violation of the constitution . . .[40]

Lord Lyndhurst's speech was a triumph of antiquarian learning; his sight was too dim to enable him to read, and he had learnt by heart the long array of black-letter authorities which he quoted to the House. He was supported by his fellow Tories and also by some Old Whigs and by three former Lord Chancellors—Campbell, St Leonards and Brougham. But the battle was not fought on party lines. Life peerages had not been intended to counter Tory hegemony in the Lords; there was no 'Tory phalanx' at that time, and the balance was held by Peelites and neutrals; Lord Derby usually lost when he challenged the government of the day on a division.[41] Opposition was by no means confined to the Tories or the House of Lords. The immediate sequel to the Lords' decision was the introduction of a Bill in the House of Commons to permit not more than four judges to sit in the House of Lords for life; the House of Commons rejected it. There were some who thought that life peerages would destroy the balance of the constitution by impairing the independence of the Lords against both Crown and Commons; some may have thought that the proposal was a stalking-horse for Prince Albert's supposed plans to turn the House of Lords into a Senate of Notables, on continental lines. Bagehot thought that a great mistake had been made. 'The House of Lords rejected the inestimable, the unprecedented opportunity of being tacitly reformed. Such a chance does not come twice.'[42] In fact, the

---

[40] H. of L., 7 and 22 Feb. 1856, cc. 265 and 1167.

[41] Olive Anderson, 'The Wensleydale peerage case and the position of the House of Lords in the mid-nineteenth century'. 82 EHR (1967).

[42] Bagehot, *English Constitution*, p. 145.

House of Lords was to be given several more chances, and it turned them all down.

In 1869, Earl Russell proposed a Bill that would have permitted not more than 28 life peers to sit in the House of Lords at any one time, with the reservation that not more than four of them should be created in any single year. Russell wished the net to be widely cast: life peers would be selected from those Scotch and Irish noblemen who did not sit in the House of Lords, from those who had sat for ten years in the House of Commons or had been in the service of the Crown at home or abroad for five years, from the judiciary, from the armed services, and from those distinguished in science, letters and the arts. The Lords refused to pass Russell's Bill, but it drew some qualified support from Lord Salisbury. He was doubtful whether what was essentially a political assembly would be strengthened by the admission of non-political figures, but he wanted the Lords to be more representative of the nation, and thus to express more diverse views and show more political antagonism to one another:

> We belong too much to one class, and the consequence is that with respect to a large number of questions we are all too much of one mind . . . We must try to impress on the country the fact that, because we are not an elective House, we are not a bit less a representative House; and not until the constitution of the House plainly reveals that fact shall we be able to retain permanently, in face of the advances of the House of Commons, the ancient privileges and constitution of this House.[43]

That was the opinion of an intelligent Conservative; for exactly opposite reasons, reform of the House of Lords would be opposed by Radicals who wished to see it ended, not mended.

The House of Lords was an effective moulder of minds; if new peers were not conservative in spirit on their creation, they tended to become so with the passing of time. Lord Granville calculated that between 1850 and 1869 the numbers of peers who took the Liberal whip had diminished by five, through

[43] H. of L., 9 April 1869, c. 465.

extinction, incapacity or conversion to Conservatism. He told the Queen, in August 1869 :

> The majority is between 60 and 70 without counting Bishops or Liberals who vote oftener for the Opposition than the Government. No one would pretend that a dozen Peers could swamp such a majority, but Her Majesty's Government requires moral support in the House. They are not cordially supported by even the small minority, of whom the most eminent are ex-place men, who many of them are not friends of Mr Gladstone and prefer the failure to the success of his colleagues. If only 3 or 4 Peers are created, they get awed by the atmosphere in which they find themselves.[44]

The splitting of the Liberal Party in 1886, and the massive defection of the Whigs from Gladstone, made it easier to accuse the Lords of party as well as class prejudice. Each successive general election after 1867 widened the social difference between the House of Lords and the House of Commons. It could still be said, on the day when Palmerston was alive and dead, that the two Houses were remarkably homogeneous in terms of class, social habits, agreement about the purposes of government, and the enjoyment of property. After 1865, there was a steady trickle of property interests away from the Liberals and towards the Conservatives; in 1886, the trickle became a gush. Gladstone, who could hardly be regarded as an inveterate foe of the House of Lords, was well aware of the dangers that might one day break up a hereditary assembly, representing a threatened form of landed property, overwhelmingly biassed towards one party, which persisted in regarding itself as the embodiment of the national will. In 1892, he warned the Queen of the possible consequences of

> the widening of that gap, or chasm, in opinion which more largely than heretofore separates the upper and more powerful from the more numerous classes of the community . . .
> As regards landed property, Mr Gladstone doubts whether Liberals now own more than one acre in 50, taking the three

[44] P. Guedalla (ed), *The Queen and Mr Gladstone* (1933), vol. i, p. 199.

kingdoms together . . . Yet, for the first time in our history, we have seen in the recent election a majority of the House of Commons . . . returned against the sense of nearly the entire peerage, and of the vast majority of the upper and leisured class.[45]

Salisbury, like Russell before him, came to argue that the Lords should be leavened with men of distinction from the world of scholarship and the arts; but this did little to resolve the problem that Gladstone had described. (Gladstone successfully recommended Tennyson for a peerage in 1884 and, ironically enough, lost his support in 1886.) Salisbury was able to elevate Sir William Thomson, president of the Royal Society, to the peerage as Baron Kelvin; but the Queen jibbed at the president of the Royal Academy and Sir Frederick Leighton had to wait for his barony until the day before his death in 1896. But the main new source of recruitment, by the end of the century, was from industry and commerce.

> The House of Lords is waiting for
> The newspaper proprietor.
> Soap, attention! Listen, Beer!
> Glory to the new-made Peer.
> Hark! the Heralds' College sings
> As it fakes his quarterings.[46]

Their lordships' period of waiting was not protracted; Alfred Harmsworth came among them as Baron Northcliffe in 1905.

From the 1880s onwards, the 'question of the Lords' was a staple article of Radical debate. Radical zealots marked down the House of Lords for the same treatment that they would give to the Church of England and denominational education, landlords and imperialists, publicans and sinners of all kinds, when the great day of reckoning came. There was, however, the constitutional difficulty that the powers of the House of Lords could only be altered by statute, and that would require the Lords' consent. There would have to be some profound convulsion before that would be forthcoming. The Queen

[45] 3 LQV, I, p. 394.
[46] Quoted in Wickham Steed, *The Press*.

greatly disliked zealots in general and popular politics in particular. She thought that the House of Lords was indispensable, because its members were not constrained to prefer their constituents' opinions to their own, or to make regrettable promises in order to be elected. There was also, as she told Gladstone, the '*great* importance (which the Queen is *sure* Mr Gladstone must himself *fully* appreciate) of maintaining a power like the House of Lords in order that it may exercise a legitimate and wholesome check upon the greatly increasing radicalism of the present day'.[47]

But one person's 'legitimate and wholesome check' might be another person's 'intolerable obstruction'. Lord Rosebery described the House of Lords to the Queen as 'a permanent barrier raised against the Liberal Party', and invited her to consider for how long a Chamber elected by six million voters would allow itself to be blocked by a Chamber not elected by anybody. The Queen had her answer to that: *England* had endorsed the actions of those Liberal peers who 'could not blindly follow Mr Gladstone's disastrous policy which split up the true Liberal Party'.[47] The Liberal Party in the 1880s and 1890s was not in a condition to confront the Lords in deadly earnestness. But there might come a day when the cup would run over, the sands begin to blossom. If the Liberal Party were to win an overwhelming election victory, would the House of Lords regard that as an unambiguous expression of the national will?

[47] 3 LQV, I, p. 76.

6

The House of Commons, Party, and Representation of the People

The House of Commons is finding more and more difficulty in passing any effective vote, except a vote of censure. It tends to lose all powers except the power to criticise and the power to sentence to death. Parliament has been called the great inquest of the nation, and for that purpose its functions have of late been rather enlarged than impaired. Nor are the inquisitors confined to any one section of the House, for while that part is played chiefly by the Opposition, the government often receives a caution from its own supporters also. If the parliamentary system has made the cabinet of the day autocratic, it is an autocracy exerted with the utmost publicity, under a constant fire of criticism; and tempered by the force of public opinion, the risk of a vote of want of confidence, and the prospects of the next election.

A. Lawrence Lowell, 1908

The House of Commons could behave with immense dignity, and it could also indulge in fits of unruliness that recalled the schoolroom rather than the grand inquest of the nation. Like all intimate assemblies, it had its own language, its own folkways, its own taboos that must not be violated, and its own peculiar standards by which it passed collective judgment upon its individual members. It could be generous, and it could be spiteful. No newcomer, however eminent, could expect to have 'the ear of the House' as a matter of course. Most of the great debaters confessed to feelings of trepidation when they rose to speak; the House could sustain a member, but it could also wither him by ignoring him, or sometimes overwhelm him with its hostility. The reception of Disraeli's maiden speech is well-known; it was unusual because it was a maiden speech, which was conventionally treated with consideration, and because those who howled at him were performing a calculated act concerted in advance. Disapproval was usually more spontaneous than that, and it was commoner to be 'coughed down' than shouted down. But the House could sometimes be very noisy indeed. Macaulay described a scene during the debate on Lord Stanley's Irish Registration Bill of 1840:

> Lord Norreys was whistling and making all sorts of noises. Lord Maidstone was so ill-mannered that I hope he was drunk . . . O'Connell was so interrupted that he used the expression 'beastly bellowings'. Then arose such an uproar as no O.P. mob at Covent Garden Theatre[1]—no crowd of Chartists in front of a hustings—ever equalled. Men on both sides stood up, shook their fists, and bawled at the top of their voices . . . At last the tumult ended from absolute physical weariness. It was past one, and the steady bellowers of the Opposition had been howling from six o'clock with little interruption.[2]

Neither the unruliness nor the physical discomforts of the House of Commons ever deterred a would-be entrant, and few who had ever sat there left the House of Commons for the last time without a feeling of deprivation. Macaulay once asked himself what the fascination was, 'which attracts men, who could sit over their tea and their books in their own cool, quiet room, to breathe bad air, hear bad speeches, lounge up and down the long gallery, and doze uneasily on the green benches till three in the morning'.[3] It was a purely rhetorical question, and Macaulay knew the answer well enough: it was the greatest of all political arenas, the place where all the governing classes of England came to a point of cohesion or collision. The balanced constitution might be a myth, but the

[1] The reference is to the 'old price' riots, when admission charges were raised at Covent Garden.
[2] G. O. Trevelyan, *The Life and Letters of Lord Macaulay* (1889 ed.), pp. 392–3.
[3] Ibid., p. 219.

elements that were supposed to be separated in harmony could all be found jumbled together on the floor of the House of Commons. It had long been established that if England were to be quietly governed it must be through the House of Commons. A writer in the *Edinburgh Review* in 1807 saw that the 'balance' was in reality a blend :

> In order to exercise their constitutional functions with safety . . . it became necessary for the King and the great families to exercise them in the lower house—not against the united Commons of England, but among them; and not in their own character and directly—but covertly, and mingled with those whom it was substantially their interest and their duty to control.[4]

Membership of the House brought status. By definition, an M.P. was a man of standing in his constituency and the opportunity was there for him to become a national figure, if he had the talent and ambition to take it. 'We come here,' Disraeli said, 'for fame.' The prize of office was beyond the reach of most back-benchers, but it could seldom be achieved by anyone who lacked parliamentary talents. In 1894, Lord Salisbury wrote to Sidney Low :

> I think that you rate too low the share which, as things are, the House of Commons possesses in the selection of the men who are placed on the Treasury bench. Of course they have no nominal or conscious share; but nevertheless, when party leaders have to select, for a certain number of the offices of the Government, members of the House of Commons who have never held office before, one of the qualifications, which they consider with the greatest care, is that of being able to speak and act in a manner acceptable to the House of Commons; and if a man who has held office before has shown a marked incapacity in this respect, the party leaders will always be glad of any decorous method of excluding him from ministerial office.[5]

---

[4] *Edinburgh Review*, 1807, pp. 411 sqq.; quoted in J. J. Park, *Dogmas of the Constitution* (1832).
[5] Low, *Governance of England*, pp. 114–15.

The House, in short, needed continuously to be managed, and managed through the spoken word. It is a commonplace to say that management through argument decayed, and was replaced by the lash of the party whips; it is easier to make the generalisation than to substantiate it. If one were to judge by what men spoke and wrote, the House of Commons was perpetually outdistancing an ever-advancing golden age of independence, always in the process of losing an initiative which a previous generation was assumed to have enjoyed.

It would be more true to say that Parliament and government were always reacting to the pressures of a changing society. There is much to be learnt here from a study of the changes in the procedure of the House: Redlich ended his great book with the remark that the rules of procedure were the political manometer, which measured the elastic strain of forces in the parliamentary machine and thereby in the whole organism of the state.[6] The Ministry was always in search of new instruments of control. Patronage took many forms. After 1832, there were not many seats in which the influence of the Crown was predominant, and the private patrons who remained were more inclined to preserve their seats for their own purposes than to place them at the disposal of Ministers. It was not always easy to find a seat for a Minister who had the misfortune not to be re-elected after taking office, as Gladstone discovered in 1845 and 1846, when he was Secretary of State for the Colonies for six months without a seat in Parliament. It seemed, throughout the century, that old means of exercising control were being removed from Ministers' hands while new responses to new demands were making controls ever more necessary for the orderly and punctual transaction of business. Gladstone was making a very familiar complaint indeed in 1882, when he spoke of the constantly increasing labours of the House and the constantly decreasing ability to perform them; he, too, looked back to a golden age. Before the Great Reform Act, 'the position of a Member of this House was one of perfect ease and convenience . . . with regard to

[6] Josef Redlich, *The Procedure of the House of Commons* (English translation, 1908); quoted in A. Lawrence Lowell, *The Government of England* (1908, 1912), vol. i, p. 355.

the physical and mental possibility of meeting the grave calls upon him'. Since then, the burden had become intolerable. The Empire had doubled in size, contacts with other nations had increased, and 'there have been changes in the ideas and views of men respecting the sphere of legislation and of government . . .' The history of the House of Commons 'is augmentation of toil and effort with progressive diminution of result'.[7]

Every Ministry left behind it, after every session of Parliament, a litter of unfinished business. 1832 was indeed the beginning of a new era : there was more for government to do, and there were more Members of Parliament who wanted to talk about what was done or not done. 'Thus, before the Reform Bill, the speaking and business of the House were in the hands of about 150 members. In 1841 there were 231 members who took part in the proceedings. In 1861 the number had gone up to 300; and in 1876 to 385 members.'[8] Another index of business was the increase in the number of public petitions from 23,283 for the years between 1828 and 1832 to 70,072 between 1838 and 1842.[9]

According to Redlich, the period between 1688 and 1832 had been that in which the least change in the rules of procedure had taken place in the whole history of the House of Commons. Its essential characteristic had been 'adherence to the historic order of business, inviolate and unimpaired by the forcible action of any majority'.[10] Forms were revered for their own sake. After 1832, custom gave way to the increasing use of standing orders. It is instructive to compare Erskine May's *Treatise on the Law, Privileges, Proceedings and Usage of Parliament*, which was first published in 1844 and had gone to a tenth edition by 1893, with its predecessor, Hatsell's *Precedents of Proceedings in the House of Commons*, last published in 1818; each edition of Erskine May harvested a

---

[7] H. of C., 20 Feb. 1882, cc. 1128–38.

[8] Alpheus Todd, *On Parliamentary Government in England; its Origin, Development and Practical Operation* (1887–9), vol. II, p. 401.

[9] T. *Erskine May's Parliamentary Practice* (15th ed., 1950, by Lord Campion), p. 819(m).

[10] Redlich, op. cit., vol. I, pp. 54, 68.

new crop of standing orders. The need for change could be seen by the appointment of committee after committee on procedure—in 1837, 1848, 1854, 1861, 1869, 1871 and thereafter: the most drastic changes came under Gladstone in 1882 and Balfour in 1902, which together tipped the balance of control over the proceedings of the House decisively in favour of the government of the day.[11]

There were many opportunities for delaying and protracting the work of the House—in 1848 there were 18 different questions for the Speaker to put for the passage of a Bill, not counting what happened to it in committee; but before the 1870s the House was not much vexed by deliberate obstruction. There were isolated instances—Gladstone spoke 29 times in vehement opposition to the Divorce Bill in 1857—but most members restrained themselves on the principles of 'do as you would be done by': in the fullness of time the Opposition would become a responsible Government. But a 'phalanx of Tory colonels' obstructed Cardwell's Army Bill, and Samuel Plimsoll used obstruction not to prevent a measure but to put pressure on the House to pass a merchant shipping Bill. But these efforts, and the subtler manoeuvres of Lord Randolph Churchill and his Fourth Party, were different in kind from the systematic obstruction practised by Irish Nationalists after 1875, which seemed directly to threaten parliamentary government itself. The prototechnician here was Joseph Biggar, of whom the *Dictionary of National Biography* says: 'Probably no member with less qualifications for public speaking ever occupied so much of the time of the House of Commons.' Disraeli, when Biggar first brought himself to the attention of the House, said to his Irish Solicitor-General: 'Mr Solicitor, is that what in your country is called a Leprechaun?' English M.P.s found very little that was funny in Irish behaviour in the years to follow. Charles Stewart Parnell took his seat in the House on 22 April 1875, the day on which Biggar spoke for four hours on an Irish Coercion Bill. Five nights later, Biggar made use of ancient custom to 'espy strangers' and demand that the galleries be cleared; this was irritating to

[11] Ronald Butt, *The Power of Parliament* (1967), p. 407.

many, since the stranger whom he had espied was the Prince of Wales. The Irish had a case, since the 'half-past twelve' rule, first introduced in 1871 and dropped in 1874, had been brought back again in 1875 for the express purpose of killing Irish Bills. Under this rule, no order of the day or notice of motion, except on a money bill, was to be taken after 12.30 a.m. if notice of opposition had been given. The effect was that Irish Bills could be blocked without even being discussed. In 1877, Parnell joined Biggar and his friends in prolonged obstruction to the South African Confederation Bill. It was then that Parnell said that 'as an Irishman, coming from a country that had experienced . . . the consequences of English cruelty and tyranny, he felt a special satisfaction in preventing and thwarting the intentions of the government in respect of this Bill'. The Chancellor of the Exchequer, Sir Stafford Northcote, moved that Parnell's words be 'taken down' as a contempt of the House; but it was argued that Parnell had said only that he would thwart 'the intentions of the government' and not 'the business of the House', and Parnell was able to resume his seat and keep the House out of bed until 5.45 a.m. by moving yet more amendments. This produced a change in the rules of procedure, to curtail the number of times in which any member might speak in a particular debate. The Irish obstructionists then organised themselves in relays.

> The new rules did not prohibit either the moving of amendments or the making of immensely long speeches and with zest Parnell and six other Irish members applied themselves to obstructing the final stages of the South Africa Bill. The sitting which ensued was without parallel in the history of Parliament. From 5.15 p.m. on 31 July until 2.10 in the afternoon of 1 August these seven Irishmen held out against some 300 British members. They were worn down in the end by sheer weight of numbers, but not until the House had sat continuously for no less than 45 hours, 21 of which had been occupied by this single piece of obstruction.[12]

[12] F. S. L. Lyons, *Charles Stewart Parnell* (1977), p. 64.

Similar methods were used in 1881 against the Protection of Person and Property (Ireland) Bill. The sitting which began on 31 January continued for 41 hours until, on 2 February, the Speaker intervened to bring it to an end by refusing to call any more members and putting the question from the chair. This had never happened before in parliamentary history. On the following day, Gladstone moved a resolution giving power to the Speaker to put the question without further delay on receiving notice from a Minister of the Crown that business was urgent, provided that this was supported by 40 Members. The resolution was easily passed, but only because 36 Irish members had been suspended from the House for disregarding the authority of the chair.

The closure was embodied in a standing order in 1882. It was accepted by the House with some misgiving: what had been devised as a counter to Irish obstruction might be used by Her Majesty's Government as a weapon against Her Majesty's Opposition. Some apprehensions were aroused by the enthusiasm with which the closure was supported by Radicals. W. T. Marriott claimed that the Birmingham Caucus wanted the closure not so much to prevent obstruction as to push its programme down the throat of the Opposition.[13] Salisbury saw in it a danger that it might make Parliament too efficient as a legislative machine. He wrote to Balfour:

It is the old story. Gladstone is master of the country but cannot manage the House of Commons . . . I hope that we shall not go too far in accepting the clôture. In my view there ought to be a strong distinction drawn between those Parliamentary functions, the performance of which is absolutely necessary to secure the working of the executive machine and those which, having no object but to change laws under which we are living quite tolerably, can be suspended certainly without serious injury and often with great advantage. For the first class of functions there ought to be within reach powers which will enable the House to decide without superfluous delay: but these only include Supply, Mutiny, Continuance Bills and such measures as may be declared in a

[13] H. of C., 20 Feb. 1882, c. 1173.

message from the Crown to be necessary for the maintenance of the public peace. I should limit the clôture to these. It is not our interest to grease the wheels of *all* legislation : on the contrary, it may do all the Conservative classes of the country infinite harm.[14]

The new rules effectively killed Irish obstruction. But, in the words of Sir Arthur Helps, the indirect results of any course of action are nearly always the most important,[15] and all governments came to use the closure as a matter of course. It was used against the official Opposition for the first time in 1887. In that year a new standing order transferred the initiative in moving the closure from a Minister to any individual member. The Speaker retained a veto where it seemed that closure would be 'an abuse of the rules of the House, or an infringement of the rights of the minority'. In 1887, the House for the first time had debate regulated by an allocation of time order—nicknamed 'the guillotine'; the closure on that occasion had to be invoked to obtain it.

The occasion for the new rules had been the behaviour of the Irish, but it is possible that it merely hastened the arrival of what was coming anyway. The tactics of the Fourth Party were not as crude as those of the Irish, but they contrived to waste a great deal of parliamentary time to no public purpose except to embarrass the government and throw its time-table into confusion. The Fourth Party consisted of Lord Randolph Churchill, J. E. Gorst and Sir Henry Drummond Wolff, with Arthur Balfour as a rather languid fellow traveller. It was a light-hearted quartet. The name 'Fourth Party' was given to them by an Irish Nationalist, and they and the House of Commons accepted it. They first went into action at the very beginning of the Parliament of 1880, over the matter of Charles Bradlaugh and the Oath of Allegiance.

Bradlaugh was one of those storm-troopers of principle who are more comfortable to live with in retrospect than in the present. He was one of the best known 'agitators' in England. He was a republican, and he had publicly praised Orsini, who

14 Add. MSS. 49688, f. 37.
15 Arthur Helps, *Thoughts Upon Government* (1872), p. 210.

had tried to assassinate Napoleon III with a bomb and had killed eight other persons instead; he had helped the Fenians to write pamphlets, and Annie Besant to write tracts on birth control, and the mob to pull down the railings of Hyde Park. He had been nominated as a candidate for election to the French National Assembly in 1870, and he had defended the Commune of Paris in 1871. He had been prosecuted for blasphemy and for sedition. This formidable crusader had been elected for Northampton in 1880. When he came to be sworn in, he claimed the right to affirm; he could not, he said, in conscience take the oath because it ended with the words 'So help me God', and he was an atheist. Speaker Brand lost his grip on the House (it must be remembered that Ministers were out of the House, awaiting by-elections on their acceptance of office), and allowed the matter to go to a select committee. Bradlaugh was repeatedly expelled from the House and re-elected; it was the Wilkes case of the nineteenth century, and it lasted all through that Parliament. Bradlaugh aroused diverse passions, and he also gave the Fourth Party a chance, which it accepted with relish, to bait the Prime Minister, show its independence of Sir Stafford Northcote, who was supposed to be the Conservative leader, and obstruct business. Gladstone sometimes laid up rods in pickle that could be used on his own back. He had written an article in the *Nineteenth Century* which had considered when parliamentary obstruction might be justified:

Now, if a great party may obstruct, it is hazardous to award narrower limits to the small one; for it is precisely in the class of cases where the party is small and the conviction strong that the best instances of warrantable obstruction may be found.

This article gave Lord Randolph and his friends a splendid debating point. Their party, they could claim, was very small and its convictions were monstrously powerful; therefore, by Gladstone's standards, its obstruction was especially warrantable. The Fourth Party found an unwitting ally in Gladstone himself. He had none of Disraeli's gift of eloquent silence, and he could never resist a challenge. It pleased Lord Randolph to portray Gladstone as Bradlaugh's supporter and thus, by association, as a friend of atheism, blasphemy and contraception. Gladstone said that this was not true, and was at pains to explain that he detested Bradlaugh's opinions but defended his right to hold them, in the name of toleration. It was very uplifting and very time-consuming. The Fourth Party enjoyed itself very much, especially on those occasions when it came down to the House after dinner, to ask the Prime Minister why the business of his government was in arrears and the management of the House out of control. Lord Hartington gave them one of the answers: in the session of 1880, Gorst had spoken 105 times and asked 18 questions, Wolff had spoken 68 times and asked 18 questions, and Churchill had spoken 74 times and asked 21 questions.[16]

If one looks at the period as a whole, three tendencies may be seen—an increase in the powers of the Speaker, the extension of ministerial control over the matter and timing of business, and the diminution of the opportunities for private members. At the beginning of the century, it would still have been possible to say that the House retained many of the essential characteristics that it had brought with it when it migrated from the Chapter House at Westminster to St Stephen's Chapel in 1547. It was still pre-eminently regarded as 'the grand inquest of the nation' (the phrase was coined by Bolingbroke), primarily concerned with voicing grievances and scrutinising the financial and administrative measures of the Crown. For Ministers, administration was more important than legislation. Private and local Bills were regarded, in the aggregate, as of great importance, and few public and general Bills were brought forward as Ministerial measures, upon which an administration would stake its existence. Private members enjoyed much the same privileges as those given to Ministers and had the same powers of initiation except in the special case of taxation. By the end of the century, the Commons had become primarily an instrument of legislation controlled by

---

[16] Robert Rhodes James, *Lord Randolph Churchill* (1959, 1969), p. 91.

Ministers in the interests of a dominant majority.[17] It is too simple to explain this transformation as a direct consequence of the development of political parties. The House was least partisan in its deliberations when it was considering changes in procedure, and many of the important developments occurred in the period between 1832 and 1867, when parties were still relatively weak. Indeed, the first sign of things to come appeared in 1811, when 'order days' were instituted: the House could not proceed to the orders of the day until notices of motion had been dealt with; orders now had precedence on Mondays and Fridays. Ministerial business was claiming priority. By 1818, the number of Cabinet Ministers in the House of Commons had risen to six. But it was 'the rage for speaking' after 1832 that made it necessary to curtail individual initiative. Debates on petitions were the first casualties; the introduction of petitions had given private members a chance to speak at large on all sorts of matters that might or might not be of general interest. Debate was precluded, first by an understanding between the two front benches, upheld by the Speaker, and then by standing orders in 1842 and 1853. In 1835, Mondays and Fridays became government order days; this was the first clear distinction made between government business and that of private members. Wednesdays became an order day for private members; on Tuesdays and Thursdays, notice days, there was a ballot.

The prime function of the House of Commons, indeed the very source of its power, had been the granting of supply, the control of the purse. That grant, historically, was made only in response to a demand from the Crown; hence the initiative in money matters lay with Ministers. In 1706, the Commons resolved 'that this House will receive no Petition for any sum of Money relating to public Service, but what is recommended from the Crown'; and this was embodied as a standing order in 1713. This did not create any new constitutional principle;

[17] On this, see Valerie Cromwell, 'The losing of the initiative by the House of Commons, 1780–1914', *TRHS*, 1968; and Peter Fraser, 'The growth of Ministerial control in the nineteenth-century House of Commons, 75 *EHR*, 1960.

it was a practical step to meet a particular difficulty, the distribution of unspent surpluses remaining in the Exchequer.

> The existence of such sums was a new phenomenon at the beginning of the eighteenth century, due primarily to the recent establishment of the practice of appropriation. In the course of the war against France the Commons had taken the step of voting specified sums for the military and naval services instead of the total produce of specified taxes; and when the taxes proved more than sufficient to cover these sums, as the officers of the Exchequer were restrained under penalties from issuing the surplus to the Crown, any such surplus remained apparently at the disposal of Parliament. Lacking any executive responsibility, the Commons could find no use of their own for this money except to apply it to the satisfaction of the claims of individuals. Petitions for pecuniary relief multiplied enormously, and the House was driven to the adoption of the standing order, which in its original form . . . applied only to petitions.[18]

This, then, was a defence against the politics of the pork-barrel. 'It extended a practice that was evolved as a defence against the extravagance of the monarch to become also a defence against the extravagance of the House.'[19] In the course of the nineteenth century, the usage developed that the House might not increase any sum proposed by Ministers, and usage was transformed into rule. In 1840, Joseph Hume was indignant when he was not permitted to amend a finance Bill by substituting 'a tax on the descent of real property' for the Chancellor of the Exchequer's proposal for 'customs and excise duties'; the political motivation was clear enough. 'Does the Chancellor mean to say,' Hume asked, 'that no man can propose a new tax in this Committee but the Chancellor of the Exchequer?'[20] That was exactly what the Chancellor of the Exchequer did mean to say, and he had a majority behind him to make his words good.

A new standing order was adopted in 1852, in the last days

[18] Erskine May, op. cit., pp. 669–70.
[19] Gordon Reid, *The Politics of Financial Control* (1966), p. 37.
[20] Ibid., p. 39.

of Derby's first Ministry. The Conservatives were anxious to dissociate themselves from the reputation that they were the party of agricultural protection—'Protection,' Disraeli had said, 'was not only damned but dead'—and they wished to avoid the embarrassment that some back-bencher who did not know when to lie down might move a motion to introduce new tariff duties. The order of 1713 was amended to read:

> That this House will receive no Petition for any Sum of Money, relating to public Service, or proceed upon any Motion for granting any Money but what is recommended from the Crown.

As Professor Reid has pointed out, 'the modern significance of the rule dates not, as is often claimed, from the time of Queen Anne, but from that amendment'.[20]

The rule of 1852 could be evaded easily enough; it was open to M.P.s to add a qualification to any Bill or amendment which they wished to propose, that any expenditure involved would be met 'out of monies to be provided by Parliament'. That loophole was closed by a new standing order of 1866; this came after the House had endured several weeks of confusion over amendments moved by private members for farmers damaged by the cattle plague to the Cattle Diseases Protection Bill. The new order (which still stands) read:

> That this House will receive no Petition for any sum relating to Public Service, or proceed upon any Motion for a grant or charge upon Public Revenue, whether payable out of the Consolidated Fund or out of monies to be provided by the Parliament, unless recommended from the Crown.

The changes, then, were rooted in politics and responses to events. They were indications that the House of Commons could no longer be relied on for rigid economy, and that pressure from their constituents might encourage private members to make new demands upon the public purse.

A financial system begun with Pitt's Consolidated Fund was carried forward by Peel and completed by Gladstone in his first great period as Chancellor of the Exchequer.

Gladstone's work was intended to create a closed circle of parliamentary control over expenditure, in the interests of rigorous economy—one business of a Chancellor of the Exchequer, in his opinion, was 'the saving of candle ends'.

> Gladstone's expenditure circle started with the Executive's presentation to the House of Commons of annual and comprehensive estimates; it ran through the long and tedious procedures for parliamentary vote and legal appropriation, the departmental spending processes, and the keeping of annual cash accounts; the next point was the audit of accounts, on behalf of Parliament, by the Comptroller and Auditor-General, to ensure that money had been spent in accordance with the appropriations made; and finally, the circle returned to Parliament via the House's Committee of Public Accounts and its follow-up enquiry into the criticisms made in the auditors' report.[21]

In fact, the House tended to move away from the close financial scrutiny of the estimates; there was little point in debating about the figures, when these could not be increased, in terms of the standing orders, or diminished, in consequence of party solidarity. Indeed, the proposal that an estimate (or a Minister's salary) be reduced became a conventional way of expressing disapproval of the policy of the government. From the middle-1850s onwards, debates on supply became the occasion for administrative criticisms; for about thirty years, the Committee of Supply was regarded as the private member's paradise. Then, debates on supply came to be regulated and controlled by the leaders of the Opposition party. The custom that proceedings in the Committee of Supply were to be regarded as an opportunity for the Opposition to criticise the general policy of the Government was formally recognised in 1896, when Balfour undertook to bring forward the more important votes in the earlier part of the year, and to give precedence to those estimates that the Opposition particularly wished to discuss. Those estimates which were not discussed were normally passed, as a formality, under the procedure of the closure.

21 Ibid, p. 58.

It was rare for an estimate to be reduced, but it was not impossible; when it occurred it was a sign that a government was in very deep trouble. But the fact that the House could carry measures against Ministers, even at the end of the century when back-benchers were supposed to have been reduced to impotence, is a corrective to the view that party discipline was absolute. It is successful governments, on the whole, that have the most obedient followers; once a government became unpopular, it was common enough for discipline to evaporate. On 14 June 1895, Lord Rosebery's government was beaten on an amendment reducing the appropriation for the buildings of Parliament by £500, as a means of calling attention to the number of rooms occupied by officials of the House. A week later, the government was beaten again on an amendment to reduce the salary of the Secretary of State for War by £100, to call attention to the supposed lack of supplies of cordite. This defeat was managed by a trick; a number of Conservatives were smuggled into the House by way of the terrace, without passing through the lobby and hence under the eye of the government whips. But at least that defeat was at the hands of the Opposition; what determined the government to use the cordite vote as an opportunity for resignation was the fear that it might be beaten on the Welsh Disestablishment Bill, where it was threatened by its own supporters. Lloyd George had put himself at the head of a group of Welsh insurgents which wanted to make the Bill more drastic and, from a different point of view, Gladstone dealt a blow at the Government from his retirement by cancelling his pair on the Welsh Church, and letting it be known, ominously enough, that he had an open mind on the subject. In 1904, Balfour's government was beaten on a snap vote to reduce the grant for the Commissioners of National Education in Ireland, as a protest against a circular limiting the teaching of the Irish language in schools. The Government simply accepted the vote, and spent £100 less that year on Irish education. In 1905, there was a more serious vote when the Government was defeated on an amendment to reduce the appropriation for the Irish Land Commission by £100, as a protest against the administration of the Irish Land Act of 1903. The vote was 199 to 196. Balfour decided to carry on; but his government was by then in hard trouble, with the Conservative Party deeply divided over tariff reform, and he resigned three months later, when Parliament was not in session.

Too much, then, can be made of the supposed domination of the party machine over the back-bencher. If back-benchers lost their opportunity for individual action, that was as much a consequence of changing thought as of the influence that whips could bring to bear. Radical thought, for instance, was switching its emphasis from individual action to collective action. In 1884, J. Guinness Rogers, in an article entitled 'Chatter versus work in Parliament', said that insistence on the rights of private members was regarded outside as mere parliamentary cant. 'The first duty of every member is to get the business of the country done . . . as expeditiously as is compatible with thoroughness, and he certainly has no rights which can be urged in contravention of that.'[22]

As early as 1854, Erskine May had suggested that the House should set up grand committees, as a means of cutting down debate on the floor of the House. The first two grand or standing committees were established as an experiment in 1882—one to consider Bills relating to law and the other for Bills on trade, subjects that were supposed to be uncontroversial between the parties. In 1888, standing committees were established as part of the ordinary machinery of the House, by standing order, and they swiftly came to be miniatures of the House itself, with the parties represented in proportion to their numbers. The standing committees were increased to four in 1907, with the provision that Bills should regularly be referred to them unless the House should direct otherwise. It was customary to keep the more controversial Bills on the floor of the House, partly because it could be assumed that all members had an interest in them, and partly because Ministers were more confident of maintaining their majority in the larger assembly.

One result of the growth of standing orders was to put more power into the hands of the Speaker; it was important, there-

<hr>

[22] 16 *Nineteenth Century* (1884), p. 404; quoted in Fraser, op. cit., p. 459.

fore, to choose men in whose impartiality all sides of the House had confidence. The feeling grew that, after his resignation from the chair, a former Speaker should not reappear in the House, either as a Minister or as a private member. The convention was established that he should be rewarded with a peerage. The precedent of Addington, a Speaker who became Prime Minister, was not repeated, although some Tories thought about Manners Sutton, Speaker from 1817 until 1835, as an alternative to Peel as the Conservative leader in the Commons. Manners Sutton was the only Speaker not to be re-elected to the chair; he was also the last Conservative to be elected as Speaker for the rest of the century. There was some Conservative resentment at this; it was felt that former Liberals, however impartial they might be from the chair, timed their resignations to coincide with Liberal majorities. There were some doubts whether Speaker Gully, elected in 1893, would be chosen again when the Conservatives returned to power in 1895; but although he was opposed in his constituency he was re-elected to the chair. Until 1855, the Speaker had no deputy; if he were ill, the House could not sit. In 1855, the Chairman of the Committee of Ways and Means, who presided over all committees of the whole House, became deputy speaker, and a·second deputy was added in 1902.

Balfour's procedural changes of 1902 were a consolidation of rules rather than a new departure. It was calculated that, in the decade between 1878 and 1888, government business had precedence on the average in 83 per cent of the sittings, and in 84.5 per cent in the following decade. This was very little less than the proportion after 1902. The new rules 'merely sanctioned by permanent standing order a practice that had long been followed in an irregular way by special resolutions adopted during the course of the session'.[23] The handing over of the parliamentary time-table to ministerial control was a necessary condition of maintaining the tradition that the King's Government must be carried on.

---

[23] Lowell, op. cit., vol. i, p. 312.

II

The origin of the phrase 'His Majesty's Opposition' is usually attributed to John Cam Hobhouse, in a speech in the House of Commons in 1826. It may have been meant as a joke (and Hansard reported 'a laugh'), but it expressed an important reality: opposition had ceased to be regarded as 'factious'. There was a Ministry, sustained by its own supporters; there was also an alternative ministry, sustained likewise. In 1812, one commentator noted that all parties, however different, claimed to rally round the constitution.[24] Party was recognised as a necessary condition of ministerial responsibility and of continuity in government.

Parties were held together by shared likes and dislikes, by common purposes, and by fidelity to leaders. Whigs and Tories were not divided by class interests, but by a different way of looking at the constitution and, perhaps, by a different interpretation of English history. Traditionally, Tories formed the party of Church and King. Whigs regarded themselves as the authors of the 'Glorious Revolution' of 1688 and of the 'balanced constitution' which it was supposed to have produced; they were Anglicans of an Erastian disposition, who were thus able to attract under their leadership Nonconformists of all kinds and all those who were hostile to the privileges of the Established Church. The two historic parties bore nicknames given in the 1680s. A Tory was an Irish outlaw, and the name was given to those who opposed the exclusion of James, Duke of York, from the succession to the crown. Whig is probably a contraction of Whiggamore, one of the Scottish Presbyterian insurgents who marched on Edinburgh in 1648. Burnet says, of the reign of Charles II: 'All that opposed the Court came in contempt to be called Whiggs.'[25] After 1832, Tories tended to call themselves Conservatives, as a means of rallying all those who felt themselves

---

[24] G. Dyer, *Four Letters on the English Constitution* (1812), p. 5.
[25] *Shorter Oxford Dictionary.*

threatened by the consequences of the Reform Act. It was
not always easy for an outsider to distinguish the difference
between them—one foreign observer of the House of Commons
said that the Conservatives sat behind Disraeli and the Whigs
were related to Lord John Russell's grandmother—; to insiders,
it was a matter of mutual recognition. The Whigs, indeed,
resembled an extended clan; they owed their majority, after
the breaking of the Old Whig party after the American War
of Independence and the creation of the second Tory party
under the younger Pitt, to the attraction of the support of
Radical reformers of all kinds—men who would go to the root
of the matter in transforming the constitution of Church and
State by legislation. Socially, the Conservatives were more
homogeneous; there was always tension on the other side
between Whigs and Radicals. The Liberal alliance was held
together with difficulty, principally by partisan hostility to the
Conservatives and by the general recognition that it was the
function of the groups and factions in the House of Commons
to combine, either to sustain a Ministry or to turn it out of
office. Cohesion was assisted by the accidental shape of the
House of Commons, which meant that Government and
Opposition faced one another as adversaries. There were conventions about where members sat. The front benches on
either side of the Speaker were for leaders, and it was regarded
as boorish of Cobbett to try to push Peel out of his recognised
place in 1833. It was a sign that a member or a group was
claiming an independence from the whips when he or it ostentat-
iously changed seats—usually to move below the gangway that ran
across the centre of the House. To 'cross the floor of the House'
was a serious matter; it meant that a man was repudiating
his party, and it usually exposed the member to the vehement
hostility of the ranks which he had quitted. The historic parties
began in Parliament; they extended themselves outwards to
the constituencies, but their final control always lay in the
hands of the parliamentary leaders. The Labour Party was
unique in that it began outside Parliament. Both the major
parties were great coalitions of interests and opinions, the
Liberals more obviously so than the Conservatives. Until the
1870s, the Liberals could usually count on the support of the

Irish Nationalists; thereafter, when Home Rule became a serious issue, the Nationalists regarded themselves as a foreign cohort. Debates on procedure were not usually regarded as the occasion for partisan speeches, but in 1902 John Redmond— a milder Irish leader than Parnell—told the House that there were two points of view, that of the loyal members of the House of Commons and that of his own followers:

> These men do not regard this House with feelings of reverence, affection, or loyalty. These men do not see any cause why they should revere the past history of this House, why they should love its traditions, or why they should be loyal to them . . . We owe nothing to this House of Commons.[26]

Party loyalty could generally be assumed; votes were given on the general merits of a government, not on that of a particular Bill. But leaders were constantly aware of the need to conciliate their own followers; Ministers' attention was focused more upon their own back-benches than upon the Opposition. Bagehot thought that there were vestiges of despotism in the Conservative leadership, and he popularised the description of the county members, apparently so docile, as 'the finest brute votes in Europe!'[27] But, although they could usually be driven, they could not be driven too far, as Peel discovered in 1846. The Conservatives broke then, over the repeal of the Corn Laws, as they had broken over Catholic Emancipation in 1829 and as they would break over tariff protection in 1903. The break of 1846 was the most important in its effects. It enriched the Liberals by the adhesion of the Peelites, and it led eventually to that long duel between Disraeli and Gladstone that was, for nearly thirty years, one of the central features of English politics.

Peel's conduct over the repeal of the Corn Laws provoked a debate on the nature of party leadership.[28] Peel never considered politics as simply a system of adversary relationships, and he always considered that the support of the executive

[26] H. of C., 6 Feb. 1902, c. 581.
[27] Bagehot, *English Constitution,* p. 158.
[28] N. Gash, 'Peel and the party system', *TRHS* 1951.

government had a higher claim than mere party advantage
on the conduct of a public man. His leadership in Opposition
was a source of strength to Ministers. He stated his creed in
his first speech in the Reformed Parliament:

> When the House of Commons was divided between two great
> parties—one of them in power and the other not, but confident
> in its principles—it was natural and right that they should
> adopt those tactics which might have the effect of displacing
> their opponents . . . But circumstances have now changed and
> I do not feel myself at liberty, holding the opinions that I do,
> now to resort to what may have been, at other seasons, the
> necessary and legitimate tactics of party. When I see the
> Government disposed to maintain the rights of property, the
> authority of the law, and, in a qualified sense, the established
> order of things against rash innovation, I shall without regard
> to party feelings, deem it my duty to range myself on their
> side . . . Believing it would be a public misfortune in the
> present crisis of the country that the hands of the Government
> should be weak, it is my determination to strengthen them as
> much as possible.[29]

In Professor Gash's words: 'Conservatism, as Peel understood
it, was not a tactical doctrine designed to draw votes to the
Tory party; the Tory party was a tactical device to make
Conservatism the basis of government.'[30] But Peel could not
escape from party pressures, and in Disraeli he found an
antagonist who used against him a deadly weapon—a charge
of apostasy in tones of ridicule. The Conservative back-benchers
had, in 1841, assumed that the Corn Laws would be maintained. By 1845, Peel had become convinced that they could
no longer be defended; they must go, lest they provoke a
dangerous collision of hostile classes. Unfortunately for himself,
Peel had changed direction once before, over Catholic
Emancipation in 1829. Thus it was easy for Disraeli to hint
at another 'betrayal', to compare Peel to the Turkish admiral
who sailed into the enemy port, to refer to 'organised hypocrisy'

[29] *Mirror of Parliament* (1833), vol. I, p. 111; quoted in Gash, op. cit.,
p. 53.
[30] Gash, op. cit., p. 56.

and to put into the mouths of Mr Tadpole and Mr Taper, in *Coningsby*, talk about a 'sound Conservative Government' consisting of Tory men and Whig measures. But, underneath Disraeli's stinging sentences, there was a real point of principle : a Minister was not only a servant of the Crown but was also in the service of his party. What was his proper course of action when the two obligations came into collision? This issue was discussed seriously, and without rancour, in the *Quarterly Review*. A party leader, the argument ran, had duties to his followers as they in turn were entitled to advise him as a condition of their support.

> A Party raises a man, or . . . affords him the footing and the force by which he raises himself, to great political distinction; the Sovereign in consequence raises him to power. What would be thought of the Minister who, *on any pretence whatsoever*, should turn against the Sovereign the power so confided? And are not gratitude and fidelity due at least equally to the Party as to the Sovereign—for the Party has been the earlier and the greater benefactor?[31]

The proper course, the writer concluded, for a Minister whose views no longer coincided with those of his party was to resign, to become a private member again, and not to promote 'a violent disruption of attachments'. The Conservative Party never forgot 1846, and its leaders were always haunted by the ghost of Peel. 'Thou shalt not split thy party' became a sort of eleventh commandment to all Conservative Prime Ministers. The memory of Sir Robert Peel was invoked when Gladstone offered the Conservatives his support on Irish Home Rule in 1886, and invoked again when Balfour refused Lloyd George's overtures for a coalition in 1910; he could not, Balfour then said, become another Peel in his party.

The most formidable threat to the primacy of the parliamentary leadership came in the Liberal Party, and it was made in Birmingham. The Birmingham Caucus, out of which the National Liberal Federation developed, had its origins deep

[31] 78 *Quarterly Review* (Sep. 1846), p. 567.

in Birmingham politics, where there had long been attempts to unite classes around common objectives. The Caucus grew out of the close collaboration, in 1866 and 1867, between the Reform League and the Liberal Association. It was an instrument for promoting class harmony in the Radical interest. It had paternalistic overtones; it was the duty of the middle classes to elevate those below them on the social ladder. 'For the artisan to be entrusted with the vote meant formal public recognition of his respectability. Hence franchise reform acquired a *mystique* that transcended politics, and Liberal support for parliamentary reform evoked a working class loyalty that was out of proportion to the political issue involved.'[32]

One result of the Reform Act of 1867 was to stimulate both parties to establish associations in the provinces, and both of them formed national bodies. The National Union of Conservative and Constitutional Associations regarded itself as having a strictly subordinate part to play. 'The Union has been organised rather as a handmaid to the party than to usurp the functions of party leadership,' said its president, Cecil Raikes, at one of its first annual meetings. Lord Randolph Churchill did use the National Union as a springboard for his own ambitions in a quarrel which he conducted with Lord Salisbury in 1884, but it never became a caucus in the Birmingham sense. The National Liberal Federation was formed in 1877; the occasion was the outburst of public sentiment over the Turkish atrocities committed upon the Bulgarians, and the chance which that gave to Liberal associations to whip up an agitation against the Conservative Government's foreign policy. But the ambitions of Joseph Chamberlain, who was the energising spirit behind the Federation, extended much further. The conference which established the new organisation met in Birmingham, and the invitations to the meeting contained a clear statement of its purpose:

The essential feature of the proposed Federation is the principle which must henceforth govern the action of Liberals as a

---

[32] Trygve R. Tholfsen, 'The origins of the Birmingham Caucus', 2 *Historical Journal* (1959), p. 176.

political party—namely the direct participation of all members of the party in the direction, and in the selection of those particular measures of reform and of progress to which priority shall be given. This object can be secured only by the organisation of the party upon a representative basis.[33]

Chamberlain, the first president, talked about the Federation becoming 'a really Liberal Parliament, outside the Imperial Legislature and, unlike it, elected by universal suffrage and with some regard for a fair distribution of political power'.[34] Lord Hartington saw the danger to the parliamentary leadership at once, and refused to have anything to do with the occasion. But there was no doubt that Gladstone, who had technically retired from the party leadership, towered over all living Liberals in public estimation. Gladstone accepted Chamberlain's invitation, spoke about the need for better party organisation, referred unfavourably to the Conservatives' preference for wealthy men, and complimented Birmingham on having 'held up the banner of a wider and of a holier principle'. Gladstone could sometimes behave naively.

The Federation claimed to represent the wishes of the Liberal activists, and thus of the Liberal electorate. Its enemies accused it of seeking to manipulate the electorate rather than reflecting it, in the interests of a Birmingham oligarchy. This was only partly true. The Federation was concerned with intestine party warfare, and it was an instrument of Radicalism in its strident and militant form. Chamberlain was being ironical when he said that 'the caucus tolerated everything—why, we even tolerate opposition'.[35] Liberalism might be a house of many mansions, but Birmingham furnished only one of them. There were still many regional jealousies as well as doctrinal variations, and Chamberlain's control over the Federation was never complete, even in its headiest days. Ostrogorski interpreted its aims—'down with the leaders and up with the people'—as 'down with the Whigs, war on the

---

[33] M. Ostrogorski, *Democracy and the Organisation of Political Parties* (1902; ed. S. M. Lipset, 1964), vol. I, p. 119.

[34] Lowell, op. cit., vol. I, p. 516.

[35] Morley, *Recollections,* vol. I, p. 157.

moderates, up with the Radicals'.[36] But all efforts to put the Liberal Party under an oligarchical leadership masquerading in democratic form would have to reckon with the still daemonic energies of Gladstone and his astonishing hold over the Liberal masses. Chamberlain never matched Gladstone in popular appeal, and Gladstone's return to active politics meant, when the challenge came, the end of Chamberlain's influence in the Liberal Party. Meanwhile, the Federation attempted to arrange the priorities of Liberal measures to be brought forward in Parliament, and some of its associations brought pressure on M.P.s who were regarded as backsliders by threatening them in their constituencies. The Bradford association quarrelled with W. E. Forster; he had never been forgiven, by Radical zealots, for the provisions in his Education Act of 1870 which favoured the Church of England. The Newcastle association made life difficult for Joseph Cowen, who had taken an independent line in the Parliament of 1885. But Cowen still headed the poll in Newcastle in 1885, though he refused to stand again in 1886, saying: 'I am under no obligation to become a party slave, or subject myself to spiteful persecution for no useful purpose. What the Caucus wants is a political machine. I am a man, not a machine . . .'[37] Those Liberals who expressed doubts about the introduction of the closure in the House of Commons were given warnings that they might find it difficult to be re-elected. There were many public men who feared that something new and menacing had appeared in English politics; but when one looks dispassionately at the practical achievements of the Caucus, what is striking is how little it accomplished. It reiterated the old war-cries—religious equality, temperance, land reform, extension of the suffrage, non-sectarian education—which had always been able to produce a reflex response of Radical approval. But when Gladstone's conversion to Home Rule became public knowledge, he regained the initiative at once. When Chamberlain broke with Gladstone in 1886, he brought to an end two decades in which Birmingham had been the

---

[36] Ostrogorski, op. cit., vol. i, p. 94.
[37] Ibid., p. 115.

focus of 'bourgeois Radicalism'.[38] Resolutions in favour of Gladstone came in from association after association—from Leicester, Halifax, Leeds, Newcastle, Derby—and in the election of 1886 not a single caucus outside Birmingham rejected a candidate because he was a Gladstonian. Chamberlain's power, it seems, stopped at the confines of greater Birmingham, and even the Birmingham caucus went back to Gladstone in 1888. (That did not signify, in electoral terms: Unionists carried every seat at every election in greater Birmingham from 1886 until 1910.) If the National Liberal Federation had aimed at transforming Liberal M.P.s into delegates controlled by an extra-parliamentary organisation, it had singularly failed. Some other explanation is needed for the steady increase in party cohesion within the House of Commons.

In his most stimulating book *Modern British Politics*, Professor S. H. Beer assembled a table of divisions in the House of Commons between 1860 and 1908, showing the state of party unity measured by 'coefficients of cohesion'.[39] In divisions where the Government put on its whips, the results were :

Year	Liberals	Conservatives
1860	58.9	63.0
1871	75.5	74.0
1881	83.2	87.9
1894	89.8	97.9
1906	96.8	91.0
1908	94.9	88.3

Each M.P. was an entity, and generalisations about parliamentary behaviour are all necessarily incomplete. However, the most plausible explanation of the increase in party solidarity is that attempted by Professor Hugh Berrington, in an important article on partisanship and dissidence in the

[38] P. C. Griffiths, 'The Cauc⸱⸱ ⸱nd the Liberal Party in 1886', *History,* 1976.

[39] S. H. Beer, *Modern British Politics* (1965), p. 257.

House of Commons. He distinguished three types of dissident
—the cross-bencher, the extremist, and the bi-partisan. Cross-
bench revolts, in his terminology, were deviations towards the
'centre of gravity' of the House, such as that of the Cave of
Adullam on reform in 1866 and of the Liberal Unionists on
Home Rule in 1886. An example of extremist revolt (in the
sense that it moved furthest from the centre of gravity) was
that of the Radicals against the Education Bill in 1870. Bi-
partisan 'revolts' are less common; often, Conservatives went,
with their leaders' support, to the assistance of Liberal Governments threatened by the defection of their Radical left wing.
The Peelites, when out of office, took up a bi-partisan approach
between 1846 and 1859. There was a tendency for Conservative dissidence to be cross-bench, Liberal to be extremist; but
there were exceptions. The Fourth Party was sometimes
bi-partisan, sometimes extremist. The Liberal Party during the
Boer War experienced both an extremist revolt of the 'pro-
Boers' and a cross-bench revolt of the Liberal Imperialists.
Looking at the period from 1880 to 1900, Professor Berrington
concludes :

> The growth of party discipline . . . is not so much the story
> of the subjugation of the courageous, moderate and spirited
> crossbencher, cowed into conformity by the sting of the party
> whip; it is rather the story of the effective absorbtion of the
> extremists into the main body of their party, of a growing
> sense of identity between the cautious leaders, and their more
> zealous followers. Parallel to this development, we have on the
> Conservative side, a lesser but still important tendency for
> crossbench dissidents to accept the restraints of party loyalty.[40]

Thus, the basic reason for the increasing importance of
party rested on a change in the habitual relationships between
the Government, the majority party and the Opposition.
Before the 1880s, the minority party by no means felt that it
was its unswerving duty to oppose on all measures; at the same
time, Governments refrained from introducing highly con-

---

[40] Hugh Berrington, 'Partisanship and dissidence in the nineteenth-
century House of Commons', 21 *Parliamentary Affairs* (1967–8), p. 349.

troversial measures unless, like the Irish Church Bill of 1869, they had recently been endorsed by the electorate or—like most of the other measures of Gladstone's first Ministry—they had long been the subject of public debate, a broad measure of support had already been identified and the question had therefore become 'ripe'. When bringing forward his unsuccessful Bill in 1859, Disraeli argued that further parliamentary reform had now reached that condition :

> In such a state of things a question in England becomes what is called a public question. Thus Parliamentary Reform became a public question; a public question in due course of time becomes a Parliamentary question; and then, as it were, shedding its last skin, it becomes a Ministerial question. Reform has been for 15 years a Parliamentary question and for 10 years it has been a Ministerial question.[41]

If a Ministry succeeded in enacting a copious programme of public measures, it was a sign either that the measures were uncontroversial or that Governments could shift alternately from the support of their own united followers to that of a section of the Opposition. Some questions could be organised into politics, and others could be organised out—tariff reform after the 1870s was an example. No one was prepared to make this a Ministerial question until Chamberlain took it up in 1903. In 1888, Lord Salisbury summoned Conservative members to the Foreign Office and asked them—secretly, he hoped—not to raise the issue of protection. In 1895, he damped down agitation again; this was the moment at which he was trying to absorb the Liberal Unionists within the Conservative Party, and there were difficulties enough in the way of that fusion without the addition of tariffs. After the election, Salisbury said that 'the character of the Government' precluded protection.[42]

The great change in the relationship between Government and Opposition began in the 1880s, with the highly con-

---

[41] H. of C., 28 Feb. 1859, c. 970.

[42] B. H. Brown, *The Tariff Movement in Great Britain, 1881–1895* (1966), passim.

troversial measures of Gladstone's Government; it was accelerated after the Liberal split in 1886 by the bitterness that accompanied that breaking of old political friendships; and it was accelerated still further when the Liberal Party came under increasing Radical influence after the Whigs had gone. Professor Beer's 'coefficients of cohesion' tell their own story; there was a new development in politics, between 1892 and 1895, a systematic, united and prolonged attack by the Opposition over the whole range of Government policy.

Professor Berrington concludes that cross-bench unity was shattered in 1886, and with it a consensus among the ruling class; new opportunities were opened to the Liberal Radical and the Tory diehard. Liberal M.P.s ceased to vote against their leaders with their previous regularity because those leaders were identifying themselves more completely with their followers' causes. Conservative leaders showed even greater fidelity, because party loyalty seemed to be the only barrier to Radical change. The decline of the independent member represented rather the transformation of leaders into the collaborators of their followers than the regimentation of back-benchers into mere lobby fodder.

III

The Whigs had framed the Great Reform Bill of 1832 as a prophylactic measure, to anticipate revolution and to give a 'final answer' to the question of the representation. It would also, they hoped, secure their own popularity and revive the Old Whig notion of 'mixed' government, in which birth, wealth and numbers would all count for something, and the Whigs would resume their eighteenth-century role as the indispensable managers of public affairs.[43] It would produce, it was hoped, a middle-class electorate that would be content under aristocratic leadership. Macaulay wrote in the *Edinburgh Review* in October 1829:

---

[43] H. J. Hanham, *The Reformed Electoral System in Great Britain, 1832–1914* (Historical Association pamphlet, 1968), p. 3.

Our fervent wish . . . is that we may see such a reform of the House of Commons as may render its votes the express image of the opinion of the middle orders of Britain. A pecuniary qualification we think absolutely necessary; and, in settling its amount, our object would be to draw the line in such a manner that every decent farmer and shopkeeper might possess the elective franchise. We should wish an end put to all the advantages which particular forms of property possess over other forms, and particular portions of property over other equal portions. And this would content us.[44]

In these words, one may see the dilemma that was to bedevil the issue of reform when it became 'ripe' again in the 1850s: how was equality to be reconciled with the protection of property? This was especially productive of debate among Radicals, as to the nature and limits of equality and the respective merits of different kinds of property, according to their origins, size, and connexions with privilege. Professor Hanham has pointed out that 'the history of electoral reform has always had a dual character, since it consists both of the history of certain measures and the history of certain ideas'.[45] Was the franchise a right or a privilege? If it was a right, could it be disposed of like any other piece of property, or was it to be exercised as a form of trust? If it was a privilege, how should it be earned, and to how many should it be accorded?

The Reform Act of 1832 made two fundamental changes in the old system: it created a new basic qualification in England and Wales—the £10 householder; and it supplemented the old forty-shilling freehold county franchise with a series of new franchises. There was a separate measure for Scotland. There was an extraordinary hotch-potch of qualifications—seventeen different ones in English counties, three in English boroughs. It was a Conservative grievance that a forty-shilling freehold in a borough, in some instances, entitled its owner to a vote in the county; urban interests, which were thought to favour the Liberals in large boroughs, thus

---

[44] Macaulay, *Works* (ed., Lady Trevelyan), vol. v, pp. 328–9.
[45] Hanham, op. cit., p. 11.

encroached upon rural interests, which favoured the Conservatives. There was no attempt to apportion representation in relation to population; the south and west, with the exception of London, were over-represented; the great towns were under-represented. The idea was still current that, in Disraeli's words, 'men are sent to this House to represent the opinions of a place and not its power'; while this endured, the old notion of 'virtual representation' could still be asserted. It was thus that Disraeli defended the retention of the borough of Arundel, often the target of 'Utopian meddlers' but important because it brought into the House a Roman Catholic of the Howard family. There were 900,000 Roman Catholics scattered about England who found a representative in Arundel. 'That is the practical working of our constitution. You talk of the small numbers of the constituency of Arundel —900,000 Roman Catholics! Why, it is more than the West Riding of Yorkshire; it is double the Tower Hamlets.'[46] Gladstone was, until the 1860s, a defender of the inequities of the electoral system. Small boroughs helped to secure the completeness and diversity of representation, by sending to Parliament men who would be unlikely to win in large and popular constituencies, where the emphasis would be on purely local affairs and the issue would be decided by local influences. But he also defended the 'nomination' boroughs—those which were 'willing to take upon trust the recommendation of candidates for Parliament from noblemen or gentlemen who may stand in immediate connexion with them. (Some cries of 'Oh!').' It was thus that Fox and Pitt, Canning and Peel (and Gladstone himself) had come young into the House. 'You cannot expect of large and populous constituencies that they should return boys to Parliament; and yet if you want a succession of men trained to take part in the government of the country, you must have a great proportion of them returned to this House while they are boys.'[47]

The question of reform became a practical question in the 1850s not because of the disturbed state of Britain but because

[46] H. of C., 28 Feb. 1859, c. 1003.
[47] Ibid., 29 March 1859, c. 1058.

of its tranquillity. The Hungry Forties were times of dangerous class antagonisms; prosperity in the 1850s took the edge off feelings of bitterness. Thus, franchise reform could be urged, as the Radicals did, as a means of achieving political change and also urged as a means of preserving political stability by absorbing the most respectable of the industrious artisans within the body politic. Gladstone's conversion to the course of reform came when he had convinced himself that 'the fixed traditional sentiment of the working man has begun to be confidence in the law, in Parliament, and even in the executive Government'. He had been deeply impressed, as Chancellor of the Exchequer, by the demeanour of a deputation from the Society of Amalgamated Engineers which had asked him to modify the rules of the Post Office savings banks to allow the Society to invest its money in them.

> . . . I venture to say that every man who is not presumably incapacitated by some consideration of personal unfitness or of political danger is morally entitled to come within the pale of the Constitution. Of course, in giving utterance to such a proposition, I do not recede from the protest I have previously made against sudden, or violent, or excessive, or intoxicating change; but I apply it with confidence to this effect, that fitness for the franchise, when it is shown to exist—as I say it is shown to exist in the case of a select portion of the working class—is not repelled on sufficient grounds from the portals of the Constitution by the allegation that things are well as they are.[48]

It was this speech which did a great deal to establish Gladstone's reputation as the working man's friend. But it was by no means as radical as it sounded in the ears of those who first heard it in Parliament, or as it appeared to those who read it without appreciating the massiveness of the qualifications.

The great difficulty of enacting a new Bill, however, was to decide where to draw a line to include the deserving, exclude the undeserving and not to seem to endanger the existing constitution. No responsible politician wanted the line to be

[48] Ibid., 11 May 1864, c. 321.

drawn too low. John Bright, the most celebrated of the advocates of a wider franchise, coined the word 'residuum' to describe the dangerous mass at the bottom of the social terrace—those for whom it would be 'better for themselves if they were not enfranchised, because they have no independence whatsoever'—who should be kept out lest their votes swamp those of the intelligent and industrious working men. 'I call this class the residuum, which there is in every constituency, of almost helpless poverty and dependence.'[49] In 1866, the Liberal Government was defeated in what had by now become familiar fashion when reform was put forward. Surprisingly, the sequel was the passing of a much more extensive Bill through the same House under a different government in the following year. The Act of 1867, which in rough terms doubled the electorate and established the principle of household suffrage in the boroughs of Great Britain (but not of Ireland), was given its shape almost entirely as a result of the struggles for party advantage, and of individual ambition, in the House of Commons. The critical factors were the determination of the Conservative leaders to get the question out of the way—to pass some Bill, almost any Bill, in that session, and thus keep their control over the consequent redistribution —and the conviction of some Radicals that the Conservatives were 'squeezable', that more could be got from them than from Gladstone, and that it was in Radical interests that the Conservatives should pass the Bill, because it would then be more likely not to be butchered in the House of Lords.

The Act of 1867 did not establish the principle of representation according to the density of population, still less did it put the working classes into power : J. S. Mill was right when he said : 'They may be able to decide whether a Tory or a Whig shall be elected; they may be masters of so small a situation as that.'[50] Like its great predecessor, the Act gave to those who were qualified the right to get themselves put on the electoral register; it did not operate automatically. Where it admitted working men to Parliament, it was by accident,

[49] Ibid., 26 March 1867, c. 637.
[50] Ibid., 13 April 1866, c. 637.

and as a result of sloppy logic in its drafting, which gave discretion to the revising barristers who were responsible for the registers in their final form. In many instances, the electorate that emerged was not that which had been expected. Some surprising groups found themselves able to be registered, such as the coal miners of the north. After some agitation in the 1870s, those who lived in tied houses in some boroughs were able to make their claims to registration good; this was how the first working men, Thomas Burt and Alexander Macdonald, entered Parliament in 1874. In Burt's case at least, it has been argued, 'this result stemmed directly from the inept drafting of the 1867 Act, which opened the way for the transformation of Morpeth from a pocket borough of the Howard family to a pocket borough of the Northumberland Miners' Union'.[51] After 1867, the Lake District had a representation in the House of Commons six times greater than that of the mining and shipping conurbation of north-east England. London, with a population of $3\frac{1}{2}$ millions, returned only 22 members. Manchester, with a population of 350,000 and an electorate of 48,000 had three members, the same number as the boroughs of Knaresborough, Petersfield and Andover, with a combined electorate of 2,500.

Another thorny question of respectable age was settled, almost wearily, in 1872 with the substitution of the secret ballot for open voting. It could still be argued that secrecy would destroy the concept that the vote was a trust; but those arguments were overborne by others drawn from practical convenience. Secrecy, some thought, might diminish the violence and intimidation that were regular features of the poll.[52] E. A. Leathem, of Huddersfield, ridiculed the notion that there were moral virtues at stake, in Ireland:

A striking tableau this, representing the dignity of open voting! In the foreground the public trustee, whining, bandaged, in the presence of his landlord; in the background,

---

[51] N. McCord, 'Some difficulties of Parliamentary reform', 10 *Historical Journal* (1967), p. 386.
[52] Donald Richter, 'The role of mob riot in Victorian elections, 1865–1885', 15 *Victorian Studies* (1971).

the military, armed, and about to drag him to the exercise of his free trust: overhead a lurid sky, charged with spiritual lightning.[53]

Bernal Osborne thought that the ballot would protect working men against the tyranny of their fellows, especially Conservative working men in the boroughs. 'They may have logical minds, but they have breakable heads.'[54] Gladstone announced his own conversion; he had previously considered that the vote was a trust and that the community had a right to see how it was performed. But the argument had been altered by the increase of the constituency: previously the vote had been in the hands of men of property, who could defend themselves; now, it had been given to men who were dependent for bread upon their daily labour. Secret voting was not an unmixed good, but the choice of the lesser of two evils.[55]

Once household suffrage had been granted to the boroughs, it was a foregone conclusion that the Liberals would extend it to the counties as soon as they were able to do so. The Act of 1884 doubled the electorate again—in round figures, it stood at five million in 1886—and for the first time Ireland was treated on the same basis as the rest of the United Kingdom. But the great break in continuity with the Third Reform Acts came with the changes in redistribution, the appearance of the single-member constituency as the norm, the recognition of the principle of numbers, and the end of the historic House of Commons. Both parties thought that they had something to gain from the new arrangements; but the gains that might have accrued immediately to the Liberals were diminished when the party split in 1886. The new system was favourable to the Conservatives—hardly surprisingly, since Salisbury was one of its architects.[56] By the 1880s, it was clear that the Conservatives had conquered suburbia; the new electoral map contained many in unchallengeable Conservative occupation.

[53] H. of C., 16 March 1870, c. 17.
[54] Ibid., c. 41.
[55] Ibid., c. 1028 sqq.
[56] Mary E. J. Chadwick, 'The role of redistribution in the making of the Third Reform Act', 19 *Historical Journal* (1976).

London may be taken as an example. Henry Pelling, in his *Social Geography of British Elections*, divided the London seats into three categories, based upon rateable value and thus, broadly, on social class. In the first category of 18 seats— predominantly middle-class—the Conservatives took 16 in 1885; then (with Liberal Unionist aid) they took all 18 in 1892 and kept them in 1895 and 1900. In the second category of 15 seats of mixed class, they took 9 in 1885, 13 in 1886, 11 in 1892, and all 15 in 1895 and 1900. In the third category, of 24 predominantly working-class seats, they took 9 in 1885, 15 in 1886, 6 in 1892, 16 in 1895 and 16 again in 1900. In the Chamberlain country of the West Midlands the consequences were even more striking. The redistribution of 1885 gave 11 seats to the Birmingham district. In 1885, 10 of them went to the Liberals. In 1886, after Chamberlain had broken with Gladstone, there were only two contested elections in Birmingham city and one more in the district, and Unionists won all three; in the other eight seats Unionists were elected unopposed. In 1892, 1895, 1900, 1906 and in both elections of 1910, Birmingham returned 11 Unionists.

The new arrangements did give a necessary stimulus to party organisation. The Conservatives were particularly successful in setting up associations in the new suburban divisions. But, as Hanham said, 'the exercise had a curiously artificial air to it. For the first time it could clearly be seen that parliamentary constituencies were merely artificial creations formed to give a basis of legitimacy to the politicans at Westminster rather than local communities. Henceforth, national and regional political issues were to be more important than local factors in deciding the result of elections.'[57]

---

[57] Hanham, op. cit., p. 26.

7

The Crisis of the Constitution, 1906–1914

A mastiff? It is the Right Honourable Gentleman's poodle.
It fetches and carries for him. It barks for him. It bites
anybody that he sets it on to.
                    Lloyd George on the House of Lords, 1907

The final test of a constitution is whether it works. To put
it another way, a successful constitution contains a 'rule of
recognition', accepted by those to whom governance is confided, which determines whether actions are regarded as having
authority. It is doubtful, to put it no higher, whether the
British constitution passed that test in the years immediately
before the outbreak of the Great War. It could be asked
whether Britain still possessed the minimum conditions
necessary for parliamentary government. Both major parties
and their ancillaries were confronted by complex issues on
which they were unable or unwilling to compromise. Each
side believed that the other had 'broken the constitution'.
The question was overtaken by the outbreak of war before it
could be answered; perhaps no answer was possible, in the
terms in which it was posed, because the 'constitution' had
come to mean different things to different parties. The argument from majorities pointed in one direction, the argument
from interests in another. In one important respect, the crisis
was more serious than it had been between 1830 and 1832.
Then, the unquestioned prerogative of the Crown was an
accepted means of resolving a political deadlock; now the
prerogative itself was a matter of dispute.
    The crisis became acute when the House of Lords rejected
the budget of 1909 and thus took the ultimate step of refusing

supplies to His Majesty's Government; but the constitution had been under increasing strain ever since the Unionists had demonstrated that they were unwilling to accept that the general election of 1906 had conferred a mandate upon the Liberal Government. The result of the election had seemed decisive enough when the seats were counted. In a House of 670, there were 400 Liberals, 157 Unionists, 83 Irish Nationalists and 40 Labour members. The pendulum had swung in a manner not seen since 1832. It seemed as though those who had come to regard themselves as the habitual governors had suddenly been stripped of power by the electorate.

It was a verdict that they were not prepared to acknowledge. At a public speech in Nottingham, in June 1906, Balfour said that it was the duty of the Unionist Party, 'in office or out of office, to continue to control the destinies of this great empire'. This was more than rhetoric; the Unionist Party would use against the Government the majority of the House of Lords, in accordance with the 'doctrine of the mandate' as elaborated by Lord Salisbury. Balfour rubbed the point in at Manchester, in October 1907 :

> The power which the House of Lords has, and which it undoubtedly ought to exercise, is not to prevent the people of this country having the laws they wish to have, but to see that the laws are not . . . the hasty and ill-considered offspring of one passionate election.[1]

This was to return to Salisbury's contention that it was impossible to deduce from an election whether any single item in a party's programme had received an endorsement. On Balfour's side, it must be said that the electorate seemed to be indifferent to the fate of Liberal legislation. There was no great public outcry when the House of Lords mutilated or rejected Bills on education, plural voting, licensing hours and the conditions of Scottish freehold. It could be argued that these were purely sectional measures, to gratify the intense minorities

---

[1] Blanche Dugdale, *Arthur James Balfour* (1935), vol. ii, p. 24.

within the Liberal Party. The House of Lords behaved otherwise when it received the Trade Disputes Bill of 1906, which
placed trade unions in a privileged position in law, and had
certainly not been proposed to the electorate in the form in
which it left the House of Commons. Nevertheless Lord
Lansdowne, the Unionist leader in the Lords, urged his
followers to pass the Bill, in language that recalled that of the
Duke of Wellington:

> . . . let us . . . be sure that if we join issue we do so upon
> ground which is as favourable as possible to ourselves. In
> this case I believe the ground would be unfavourable to this
> House, and I believe the juncture is one when, even if we
> were to win for the moment, our victory would be fruitless
> in the end. I shall not vote against the Bill. I regard it as
> conferring excessive privileges upon the Trade Union, as
> conferring dangerous privileges on one class and on one class
> only . . . but I also hold that it is useless for us, situated as we
> are, to oppose this measure.[2]

In short, the Unionists were prepared to ignore their 'doctrine
of the mandate' when an insistence upon it might bring them
into direct conflict with organised labour. In other matters,
however, they reverted to challenging the Government to put
their measures, one by one, to the judgment of a general
election. That this would be a pattern of conduct throughout
the Parliament had become plain by the end of the first
session. Campbell-Bannerman threatened the House of Lords,
when he withdrew the Education Bill, in December 1906,
because the Lords had insisted upon their wrecking amendments:

> The resources of the House of Commons are not exhausted,
> and I say with conviction that a way must be found, and a
> way will be found, by which the will of the people, expressed
> through their elected representatives, will be made to prevail.

For the moment, however, such words seemed no more than
a variant of 'filling up the cup'. The rejection of the Education

[2] Lord Newton, *Lord Lansdowne* (1929), p. 359.

Bill was hardly an issue upon which the Liberals could go to the country, especially as the intelligence from the constituencies was that the country seemed hardly to care. The House of Lords had, indeed,

> left the Government in a serious dilemma. Were they to dissolve and risk their great majority before it had done more than touch the fringe of its work, or were they to 'take it lying down', and earn the discredit which falls on every Administration which is unable to resent an injury? A few, a very few, voices were for dissolution. The great majority were of opinion that the Education Bill was not big enough for the great issue which must be raised before the final battle was joined.[3]

Ministers were not agreed among themselves about what should be done about the House of Lords. Should the composition of the Lords be changed, so as to remove their partisan majority, or should their powers be curbed—and, if so, how— or should both these things be attempted at the same time? A committee of the Cabinet, in 1907, proposed that disputes between the Houses should be resolved by a joint sitting of the House of Commons as a whole and one hundred peers, including all members of the Government. Campbell-Bannerman used his authority as Prime Minister to reject this, and propose instead that the power of the Lords to reject a Bill should be transformed into a suspensory veto. A resolution to this effect was passed in the House of Commons in 1907 after a debate of unusual acrimony. Arthur Henderson, on behalf of Labour, moved unsuccessfully an amendment that 'The Upper House, being an irresponsible part of the legislature, and of necessity representative only of interests opposed to the general well-being, is a hindrance to national progress and ought to be abolished.'[4] Lloyd George described the House of Lords as Balfour's poodle,[5] and Winston Churchill called it 'a one-sided, hereditary, unpurged, unrepresentative, irres-

---

[3] J. A. Spender, *Campbell-Bannerman,* vol. II, p. 312.
[4] H. of C., 25 June 1907, c. 1193.
[5] Ibid., 26 June, c. 1429.

ponsible absentee'. How, he asked, could one defend the
bishops?

> By what violation of all ideas of religious equality the leaders
> of one denomination only should be represented, I do not
> pause to inquire; but no doubt when such very delicate
> and ticklish questions as Chinese labour and the prevalence
> of intemperance, and great questions of war and the treatment
> of native races beyond the seas come up, it is a very con-
> venient thing to have the bishops in the House of Lords in
> order to make sure that official Christianity shall be on the
> side of the upper classes.[6]

The resolution in favour of a suspensory veto was adopted
by the House of Commons by 432 votes to 147, and the
House of Lords went on its way undeterred.

The rejection of the budget of 1909 was a challenge that
the Government could not ignore. It has sometimes been
argued that the budget was framed in order that it might be
rejected, so that the 'inevitable conflict' with the House of
Lords might take place on the most favourable ground that
the Liberals could find—a breach of ancient custom, denying
benefits to the poor for the sake of privileges for the rich.
There is no evidence for this. Asquith, who had succeeded
Campbell-Bannerman as Prime Minister in 1908, would not
and could not have acted in such a way. In financial terms,
the needs of the Government in 1909 were much what they
had been in 1908, plus the cost of eight new dreadnoughts.
The additional sum to be raised in taxation was £16,000,000.
Lloyd George, as Chancellor of the Exchequer, proposed to
find this by increasing the duties on spirits, tobacco and liquor
licences, by increases in death duties and income taxes, by
supertaxes on incomes of over £5000 and—the most controversial of all—a set of land taxes which seemed aimed at
eventually bringing to the state the 'unearned increment'.
Lloyd George was faced with the problem that had beset his
predecessors ever since the annual national expenditure had

[6] Ibid., 25 June, c. 1248.

begun to rise steadily in the 1880s: how were they to find new sources of income without abandoning free trade? But whereas free trade had, in the past, been common ground between the parties, now important groups had been converted to tariff protection. One reason why Lloyd George's budget was so unpopular was that it offered an alternative to tariff protection as a means of financing an expanding state expenditure; it was this which encouraged men of the stamp of Chamberlain and Milner to encourage rejection. At the same time, there was resentment at the new taxes, fears about the proposals for land valuation, and general resentment at Lloyd George: he had talked earlier of having to 'rob someone's hen roost next year'. Certainly, the budget was an instrument of party warfare as well as of financial necessity. It was intended to encourage the Liberals, to accomplish some social purposes and indicate to the obstructionists in the House of Lords that they might have to pay for their pleasures. The budget was meant to pass. It was discussed to an unusual degree in Cabinet—it was the principal business at 14 meetings between 17 March and 26 April, and on 19 March the Cabinet rejected Lloyd George's proposals to tax the ground-rents of built-up land because they would have meant interference with existing contracts.[7]

Once the possibility was there that the House of Lords would reject the budget, Lloyd George certainly used provocative language, to the fury of the Lords and the distress of the King. Asquith, on the other hand, refused even to discuss contingency plans; it would be incredible if the Lords were to act so irresponsibly. Churchill was rebuked with unusual severity for his statement in Edinburgh that if the Lords did not pass the budget there would be an immediate dissolution of Parliament. At the Cabinet of 21 July, Asquith

> with the general assent of his colleagues, pointed out that unauthorized statements of matters of high policy, made by an individual Minister, without previous consultation, and purporting to speak on behalf of the Government, are

[7] RA R29/98.

quite indefensible, and altogether inconsistent with Cabinet responsibility and Ministerial cohesion.[8]

In November 1909 the House of Lords rejected the Finance Bill on second reading by 350 votes to 75. The arguments used by the Unionist majority were familiar enough in general; all that was new was that the concept of the mandate had not before been applied to a money Bill. The advice and consent of the Lords spiritual and temporal, Lansdowne said, was not 'some mere musty anachronism'. The Bill was a 'kind of hotch-potch of financial legislation' in which had been embedded the essentials of measures, such as licensing and land valuation, which the Lords had already rejected or amended. On that principle, could not an Irish Home Rule Bill be grafted on to the budget? The House of Lords would not pass the Bill 'until it has become aware that the people of this country desire that this Bill should become law'. That might produce a deadlock between the two Houses, but that need not last for very long. 'Is your Budget so perishable that it will not keep for six weeks?'[9]

Loreburn, the Lord Chancellor, said that the Lords could reject the budget legally but not constitutionally:

> . . . it is not to the letter of the law itself that those who wish to govern this country as this country has been governed in the past must look. They must look even more to custom, usage, convention—call it whatever you please—by which inveterate practice had so modified the hard law itself that we are governed more by custom in this country in great matters than we are even by the law.

It was the Lords who were breaking that custom. He looked back mordantly to the fate of the Licensing Bill in 1908, considered at length in the Commons and then rejected by the Lords, after brief debate and after it had already been condemned at a party meeting at Lansdowne House. That Bill, he said, 'was not alive when it came here. It had perished

[8] RA R/30/45.
[9] H. of L., 22 Nov. 1909, cc. 731 sqq.

by the stiletto in Berkeley Square before it ever saw this House.'[10]

The King had used his personal influence with Balfour and Lansdowne; he summoned them to Buckingham Palace and asked them to persuade the House of Lords to pass the budget. He found them 'stiff and uncommunicative'.[11]

Asquith asked for and obtained a dissolution of Parliament. Once the Lords had rejected the budget, the Cabinet had been faced with an unprecedented situation. Refusal of supply was only one step removed from the ultimate 'appeal to Heaven'. One possibility was to reintroduce the Finance Bill in the Commons and send it back to the Lords with the threat that if it were rejected again the King would be advised to create peers, on the precedent of 1832. But this time 500 peers would be needed, and it was not certain that the King would agree to a step as drastic as that which the Lords had taken themselves. The Cabinet did for a moment consider whether to advise the King to transfer into the hands of the Prime Minister the prerogative of creating peers; Lord Knollys said of this proposal, when he heard of it through Lord Esher, that it 'would be better that the King should abdicate than agree to it'. A second proposal that had been tentatively discussed was that the King should give a pledge, to be made public before the election, that he would create enough peers to pass a Bill curbing the powers of the House of Lords if the Liberals should win. It is clear that King Edward would not willingly have agreed to either of these proposals. Knollys told Esher that he did not propose to show the letter to the King, 'at any rate for the present', because it would be a 'a mistake to set him still more against his Ministers'.

On 15 December, the King sent Lord Knollys to inform Vaughan Nash, Asquith's private secretary, that he would not agree to a creation of peers until the question had been put specifically to the country at a second general election.[12]

It is difficult to see the general election of January 1910 as giving anyone a mandate for anything. The Liberals lost

[10] Ibid., c. 759.
[11] Philip Magnus, *King Edward the Seventh* (1964), p. 437.
[12] Ibid., pp. 438–40.

about a hundred seats, the Unionists gained them, and the other parties remained much as before. The new House contained 275 Liberals, 273 Unionists, 82 Irish Nationalists and 40 Labour. Under the most favourable conditions, there was still an anti-Unionist majority of about 120. The votes of the Irish and of Labour could not be taken for granted, but it was unlikely that ·either of these parties would wish to turn out Asquith to put Balfour in; nevertheless it seemed that John Redmond had come to hold the balance of power in the House of Commons—had achieved that pivotal position which had eluded Parnell. Redmond tested his bargaining strength at once. The Irish disliked parts of the budget, especially the spirit duties, and warned that they might vote against it when it was reintroduced unless they were given assurances that the Government would bring forward a Bill to curb the powers of the House of Lords during the session of 1910.[13] It was clear enough that with the obstruction of the Lords removed, the way would be open for the granting of Home Rule to Ireland. Some members of the Cabinet suggested, indeed, that the Government should resign, since it could not rely upon a stable majority; however, these waverers had recovered their nerve by the next morning, and on 26 February the Cabinet authorised the Master of Elibank, the chief whip, who was present by invitation, to tell Redmond that there would be no deal.[14] Asquith reported to the King that Ministers were 'strongly and unanimously of the opinion that to purchase the Irish vote by such a concession would be a discreditable transaction, which they could not defend'.[15]

Politics had reached a state of halting uncertainty. As Churchill put it in one of his formal letters to the King on the daily sessions of the House of Commons, the Cabinet felt that it was living 'from day to day under the shadow of the axe'.[16] There was an air of the artificial and the provisional. 'Your Majesty's new Parliament has been born in a trance. Two prevailing impressions are in everyone's mind—that its

[13] RA R30/91.
[14] RA R/30/108.
[15] RA XII/28.
[16] RA XII/21.

hours are numbered, and that in the pass to which we are come, speeches are but words.'[17] The Irish gained no concessions on the budget, which was reintroduced in the House of Commons and passed the Lords without a division; if one thing was clear, it was that the Unionists had not won. It was equally clear that the Government would now have to do something about the House of Lords. But what, and how? By March, the Cabinet was considering printed extracts from and digests of the works of constitutional authorities—Erskine May's *Constitutional History*, Anson's *Law and Custom of the Constitution*, Dicey's *Law of the Constitution* and Lecky's *History of England in the Eighteenth Century*. Still, they could not agree upon details. By April, they had decided to propose resolutions in the House of Commons to the effect that the 'will of the electorate as determined at the polls' should be able to transform itself into law within the period of a single Parliament. That the Lords would reject these resolutions could be taken as a foregone conclusion, and the Cabinet then made up its mind, in a cloudy way, about what it would do next.

> They came to the conclusion that, in that event, it would be their duty at once to tender advice to the Crown as to the necessary steps—whether by the exercise of the prerogative, or by a referendum *ad hoc*, or otherwise—to be taken to ensure that the policy, approved by the House of Commons by huge majorities, should be given statutory effect in this Parliament. If they found that they were not in a position to accomplish that object, they would then either resign office, or advise a dissolution of Parliament; but in no case would they feel able to advise a dissolution, except under such conditions as would secure that in the new Parliament the judgement of the people, as expressed at the elections, would be carried into law.[18]

This conclusion, quoted here in the manner in which it was transmitted to the King, was curiously loose and ambiguous. Asquith had known since the previous December

[17] RA R/39/123.
[18] RA XII/28.

that the King would not create peers until after another general election. The Cabinet decision, then, looked like a warning; the alternative to a dissolution, with some sort of guarantee given by the King in advance, might be a resignation of Ministers in circumstances that could look like a dismissal. The decision, so far as the conditions relating to a dissolution went, was converted into a public pledge when Asquith repeated its substance in the House of Commons on 14 April 1910.

Here, then, was publicly raised the question of 'contingent guarantees'—pledges in advance from the King that he would act in a certain way in hypothetical circumstances. But Asquith knew already what the King's attitude was : hold another election, and see what happens. Why, then, did he use the language of menace? Was the Cabinet deliberately resolving to coerce the King—to decide, as Balfour put it later, to behave like bullies in the Royal Closet? Asquith may have encountered from the King a resistance that is not reflected either in the royal archives or in contemporary memoirs; but it is more likely that both the Cabinet decision and the parliamentary pledge were intended to appease the hostility to the Prime Minister that was showing itself on the Liberal back benches. There had been discontent there when it was learned, after the election in January, that the House of Lords was to be dealt with in two stages. Asquith's admission in the House of Commons on 21 February that he had neither asked for nor received a promise that peers would be created had been received with angry dismay; by 13 April, he evidently felt that he would have to placate his party, even at the expense of the King. The most plausible explanation of Asquith's interpretation of events was that given by Vaughan Nash in a review of the whole episode which he sent to Lord Knollys 15 months later :

The House of Commons was overshadowed and almost paralysed by a sense of its helplessness and futility. It, or rather the majority, saw itself stultified in the eyes of the country : people in the House and out of it asked themselves what was the use of elections if nothing was to come of them;

what would be the force of another election (which was seen to be impending) if the same issue was to be put to the country with the same results, and what was the good of doing work in the House of Commons which the House of Lords occupied itself in destroying? The position was perilous in an extreme degree not merely for the Government but for the authority and standing of our Parliamentary procedure and institutions.[19]

It seemed that the political clock had been turned back to 1832. Was the King bound to accept his Ministers' advice, or could he find another administration that would be prepared to take office? Discreet enquiries were made. At Lord Knollys's request, the Archbishop of Canterbury acted as host at a meeting on 27 April, at which were present Knollys, Balfour and Lord Esher, that tireless go-between. The record, drawn up by Esher and magniloquently headed 'Lambeth Conference', quoted Balfour as saying that, if Asquith resigned, he would be prepared to form a government and would at once ask for a dissolution. According to this testimony, Balfour was prepared to play the role of Peel to King Edward's William IV and to reenact the events of 1835—not an auspicious precedent. Knollys sent this news to the King on 29 April; clearly it was not regarded as urgent. From there, it went no further. On 6 May, King Edward died. Neither Knollys nor Esher, it seems, mentioned the matter to the new King.

King George V's reign began with a sort of Truce of God, during which the elders of both major parties tried unsuccessfully to agree in private on what the proper functions of a reformed Second Chamber ought to be. The Liberals were represented by Asquith, Lloyd George, Crewe and Birrell, the Unionists by Balfour, Lansdowne, Austen Chamberlain and Lord Cawdor. No Irish or Labour representatives were invited. They met first in the Prime Minister's room in the House of Commons, but then found a more congenial venue; the whole set of meetings, which continued sporadically from June until November, is usually called the Lansdowne House conference. The President of Columbia University, Dr Nicholas

19 Ibid.

Murray Butler, was invited in on one occasion to explain the workings of the American Constitution.[20] These discussions were enlivened by a proposal from Lloyd George for a latter-day Ministry of All the Talents, a coalition to deal with all outstanding difficulties by agreement between the two front benches; this would have entailed treating the party system as though it did not exist, and it did not find favour with the whips. Balfour was put in mind again of the spectre of Sir Robert Peel.[21] Having dismissed the idea of a coalition, the conference failed to agree on what was to be regarded as 'constitutional' legislation, on which the Lords might keep their veto, and 'ordinary' legislation, where the majority in the Commons should prevail. The stumbling block was the classification of Home Rule, regarded as 'ordinary' by the Liberals, 'constitutional' by the Unionists.

On 9 October, Balfour wrote a memorandum enumerating the choices that would be open to the King if the conference failed.[22] This is in the Royal Archives, and it bears a note in Lord Esher's hand saying that he had sent it to Lord Knollys. Balfour began with the assertion that a demand that the King should give a promise in advance, extorted by the threat of resignation, to use his prerogative to destroy the powers of the House of Lords could 'neither be constitutionally made not [sic] constitutionally conceded'. The proper constitutional course would be for the King to tell the Prime Minister that he could not commit himself until the necessity had arisen. But what if the Prime Minister then resigned? As he himself was at present advised, Balfour went on, the Leader of the Opposition would not be justified in accepting office, even for the purpose of taking responsibility for advising an immediate dissolution of Parliament. What expedients then remained? Balfour suggested two. Either the King could send for a 'neutral' statesman and ask him either to form a government or advise a dissolution (and for this office, in Balfour's opinion, Lord Rosebery was the only candidate); or else the King could try 'a wholly new, but perfectly constitutional

[20] J. A. Spender, *Great Britain, 1886–1935* (2nd ed., 1935), p. 382.
[21] Dugdale, op. cit., p. 54.
[22] RA G.V K/2552/88.

experiment, and give the Heads of Departments, or some of them, such official rank as would enable them legally to secure a Dissolution, and to carry on the routine work of their Offices, until the result of that Dissolution were known'.

Whoever saw that paper might reasonably conclude that there was no comfort for the King to be had from the Leader of the Opposition. Balfour had clearly thought better of his earlier offer, made at the 'Lambeth Conference'. Now, his suggestion about elder statesmen, still more his idea of a King-in-Council with civil servants, would have taken executive government so far outside the established patterns as to make it certain that any King who followed Balfour's advice would be attacked for creating precedents or for reviving powers that had been dormant for a very long time indeed.

On 11 November, after the Lansdowne House talks had broken down, Asquith saw the King at Sandringham. Asquith's extensive note of this conversation makes it clear that he did not, at that meeting, ask for a guarantee. He reviewed in a general way the whole constitutional problem, and said that if the Government had an adequate majority in the new House of Commons, after the election that was now inevitable, 'the matter should be put in train for final settlement'.[23] The note of the conversation made by Sir Arthur Bigge (who now shared with Knollys the office of private secretary to the King) reported Asquith as saying that he 'did not come to ask for anything from the King: no promises, no guarantees during this Parliament'. The House of Lords, Asquith continued, 'would have to give way. It cannot be dissolved: it cannot be reduced (for he does not admit the legality of withholding writs of summons): it can only be increased in numbers . . .' He did not think that it would be necessary to proceed from a threat of creation to its execution. 'There could, in Mr Asquith's opinion, be no doubt that the knowledge that the Crown was ready to use the Prerogative would be sufficient to bring about an agreement, without any necessity for its performance.' What Asquith was suggesting (although he did not use the analogy) was that the information about the King's

[23] Harold Nicolson, *King George V* (1952), p. 134.

intentions could be used to deter the Opposition, much as Lord Derby had used the information that the Queen would not refuse him a dissolution in 1859.

This was vintage Asquith—the absence of any sense of urgency, the assumption that reasonable men would always behave reasonably, the comfortable conviction that a judicious consideration of all the circumstances would lead men on either side of a controversy to substantially the same conclusion. Asquith did not, in politics at least, appreciate the forces of passion. It was this confidence in other men's rationality that had led him to the conclusion that the House of Lords was bluffing on the budget in 1909, that it was bluffing again on further resistance, and it would lead him to the conclusion that Bonar Law, Carson and Craig were bluffing on out-and-out opposition to Home Rule. It is this consistency in Asquith's conduct that leads one to disagree with Harold Nicolson, King George V's biographer, when he suggests that on 11 November Asquith was merely preparing the King for more definite and disagreeable advice that would follow later. It is more likely that Asquith said what he then thought when he said that he was not asking for guarantees; and that when he changed his mind, as he did within four days, it was because he had once more been threatened with the wrath of his party. The Master of Elibank told him:

> You must get your guarantees, otherwise :—
> (1) You break faith with your Party, or
> (2) You must say that you have asked for guarantees and the King has refused,
> (3) You leave the country to conjecture that the King has refused.
>   The Socialists and Irish will be indignant with the King and drag his name into the controversy.[24]

The Master of Elibank stressed party considerations in a letter to Lord Knollys of 14 November. He was, he said, searching for a formula that would make clear to the public that Asquith had asked for contingent guarantees even if the

[24] Master of Elibank to Asquith.

King refused to give them. He wanted a form of words 'which will strictly define His Majesty's attitude as correct and constitutional while at the same time safeguarding the Prime Minister'. The Master was plainly seeking for assurances that he could give, as chief whip, to those Liberal back-benchers who were muttering that Asquith had been too soft on Edward VII and was going to be too soft on George V:

> I am sure you will recognise that the Prime Minister has come through a year of unexampled difficulty, and that, in arranging and entering the [Lansdowne House] Conference, he strained the loyalty of his Party to a very strong degree, and if there is a feeling in the country that he is in any way flinching now that the crisis is upon us again, it would only serve as help and encouragement to the Socialist and extreme forces in the country. A very nasty spirit of unrest pervades the working classes at this moment, and I am particularly anxious that nothing should occur to drag the King into the vortex of our political controversies.[25]

It might be regarded as a curious way of keeping the King out of the vortex of controversy to push him into alignment with Liberal 'feeling in the country' as interpreted by the party's chief whip. Bigge, who saw the letter, retorted indignantly that when the time came after the electorate had voted, 'The King will do what is right.' To the King, Bigge wrote 'It is not His Majesty's duty to save the Prime Minister from the mistake of his incautious words on 14 April.'[26]

On 14 November, after the Cabinet had met, Asquith sent the King a memorandum outlining the possible actions which he might advise him to take if (or, rather, when) the Lords rejected the resolutions which would be moved in the Commons on the limitation of their powers: (1) Creation of peers, without a dissolution; (2) Dissolution, preceded by an assurance from the King that he would create peers if the Government were returned with an 'adequate majority' which the Government would be allowed to make public at once; (3) The same

---

[25] RA G.V K2552 (1)/50.
[26] Nicolson, op. cit., pp. 137, 138.

as (2) but with no public announcement; (3) Dissolution, with
no assurance precedent, but with 'a clear understanding' that
the King would create peers if the Government came back
into office.[27]

It was at this stage that the King received conflicting
counsels from Bigge, who was with him at Sandringham, and
Knollys, who was in London. It seems that the Master of
Elibank had convinced Asquith, and both of them had convinced Knollys, that the King should give the guarantees at
once. On 14 November, reporting to the King a meeting
which he had just had with Asquith, Knollys wrote:

> He asked me to see the Master of Elibank, who came to
> No. 10. He [*sc.* the Master] also strongly supported this latter
> idea, as he said unless it was done the country, after the
> speech of 14 April, would imagine he was 'playing with them'.
> I told both him and Asquith that you could not agree to
> contingent guarantees and that if on this the Cabinet resigned
> you would send for Balfour . . .
> I understand that you had already practically told him you
> would agree to the creation of Peers, but this consent was not
> to be made public. I presume I may take it for granted that
> you will agree to No. 3 in Asquith's paper.[28]
> If the Prime Minister were to insist on guarantees, the King
> would refuse them and his resignation would be the only
> alternative. Mr Balfour would be sent for, he would be unable
> to form a government, and dissolution would follow, though
> no doubt the King would be blamed for this delay in appealing
> to the country.[29]

If there were to be blame, the King was prepared to take
it. On 15 November, Bigge telegraphed to Asquith's private
secretary: 'His Majesty regrets that it would be impossible
to give contingent guarantees and he reminds Mr Asquith of
his promise not to seek for any during the present Parliament.'[30]

The crisis was now acute, and it seemed that a parting of
the ways had been reached. On 15 November Asquith sent to

[27] RA G.V K2552 (1)/46.
[28] RA G.V K2552 (1)/47.
[29] Ibid.
[30] Nicolson, op. cit., p. 134.

the King a formal Cabinet minute. Ministers now advised a dissolution as soon as necessary business had been completed in the House of Commons, no matter what the Lords did with the resolutions. But they could not 'take the responsibility of advising a dissolution' unless they knew that the King would be 'ready to exercise his constitutional powers' if the Government were returned.

> His Majesty will doubtless agree that it would be undesirable, in the interests of the State, that any communication of the intentions of the Crown should be made public, unless and until the actual occasion should arise.[31]

This was an ultimatum, and Knollys urged the King to accept it. This was, he said, 'a great compromise on the part of the Cabinet, made entirely to fall in as far as possible with your wishes and to enable you to act conscientiously'. The King found it hard to see why a contingent guarantee should be given at all, if it were not to be made public, unless the Cabinet plainly had no confidence that he would act 'constitutionally' when the time came. He asked this question on 16 November when Asquith, accompanied by Lord Crewe, saw him at Buckingham Palace. They told him plainly that the Cabinet would resign unless the guarantee were given there and then. It would, they said, 'be considered an absolute secret by the Cabinet and would never be made public: if any member of the Cabinet violated this secrecy he would be regarded "as a man who had cheated at cards".' The King wanted to know why a private assurance from him to Asquith and Crewe would not be enough, without a formal pledge. 'But what reply,' they answered, 'can be given to the Cabinet who are waiting to know the results of our interview?' Asquith and Crewe repeated the arguments already used by the Master of Elibank; they 'feared that there was a serious state of unrest among the working classes and if the King did anything to bring about a resignation of the Government it might do great harm to the Crown'.[32]

[31] Ibid., p. 136.
[32] RA G.V K/2552 (1)/66.

At last and with great reluctance, the King gave way to unusual, if not unprecedented, ministerial pressure; it would not be unreasonable to call this an act of coercion. He agreed to give a secret guarantee to create peers. It was a decision that he was to regret for the rest of his life. Twenty-one years later, when he received Lord Crewe's final resignation, he harked back to that day in 1910:

> The King said that this forcing of His Majesty's hand against his better judgment was the dirtiest thing ever done. What right had Asquith to bring a colleague with him on this occasion to browbeat His Majesty? . . .
> The King said he wished he had then the experience he has now. He ought to have said: 'All right, Mr Asquith— put everything on paper and I will give you my answer by 12 noon tomorrow.[33]

There has been some controversy over the ethics of Lord Knollys's behaviour during this crisis. The King admitted that he was much influenced by Knollys—'Francis strongly urged me to take this course and I think his advice is generally very sound. I only trust and pray he is right this time.'[34] Roy Jenkins wrote: 'Knollys only got his way by keeping a vital piece of information from the King'—that Balfour had said, at the "Lambeth Conference", that he would be prepared to form a government—and 'there was no evidence that Balfour had changed his mind in the meantime'.[35] It is strange that the King knew nothing about that gathering until more than three years after it had happened. On 7 January 1914, the King wrote in his own hand upon the Lambeth papers: 'It was not until late in the year 1913 that the foregoing letters and memoranda came into my possession. The knowledge of their contents would undoubtedly have had an important bearing and influence upon my decision with regard to Mr Asquith's request for guarantees on 16 November 1910.'[36]

[33] RA G.V K/2552 (2)/99.
[34] Nicolson, op. cit., p. 138.
[35] Roy Jenkins, *Asquith* (Fontana ed.), p. 244–5.
[36] RA G.V K/2552 (2)/89.

There is, moreover, a letter from Balfour to Lord Stamfordham (as Bigge had become) written on 1 August 1911 and referring to reports that, when Asquith obtained the guarantees, the King had been told that Balfour was not willing to take office. First, said Balfour, he was never asked; secondly, he was in complete ignorance of what was going on between the King and his Cabinet:

> If I had been told that the King was being pressed to give a promise to coerce the House of Lords into passing a Parliament Bill, seven or eight months before the Parliament Bill could reach the final stages, and if I had been requested to form a Government, I should have of course complied, though with very grave doubts as to the view which the country would have taken on the subject. Had I been asked, on the other hand, to form a Government in order to protect His Majesty from giving a promise, not merely that a Parliament Bill should be passed over the heads of the Lords, but that it should be passed in a form which by implication carried Home Rule with it, I should not only have formed a Government, but I should have had great hopes of carrying the country with me.[37]

This was hindsight. A letter written in August 1911 is no sure guide to how its author would have acted in November 1910. Balfour's memory was notoriously bad. In his letter to Stamfordham, he wrote in general terms and made no specific mention of the meeting at Lambeth. Should Lord Knollys have isolated that particular episode from all that had happened since and brought it to King George V's attention? Since then, among much else, Knollys had seen Balfour's memorandum of 9 October 1910 which contained, along with strange matter about elder statesmen and civil servants, his own unequivocal statement that he would not be justified in taking office. So far from Knollys concealing information from the King, for however high-minded a reason, he had left the King with an exact impression of Balfour's intentions as expressed in his most recent communication. As for Balfour's letter of 1 August

1911, it is reasonable to point out that it is a good example of its author's mastery of debating points. It does not accord with what Balfour said either in October 1910 or in January 1911 when Lord Knollys, with Asquith's knowledge, asked him what he would have done if the King had sent for him in December 1910, after the election. Balfour then said that he would have tried to form a government, but with no hope of success. Knollys's report to the King continued:

> The result would therefore have been that after you had been reviled by the Radical Press, and hostilely criticised by the Liberal Parliamentary candidates, besides having your name brought forward, in a friendly spirit by one Party and in the reverse spirit by the other side, you would have been obliged to call back the present Ministers, who would have returned very sore with you and with their followers triumphant and bitter. He [*sc.* Balfour] could not think that such a state of affairs could do anything but harm to the Crown and to you personally.[38]

It is a fair conclusion, then, that the King never had a chance of finding an alternative government and that therefore he had no effective way of resisting Asquith's demands, once those were backed by a threat of resignation. The pledge which Asquith had extorted was vague and ambiguous. The King had bound himself to act in a particular way in a future situation that was only partly defined. His pledge was to be fulfilled if the Government had an 'adequate majority': did that mean a purely Liberal majority or only with the aid of a third or a fourth party? What if the Liberals won substantially fewer seats than the Unionists, but could still govern with the support of the Irish? As it happened, the election of December 1910 reproduced almost exactly the results of the previous January; the Liberals had three fewer seats and the Unionists one, leaving them level at 272 each.

There remains the Cabinet's promise to keep the guarantees secret. That might have been kept to the letter, but hardly to the spirit. Once Asquith had said that he stood by his statement

[38] RA G.V K2252 (1)/76.

of 14 April and then announced that Parliament would be dissolved, it was not difficult to put two and two together. The leading article of *The Star* of 19 November was headed: 'We have got the guarantees.' *The Daily News* of 21 November reported Lloyd George as saying: 'Does any man, in his senses, think that we would provoke another election unless we were certain that if we can get a majority it will be a final one?'

The guarantees served no constitutional purpose: once the results of the election were known, the King had no alternative choice open to him, whether he had given guarantees or not. They were insisted upon for purely party reasons, for the advantage of Asquith and his Cabinet in their relations with their back-benchers. As it was, no alternative government was in sight, a third election was out of the question, and therefore the King was in a position where, as Balfour put it, the Cabinet 'within rather wide limits . . . can compel him to take any course they please by threatening resignation'.[39] Such a situation had not been 'known to the constitution' at least since George IV had given way on Catholic Emancipation in 1829, but Wellington had then asked for immediate, and not contingent, action. A nearer precedent for Asquith's action would have been Derby's request for a dissolution in 1859, but the essence of the Queen's acquiescence then had been that her decision should be discreetly used to deter the Opposition. The novelty of Asquith's action was that the demand was made, under pressure from his chief whip, for reasons that made sense only if the secret were in some manner shared with his followers.

The King kept his side of the bargain, until Asquith released him from the pledge of secrecy by announcing on 20 July 1911 that the guarantees had been given. In the intervening seven months, the King was in an unhappy, even in a false, position; he had something to hide, and he was inhibited from those confidential discussions which his predecessors had always regarded as legitimate. One example will suffice for many. On 11 January 1911, the Archbishop of Canterbury,

[39] RA G.V K2552 (1)/76.

Randall Davidson, who had every reason to regard himself as a confidant of the King's father and grandmother, sent him a memorandum, arguing that it would be wrong for the King to give a pledge in advance because it would

> be most unfair to the Unionists were a discussion to take place, the issues of which were apparently undecided, while all the while the Prime Minister had in his pocket or his memory a declaration made by the King before the debates began, to the effect that His Majesty would, in the end, whatever happened, give full weight to the wishes of the Government.[40]

It must have been galling for the King to recognise that the Archbishop was warning him against something which he had already done. What rankled with the King—as his conversation with Crewe, years afterwards, made plain—was that Asquith had not trusted him. Margot Asquith, in her *Autobiography*, quoted the King's question on 16 November—'Is this the advice that you would have given to my father?'—and her husband's reply: 'Yes, Sire, and he would have taken it.' One may be more sceptical than Asquith was about Edward VII's reactions; he had not been taught, like his son, that the monarchy was the dignified rather than the efficient part of the constitution. As Duke of York, George V had been instructed in English history and government by J. R. Tanner, a Fellow of St. John's College, Cambridge, and later a notable editor of constitutional documents. Under this tutelage, the Duke had summarised Bagehot's *English Constitution*: one of his extracts was that the 'existence of the Crown serves to *disguise* change and therefore to deprive it of the evil consequences of revolution . . .'[41] But Bagehot's knowledge of what the monarch actually did in his own time was not extensive; and Balfour certainly had a point when he denied that the King could properly be asked, without public debate, to make an irreversible change in the constitutional conventions:

[40] RA G.V K2552 (1)/78.
[41] Nicolson, op. cit., p. 62.

No action on the part of the Sovereign can be part of the accepted machinery of the Constitution unless it is capable of repetition under similar circumstances. Now I take it that even those who think it within the proper limits of the Constitution to turn an Assembly of six hundred into an Assembly of one thousand would hardly think the same of a subsequent scheme for converting an Assembly of one thousand into an Assembly of (say) eighteen hundred.[42]

The justification for Asquith's behaviour must lie in his appreciation of the felt necessities of the moment. The relatively novel claims of party had produced strains that could not be contained within the framework of existing conventions. But if Asquith really believed that secrecy would shield the King from political controversy, then his action was as naive as it was nugatory. The reaction of the Unionists was that if one party could make unusual demands on the King, so could the other.

II

In spite of the resistance of the Diehards under Lord Halsbury, enough Unionist peers either abstained or voted with the Government to allow the Parliament Bill of 1911 to pass the House of Lords by 131 votes to 114. The Lords of 1911, like those of 1832, had been faced with the choice of having to accept a disagreeable measure with a creation of peers or having to accept it without a creation of peers. They decided against being swamped. (*Punch*, of 2 August 1911, published a cartoon of Lord Halsbury dragging forward a Trojan horse labelled 'To hold 500 Liberal peers'. The captions read: 'Lord Lansdowne: "Don't lug that infernal machine into the citadel. The thing's full of enemies." Lord Halsbury: "I know. That's where my heroism comes in." ') The Parliament Act provided that a money Bill, so certified by the Speaker, should be deemed to have passed the Lords unless they had passed it without amendment within one

42 RA G.V K2552 (1)/71.

month; and that any other Bill (except one to extend the life of Parliament beyond the new limit of five years) should be deemed to have passed the Lords after having been passed by the House of Commons in three successive sessions, provided that at least two years had elapsed between the second reading in the first session and the third reading in the third. The House of Lords had been deprived of an outright veto, but it still had its Unionist majority and it still had powers enough to make it a formidable opponent in certain circumstances. Bonar Law wrote in a letter to *The Times* of 26 July 1911, that the House of Lords might still be able to force a general election:

> They can delay for instance the Expiring Laws Continuance Bill or the Army Annual Bill, and such action on their part would undoubtedly make the continuance of the Government impossible and compel an election . . . It might or might not be wise to use this power, but if I am right in thinking that the House of Lords would have the means of compelling an election before Home Rule became law, that surely is not a power which ought to be lightly abandoned.[43]

The reference to Home Rule goes to the heart of the bitterness that was to characterise the party struggle during the next three years. The anger of the Unionists over the Parliament Act was compounded by their knowledge that there was now no constitutional barrier to Home Rule. They convinced themselves that Asquith had first perverted the constitution and then entered into a corrupt bargain with the Irish Nationalists, in which Home Rule was the price of the Liberals' continuance in office. Lord Curzon spoke for many Unionists when he accused the Government of dismembering the United Kingdom behind the backs of the people:

> There is a phrase in one of the Letters of Junius to the Duke of Grafton in which he says—'You began by betraying the people; you ended by betraying the King.' We do not in these days use the rather full-blooded language of the

[43] Robert Blake, *The Unknown Prime Minister* (1955), p. 70.

eighteenth century; but, my Lords, if any modern Junius were
to arise and were to address His Majesty's Ministers at this
moment and say to them—'You inverted the process. You
began by coercing the King; you ended by betraying the
people', I, at any rate, should not quarrel with him either for
his language or his sentiments . . . You are going to usurp
the Prerogative of the Crown in order to deny and extinguish
the Prerogative of the People.[44]

Bonar Law had succeeded Balfour as Unionist leader in the
Commons in 1911. He too felt that he had to satisfy his
followers. As he and Asquith were walking away side by side
after listening to the King's speech at the opening of the
session of 1912, Bonar Law said: 'I am afraid I shall have to
show myself very vicious, Mr Asquith, this session. I hope you
will understand.'[45] During the next three years, he demonstrated that he was prepared to go to almost any lengths to
prevent Home Rule. The Unionists' tactics were to skirmish
on several fronts—to persuade the Government to change its
mind, by action in and out of Parliament; to encourage armed
resistance in Ireland; to force a general election; to put
pressure on the King to dissolve Parliament, or to dismiss his
Ministers, or to refuse assent to a Home Rule Bill when it
was presented to him.

The Parliament Act of 1911 had been lumbered, in the
manner of the eighteenth century, with a preamble which
stated an intention, some time in the future, of reconstituting
the composition of the House of Lords—'whereas it is intended
to substitute for the House of Lords as it at present exists a
Second Chamber constituted on a popular instead of hereditary
basis, but such substitution cannot be immediately brought
into operation . . .' This clumsy passage, which had no effect
in law, had been added to appease Sir Edward Grey. It was
the existence of this preamble that enabled the Unionists to
argue that the passing of the Parliament Act had created a
'gap in the constitution'; until the presaged reform had been
accomplished, one of the traditional balances of the constitution

[44] H. of L., 8 Aug. 1911, cc. 823, 832.
[45] Blake, op. cit., p. 96.

would be lacking; and in the interim the lost powers of the
Lords must therefore have devolved upon the King. In
particular, they argued, the King had recovered the power to
dissolve Parliament, without the advice of Ministers, as part
of the prerogative. This was an ingenious blend of High Tory
and Old Whig doctrines; it served as a justification for the
appeals which they made to the King. It became a commonplace of Unionist rhetoric to accuse Asquith of having made a
squalid bargain with Redmond. Thus Bonar Law could say,
in Belfast on 9 April 1912:

> In order to retain for a little longer the ascendancy of their
> party, to remain a few months longer in office, they have sold
> the constitution, they have sold themselves . . . [46]

Lord Hugh Cecil, in the House of Commons, talked about
'a sordid chain of coercion—the Irish Party coercing the Prime
Minister, and the Prime Minister coercing Parliament'.[47] It
was this feeling in each party that the other was no longer
observing the conventions of the constitution that explains the
extreme behaviour of those who howled down the Prime
Minister in the House of Commons, incited Ulster to resistance
and the British Army to mutiny and, on the other side, threatened to use the Royal Navy against Belfast.

The King behaved with his customary seriousness. He consulted constitutional authorities on the prerogative; the answers
he received reflected the political sympathies of the respondents.
Grant Robertson told him that the personal prerogative of
dissolution had been extinguished by time and circumstance;
its last use had been in 1680, but then 'there was no modern
Cabinet and all that that implies'.[48] Sir William Anson thought
that the prerogative of refusing assent to a Bill undoubtedly
existed and could be compared to the power to create peers—
'a discretionary prerogative in the use of which the King may
sometimes consider whether the advice of his ministers is in
accordance with the wishes of his people . . . It is worth

[46] Ibid., p. 95.
[47] H. of C., 8 Aug. 1912, c. 977.
[48] RA G.V K398/6.

bearing in mind that the last use of the royal veto on legislation was only five years earlier than the last use of the power to create peers in order to determine a vote in the Lords.'[49] (Anson was referring to Queen Anne's veto of a Scotch Militia Bill in 1707, and the creation of 12 peers to pass the Treaty of Utrecht in 1712.) Balfour, in a memorandum written in 1913, argued that the fact that a prerogative power had not been used for a long time was a reason why, on logical grounds, it had not become obsolete: 'It is surely obvious that if a prerogative *ought* rarely to be used, it cannot become obsolete *merely because* it is rarely used.'[50]

Bonar Law tried to make the King's flesh creep. On 4 May 1912, he told Austen Chamberlain that he had given the King 'the worst five minutes that he has had for a long time', when he warned him, after dinner, that his 'only chance' was that the Government should resign within two years. 'If they don't you must either accept the Home Rule Bill or dismiss your Ministers and choose others who will support you in vetoing it—and in either case half your subjects will think that you have acted against them.'[51] Meanwhile, Bonar Law said in public that there were 'things stronger than parliamentary majorities', and assured the Ulstermen that there were no lengths to which they might go in resistance to Home Rule in which he would not support them. In 1913, he was seriously considering using the power of the Lords to amend the annual Army Bill in such a way that the forces of the Crown could not be used in Ulster until after a general election. On 16 November 1912, he told Lord Stamfordham that 'if the tension does not come to a head in some other way, we shall have to decide between breaking the Parliamentary machine and allowing these terrible things to happen. When faced with a choice of such evils as these, we shall not, I think, hesitate in considering that the injury to the House of Commons is not so great an evil as the other.'[52]

By 1913, both sides had come to the despairing conclusion

[49] RA G.V K398/7.
[50] RA G.V K2553 (2)/50.
[51] Blake, op. cit., p. 133.
[52] RA G.V K2553 (1)/8.

that a general election would settle nothing : Ulster would not accept the result if it went one way, and southern Ireland would not accept it if it went the other way. It seemed that both the Unionists and the Liberals had become the prisoners of their Irish allies. Asquith, when he saw the King at Balmoral in August 1913, said that he saw no way out of the *impasse* except by a change of heart in Ulster. He admitted that the Government had not expected such extreme reactions when the Home Rule Bill was drafted; but, events having taken their course, an election offered no solution. 'What would be the use of it, since Sir Edward Carson says Ulster would not accept its verdict if the Government was returned to power. If, on the other hand, the Opposition win, the South and West of Ireland will be in revolt, and the new Government will be "up against Home Rule again".'[53] Asquith was equally discouraging to those who wanted a referendum. That, he said, would undermine the foundations of representative government, and give only a misleading result since it would be conducted on purely party lines, and would therefore be as meaningless as an election.

All this bore hardly upon the King. He had indeed been placed, through no volition of his own, at the vortex of controversy. Bonar Law's words to him had sunk deep. Again and again, in his correspondence with the Prime Minister, the King returned to the point that, whether he took some action of his own or whether he simply followed his Ministers' advice, he would offend half his subjects. Asquith's standard reply was that the King acted only upon the advice of his Ministers and therefore could not be held personally responsible for the result. But the stubborn fact, as the King saw with agonised clarity, was that in this dilemma a disturbing number of his subjects had demonstrated that they *would* hold him personally responsible. He produced a list of formidably hard questions for his Prime Minister to answer : the reply amounted to a reiteration of the diagnosis that there were some questions to which the verdict of the electorate, refracted as it must be by party allegiance, prejudice, and the impossibility of singling

[53] RA G.V K2553 (2)/60.

out a particular issue, would be no answer. The King increasingly felt that the Prime Minister was drifting towards an abyss—and taking the King with him.

In spite of Asquith's objections, the King's mind turned more and more towards an election; he began, too, seriously to consider whether, if no election were held, he could properly assent to Home Rule. He wrote a long memorandum in his own hand; it is undated, but internal evidence suggests that it was completed before May 1914, the earliest date on which the Home Rule Bill could pass, under the Parliament Act.[54]

Before the passing of the Parliament Act, the King wrote, it was clear that the House of Lords 'had the power to compel a Government to refer to the country any measures which they regarded as not having been fully put before the electorate. But *now* it is the King alone that stands between the Commons and the Electors.' It was an open question whether Home Rule had ever been put before the electorate. 'The actual Bill itself certainly has *not* been.' When the Bill was presented for his assent, 'I shall then remember how it was forced through the House of Commons, pages of it never even discussed, and yet rejected three times by the House of Lords.' He reverted once more to the chilling predicament which Bonar Law had described :

> *Never* has a British sovereign in more recent times been placed in such an odious and mortifying position . . . Whichever course I follow, never again shall I be able to set foot in Ireland. Is it right, is it just, to place the Sovereign in such an intolerable predicament? Whether Home Rule should be given to Ireland or not is a matter on which I have no opinion. But there *is* an opinion yet unsought, the opinion of my people, and I maintain that, in an appeal to it, is to be found the only sound solution of this momentous question.

But that was an appeal which Asquith could not allow. On 5 February 1914, the King gave the Prime Minister a clear warning that he would 'feel it his duty to do what in his own

[54] RA G.V K2553 (5)/98B.

judgment was best for his people generally'. Asquith replied that he hoped that the King was not thinking of refusing assent. 'Such a thing had not been done since the reign of Queen Anne, and it would undoubtedly prove disastrous to the Monarchy.' It would be the lesser evil if the King were to dismiss his Ministers.[55]

The King's final decision was taken after he had received advice from Lord Loreburn, who had retired as Lord Chancellor and whom the King consulted in Loreburn's capacity as chancellor of the Duchy of Cornwall. Loreburn's opinion was that the King should give his assent to the Home Rule Bill, but only after he had received written advice from his Ministers that he should do so, given in a form that could be published.[56] On 31 July 1914, after the last attempts at compromise seemed to have failed, the King drew up a letter to the Prime Minister, with Loreburn's help. It said that the refusal of assent had been considered : but

> . . . the King feels strongly that that extreme course should not be adopted in this case unless there is convincing evidence that it would avert a national disaster, or at least have a tranquillising effect on the distracting conditions of the time. There is no such evidence.

Therefore, the King asked that Ministers should provide him with a full statement of the reasons why they advised him to grant his assent, to be presented 'in a form which can be put on record for the use of his successors and referred to if any necessity should hereafter arise'.[57]

The letter was never sent. Events on the continent of Europe supervened, and in the British Isles one set of passions was replaced by another. The great constitutional quarrel between the parties was not resolved; it was adjourned, to the indefinite future.

[55] Nicolson, op. cit., pp. 233–4.
[56] RA G.V K2553 (5)/103.
[57] Nicolson, op. cit., p. 234, n.l.

Chronology

1827 End of Liverpool's Ministry. April : Canning prime minister. Break-up of Tory Party
August : death of Canning. Goderich prime minister

1828 February : resignation of Goderich. Wellington prime minister

1829 Roman Catholic Relief Bill passed

1830 June : death of George IV; accession of William IV. General election. July : revolution in France
November : resignation of Wellington; Grey prime minister

1831 1st Reform Bill defeated in House of Commons. General election; Grey returned to office. 2nd Reform Bill defeated in House of Lords

1832 3rd Reform Bill amended in House of Lords. Resignation of Grey; Wellington fails to form a ministry; Grey recalled. Reform Act passed. General election; Grey returned to office

1834 Resignation of Grey, Melbourne prime minister
Melbourne dismissed; Peel prime minister

1835 General election. Resignation of Peel; Melbourne prime minister

1837 Death of William IV; accession of Queen Victoria. General election; Melbourne returned to office

1838 Publication of the People's Charter. Formation of Anti-Corn-Law League

1839 Resignation of Melbourne. 'Bedchamber crisis.' Peel declines to form a ministry; Melbourne resumes office

1840 Marriage of Queen Victoria

1841 Melbourne's ministry defeated in House of Commons. General election; Peel prime minister

1846 Repeal of the Corn Laws. Peel's ministry defeated in House of Commons; Russell prime minister

1847 General election; Russell returned to office

1848 Chartist demonstration in London
1850 Death of Peel
1851 Great Exhibition in the Crystal Palace
Palmerston dismissed from Foreign Office
1852 Russell's ministry defeated in House of Commons; Derby prime minister. General election; Derby continues in office. Derby's ministry defeated in House of Commons; Aberdeen prime minister
1852 Death of Wellington
1854–6 Crimean War
1855 Resignation of Aberdeen; Palmerston prime minister
1857 Vote of censure on Palmerston's ministry carried in House of Commons. General election; Palmerston returned to office. Outbreak of Indian Mutiny
1858 Palmerston's ministry defeated in House of Commons. General election; Derby prime minister
1859 Derby's ministry defeated in House of Commons. General election; Palmerston prime minister
1860 Paper Duties Repeal Bill rejected by House of Lords
1861 Paper duties repealed (incorporated in Finance Act). Death of Prince Albert
1865 General election : Liberal majority. Death of Palmerston; Russell prime minister
1866 Russell's ministry defeated on Reform; Derby prime minister
1867 Second Reform Act passed
1868 Resignation of Derby; Disraeli prime minister. April : Disraeli's ministry defeated on Irish Church question
November : general election. Liberal majority. Gladstone prime minister
1869 Disestablishment of Irish Church
1870 Forster's Education Act
1872 Ballot Act
1873 Gladstone resigns but resumes office
1874 General election. Conservative majority. Disraeli prime minister
1876 Queen proclaimed Empress of India
Disraeli created Earl of Beaconsfield
1880 General election. Liberal majority. Gladstone prime minister
1881 Death of Lord Beaconsfield. Closure first used in House of Commons
1882 Phoenix Park murders. Occupation of Egypt
1884–5 Third Reform Bill

1885   Fall of Khartoum and death of Gordon. Gladstone's ministry defeated in House of Commons. Salisbury prime minister. General election

1886   Salisbury's ministry defeated in amendment to the Address; Gladstone prime minister
First Home Rule Bill. Gladstone's ministry defeated in House of Commons. General election. Liberal Unionists hold the balance of power. Salisbury prime minister

1887   Queen's Golden Jubilee

1890   Parnell divorce case

1891   Death of Parnell

1892   General election. Irish Nationalists hold balance of power. Gladstone prime minister

1893   Second Home Rule Bill defeated in House of Lords
Independent Labour Party formed

1894   Resignation of Gladstone; Rosebery prime minister

1895   Rosebery's ministry defeated in House of Commons; Salisbury prime minister. General election. Unionist majority

1897   Queen's Diamond Jubilee

1899–1902   Boer War

1900   Formation of Labour Representation Committee. General election; Unionist majority

1901   Death of Queen Victoria; accession of Edward VII

1902   Resignation of Salisbury; Balfour prime minister

1903   Resignation of Chamberlain. Opening of tariff reform campaign

1905   Resignation of Balfour; Campbell-Bannerman prime minister

1906   General election; Liberal majority

1908   Resignation of Campbell-Bannerman; Asquith prime minister

1909   Rejection of the Budget in the House of Lords

1910   January: general election. May: death of Edward VII; accession of George V. December: general election

1911   Parliament Act passed

1912   Third Home Rule Bill passed in House of Commons

1913   Home Rule Bill passed in House of Commons

1914   Home Rule Act passed under provisions of Parliament Act; its operation suspended for the duration of the war

Principal Persons Mentioned in the Text

(Names in brackets after ministerial offices refer to the prime ministers under whom those offices were held.)

ABERDEEN : George Hamilton-Gordon, 4th Earl of Aberdeen (1784–1860). Foreign Secretary, 1828–30 (Wellington). Secretary of State for War and the Colonies, 1834–5, and Foreign Secretary, 1841–6 (Peel). Prime Minister, 1852–5.

ADDINGTON, Henry (1757–1844). Speaker of the House of Commons, 1789–1801. First Lord of the Treasury and Chancellor of the Exchequer, 1801–4. Created Viscount Sidmouth, 1805. Lord President of the Council, 1805 (Pitt). Lord Privy Seal, 1806, and Lord President of the Council, 1806–7 (Grenville). Home Secretary, 1812–22 (Perceval and Liverpool). Cabinet Minister without office, 1822–4 (Liverpool).

ALTHORP : John Charles Spencer, Viscount Althorp and 3rd Earl Spencer (1782–1845). Chancellor of the Exchequer, 1830–4 (Grey and Melbourne). His succession to his father's peerage and consequent departure from the House of Commons precipitated the dismissal of Melbourne's first Ministry.

ASQUITH, Herbert Henry (1852–1928). Barrister. Home Secretary, 1892–5 (Gladstone, Rosebery). Chancellor of the Exchequer, 1905–8 (Campbell-Bannerman). Prime Minister, 1908–16.

BAGEHOT, Walter (1826–1877). Editor of *The Economist*, 1860–77. Published *The English Constitution, Physics and Politics, Lombard Street, The Depreciation of Silver*, and numerous essays.

BALFOUR, Arthur James (1848–1930). Nephew of 3rd Marquess of Salisbury. M.P. 1874. Loosely attached to the 'Fourth Party',

1880–5. President of the Local Government Board, 1885; Chief Secretary for Ireland, 1887–91; First Lord of the Treasury and Leader of the House of Commons, 1891–2 and 1895–1902 (Salisbury). Prime Minister, 1902–5. Resigned as Leader of the Conservative–Unionist Party, 1911. First Lord of the Admiralty, 1915–16 (Asquith). Foreign Secretary, 1916–19; Lord President of the Council, 1919–22 (Lloyd George). Lord President of the Council, 1925–9 (Baldwin). Author of the Balfour Declaration in favour of a Jewish national home in Palestine, 1917. Created Earl of Balfour, 1922. Author of *Defence of Philosophic Doubt, Foundations of Belief, Theism and Humanism, Theism and Thought*, etc.

BENTHAM, Jeremy (1748–1832). Founder of that variation of utilitarian philosophy known as Benthamism. Wrote voluminously and attracted many disciples, including several eminent administrators. His skeleton was preserved in University College, London.

BIGGE, Arthur John; Baron Stamfordham (1849–1931). Private Secretary to King George V from 1910.

BLACKSTONE, Sir William (1723–1780). Legal scholar and judge. First Vinerian Professor of English Law at Oxford, 1758–66. His lectures are said to have inspired Bentham to attack him in print. Author of *Commentaries on the Laws of England*, etc.

BRIGHT, John (1811–1889). Radical politician. A principal member of the Anti-Corn-Law League. M.P. 1843. President of the Board of Trade, 1868–70; Chancellor of the Duchy of Lancaster, 1873–4 and 1880–2 (Gladstone). One of the most notable public orators of his time.

BRYCE, James (1838–1922). Regius Professor of Civil Law, Oxford, 1870–93. M.P. 1880. Under-secretary for Foreign Affairs, 1886; Chancellor of the Duchy of Lancaster, 1892–94 (Gladstone). President of the Board of Trade, 1894–95 (Rosebery). Chief Secretary for Ireland, 1905–6 (Campbell-Bannerman). Ambassador to the United States, 1907–13. Created Viscount Bryce, 1914. Author of *Studies in History and Jurisprudence, The American Commonwealth*, etc.

CAMBRIDGE: H.R.H. George William Frederick Charles, 2nd Duke of Cambridge (1819–1904). Grandson of King George III and first cousin of Queen Victoria. Commanded a division in the Crimea, 1854. Commander-in-Chief of the British Army, 1856–95.

CAMPBELL-BANNERMAN, Sir Henry (1836–1908). Chief Secretary for Ireland, 1884–5; Secretary of State for War, 1886 (Gladstone). Secretary of State for War, 1892–5 (Gladstone and Rosebery). Leader of the Liberal Party in the House of Commons, 1898. Prime Minister, 1905–8.

CANNING, George (1770–1827). Treasurer of the Navy, 1804–6 (Pitt). Foreign Secretary, 1807–9 (Portland). President of the Board of Control, 1816–21; Foreign Secretary, 1822–7 (Liverpool). Prime Minister, April–August, 1827. Notable writer of satirical verse.

CHAMBERLAIN, Joseph (1836–1914). Unitarian. Went into business in Birmingham at 16 and retired with a substantial fortune at 38. Chairman of National Education League of Birmingham, 1868; National Chairman, 1870. Mayor of Birmingham, 1873–5. M.P. 1876. Founded the National Liberal Federation, 1877. President of the Board of Trade, 1880–5; President of the Local Government Board, 1886 (Gladstone). Broke with Gladstone over Irish Home Rule, 1886. Colonial Secretary, 1895–1903 (Salisbury, Balfour). Resigned to campaign for tariff reform, 1903. Incapacitated by a heart attack, 1906.

CHURCHILL, Lord Randolph (1849–1895). Younger son of the 7th Duke of Marlborough. M.P. 1874. Practised a subtle form of obstruction in the Parliament of 1880–5 as leader of the 'Fourth Party'. Secretary of State for India, 1885; Chancellor of the Exchequer and Leader of the House of Commons, 1886 (Salisbury). Resigned in December 1886 and was never offered office again.

CHURCHILL, Winston Leonard Spencer (1874–1965). Son of Lord Randolph Churchill. Trained as a soldier. M.P. (Conservative–Unionist) 1900. Left the Conservative Party over free trade, 1904. Under-secretary for the Colonies, 1906–08 (Campbell-Bannerman). Entered Cabinet as President of the Board of Trade, 1908; Home Secretary, 1910–11; First Lord of the Admiralty, 1911–15; Chancellor of the Duchy of Lancaster, 1915 (Asquith). Minister of Munitions, 1917–19; Secretary of State for War and Air, 1919–21; Secretary of State for Air and Colonies, 1921; Colonial Secretary, 1921–2 (Lloyd George). Chancellor of the Exchequer, 1924–9

(Baldwin). First Lord of the Admiralty, 1939–40 (Chamberlain). Prime Minister and Minister of Defence, 1940–5; Prime Minister, 1951–5 (Minister of Defence, 1951–2). Published one novel (*Savrola*), accounts of campaigns in India, the Sudan and South Africa; biographies of Lord Randolph Churchill and of the 1st Duke of Marlborough, autobiographical histories of the First and Second World Wars, etc.

CLARENDON : George William Frederick Villiers, 4th Earl of Clarendon (1800–1870). Ambassador at Madrid, 1833–9. Lord Privy Seal, 1839–41 (Melbourne). President of the Board of Trade, 1846 (Russell). Lord-Lieutenant of Ireland, 1847–52. Foreign Secretary, 1853–8 (Aberdeen and Palmerston); 1865–6 (Russell); and 1868–70 (Gladstone).

DAVIDSON, Randall Thomas (1848–1930). Dean of Windsor, 1883–91. Bishop of Rochester, 1891–5. Bishop of Winchester, 1895–1903. Archbishop of Canterbury, 1903–28 (a longer period than any of his predecessors since William Warham, 1504–32). Created Baron Davidson of Lambeth, 1928.

DERBY : Edward George Geoffrey Smith Stanley, 14th Earl of Derby (1799–1869). M.P. 1822. Called up to the Lords as Lord Stanley, 1844; succeeded his father as Earl of Derby, 1851. Under-secretary for the Colonies, 1827 (Canning). Chief Secretary for Ireland, 1831–3; Secretary of State for War and the Colonies, 1833–4 (Grey); and 1841–5 (Peel). Prime Minister, 1852, 1858–9 and 1866–8. Translated the *Iliad* into blank verse.

DERBY : Edward Henry Stanley, 15th Earl of Derby (1826–1893). M.P. 1848. In his father's Ministries, he was Under-secretary for Foreign Affairs, 1852; Colonial Secretary, 1858; President of the Board of Control, 1858–9; Foreign Secretary, 1866–8. Refused the Greek throne, 1863. Foreign Secretary, 1874 until his resignation in 1878 (Disraeli). Left the Conservative Party in 1880. Colonial Secretary, 1882–5 (Gladstone). Joined Liberal Unionists 1886, and led them in the House of Lords until 1891.

DICEY, Albert Venn (1835–1922). Vinerian Professor of English Law, Oxford, 1882–1909.

DILKE, Sir Charles (1843–1911). Under-secretary for Foreign Affairs, 1880–82; President of the Local Government Board,

1882–5 (Gladstone). Ally of Joseph Chamberlain. His career was broken when he was cited in the Crawford divorce case in 1886.

DISRAELI, Benjamin (1804–1881). Son of Isaac D'Israeli, author. Baptised, 1817. Privately educated. Articled as a solicitor, 1824. Published *Vivian Grey*, 1824, the first of a dozen novels. Wrote, also, *Vindication of the English Constitution, The Spirit of Whiggism, Life of Lord George Bentinck*, etc. M.P. 1837. Attacked Peel, 1843–6, on the issue of the repeal of the Corn Laws. Leader of the Conservative Party in the House of Commons, 1847–68. Chancellor of the Exchequer, 1852, 1858–9, 1866–8 (Derby). Prime Minister, 1868 and 1874–80. Created Earl of Beaconsfield, 1876.

EDWARD VII : King of Great Britain and Ireland and of the British Dominions beyond the Seas, Emperor of India (1841–1910). Eldest son and second child of Queen Victoria. Married, 1863, Princess Alexandra, daughter of Prince Christian of Schleswig–Holstein–Sonderburg–Glucksburg. Succeeded to the throne, 22 January 1901.

GEORGE V : King of Great Britain and Ireland and of the British Dominions beyond the Seas, Emperor of India (1865–1936). Second son of Edward, Prince of Wales, later Edward VII. Succeeded his elder brother, Edward Duke of Clarence, as second in succession to the throne, 1892. Trained as a naval officer. Married Princess Victoria Mary of Teck (who had been betrothed to his brother), 1893. Succeeded to the throne, 6 May 1910.

GLADSTONE, William Ewart (1809–1898). M.P. 1832. Under-secretary for War and the Colonies, 1835; Vice-president of the Board of Trade, 1843; resigned 1845; Secretary of State for War and the Colonies (without a seat in Parliament), 1845–6 (Peel). 1852–5, Chancellor of the Exchequer (Aberdeen). Chancellor of the Exchequer, February 1855; resigned (Palmerston). Chancellor of the Exchequer, 1855–9 and 1859–65 (Palmerston). Chancellor of the Exchequer and Leader of the House of Commons, 1865–6 (Russell). Prime Minister, 1868–74 (Chancellor of the Exchequer, 1873–4); 1880–5 (Chancellor of the Exchequer, 1880–2). Prime Minister and Lord Privy Seal, 1886 and 1892–4.

GRANVILLE : Granville George Leveson-Gower, 2nd Earl Granville (1851–1891). Paymaster-General, 1851; Foreign Secretary,

1851–2 (Russell). Lord President of the Council, 1852–4 (Aberdeen). Lord President of the Council, 1855–8 (Palmerston). Lord President of the Council, 1859–66 (Palmerston, Russell). Colonial Secretary, 1868–70; Foreign Secretary, 1870–4 and 1880–5; Colonial Secretary 1886 (Gladstone). Leader of the Liberal Party in the House of Lords from 1855.

GREY: Charles, 2nd Earl Grey (1764–1845), 'Lord Grey of the Reform Bill'. One of the managers of the impeachment of Warren Hastings, 1788. First Lord of the Admiralty, 1806; Foreign Secretary, 1806–7 (Grenville). Prime Minister, 1830–4.

HARCOURT, Sir William George Granville Venables Vernon (1827–1904). M.P. 1868. Whewell Professor of International Law, Cambridge, 1869–87. Solicitor-General, 1873–4; Home Secretary, 1880–5; Chancellor of the Exchequer, 1880–5 (Gladstone). Chancellor of the Exchequer, 1892–5 (Gladstone, Rosebery). Disappointed of the premiership on Gladstone's retirement. Leader of the Liberal Party in the House of Commons, 1894–8.

HARTINGTON: Spencer Compton Cavendish, Marquis of Hartington and 8th Duke of Devonshire (1833–1908). M.P. 1857. Junior lord of the Admiralty, 1863 (Palmerston). Under-secretary, War Office, 1863–6 (Palmerston, Russell). Secretary of State for War, 1866 (Russell). Postmaster-General, 1868–70; Chief Secretary for Ireland, 1870–4 (Gladstone). Succeeded Gladstone as Leader of the Liberal Party in the House of Commons, 1875. Refused to form a government, 1880, 1885, 1886. Secretary of State for India, 1880–2; Secretary of State for War, 1882–5 (Gladstone). Broke with Gladstone over Home Rule, 1886, and led the Liberal Unionists in the House of Commons from 1886 until he succeeded to his father's dukedom in 1891. Lord President of the Council, 1895–1903 (Salisbury, Balfour). Opponent of tariff reform.

KNOLLYS, Francis, 1st Viscount Knollys (1837–1924). Private secretary to the Prince of Wales from 1875. Continued as private secretary after the Prince's accession as Edward VII in 1901. Joint private secretary to King George V, 1910–13.

LANSDOWNE: Henry Petty-Fitzmaurice, 3rd Marquis of Lansdowne (1780–1863). Chancellor of the Exchequer (as Lord Henry Petty), 1806–7 (Grenville). Cabinet minister without office,

1827 (Canning). Home Secretary, 1827–8 (Canning, Goderich). Lord President of the Council, 1830–4 (Grey, Melbourne); 1835–41 (Melbourne); and 1846–52 (Russell). Cabinet minister without office, 1852–5 (Aberdeen); and 1855–8 (Palmerston).

LANSDOWNE: Henry Charles Petty-Fitzmaurice, 5th Marquis of Lansdowne (1845–1927). Governor-General of Canada, 1883–8. Viceroy of India, 1894. Secretary of State for War, 1895–1900 (Salisbury); Foreign Secretary, 1900–5 (Salisbury, Balfour). Leader of the Conservative Opposition in the House of Lords, 1906–15. Cabinet minister without office, 1915–16 (Asquith).

LAW, Andrew Bonar (1858–1923). Born in Canada, son of a Presbyterian minister from Ulster. Brought up in Scotland from age of 12. Joined firm of iron merchants. M.P. 1900. Parliamentary secretary to the Board of Trade, 1902 (Balfour). Proponent of tariff reform. Succeeded Balfour as Leader of the Conservative–Unionist Party in the House of Commons, 1911. Colonial Secretary, 1915–16 (Asquith). Chancellor of the Exchequer, member of the War Cabinet, and Leader of the House of Commons, 1916–18 (Lloyd George). Lord Privy Seal, 1919–21 (Lloyd George). Resigned, 1921. Prime Minister, October 1922–May 1923.

LIVERPOOL: Robert Banks Jenkinson, 2nd Earl of Liverpool (1770–1828). Foreign Secretary (as Lord Hawkesbury), 1801–4 (Addington). Home Secretary, 1804–6 (Pitt) and 1807–9 (Portland). Succeeded his father as Earl of Liverpool, 1808. Prime Minister, 1812–27.

LLOYD GEORGE, David (1863–1945). Educated at Church of England elementary school. Solicitor. County councillor, 1889. M.P. 1890. Opponent of the Boer War and of Balfour's Education Act of 1902. President of the Board of Trade, 1905–8 (Campbell–Bannerman). Chancellor of the Exchequer, 1908–15; Minister of Munitions, 1915–16; Secretary of State for War, 1915–16. Prime Minister, 1916–22. Created Earl Lloyd-George of Dwyfor, 1945.

LOREBURN: Robert Threshie Reid, 1st Earl Loreburn (1846–1923). Solicitor-General, 1894 (Gladstone). Attorney-General, 1894–5 (Rosebery). Lord Chancellor, 1905–12 (Campbell-Bannerman, Asquith). Established the Court of Criminal Appeal, 1907.

LOWE, Robert, 1st Lord Sherbrooke (1811–1892). Fellow of Magdalen College, Oxford, 1835–6. Member of the Legislative Council, New South Wales, 1843–50. M.P. 1852. Vice-president of the Committee of the Council on Education, 1859 (Palmerston); resigned, 1864. Opposed Russell's Reform Bill of 1866, as one of those Liberals whom Bright described as dwelling in the Cave of Adullam, where King David gathered 'every one that was in distress . . . and every one that was discontented' (I Samuel, xxii). Chancellor of the Exchequer, 1868–73 (Gladstone). Unsuccessfully attempted to introduce a match tax, and proposed that the label should read 'Ex luce lucellum, Out of light a little gain'. Home Secretary, 1873–4 (Gladstone).

LOWELL, Abbott Lawrence (1856–1943). Professor of Political Science, Harvard University, 1900–9. President of Harvard, 1909–33. Author of *The Government of England*, etc.

LYNDHURST: John Singleton Copley, 1st Earl of Lyndhurst (1772–1863). Barrister. M.P. 1818. Solicitor-General, 1819–24; Attorney-General, 1824–6 (Liverpool). Master of the Rolls, 1826. Lord Chancellor, 1827–30 (Canning, Goderich, Wellington); 1834–5 and 1841–6 (Peel). Successfully opposed introduction of life peerages, 1856.

MACKINTOSH, Sir James (1765–1832). Philosopher. Author of *Vindiciae Gallicae* (1791), a reply to Burke's *Reflections on the French Revolution*. Recorder of Bombay, 1804. M.P. 1819.

MACAULAY, Thomas Babington (1800–1859). Fellow of Trinity College, Cambridge, 1824. Contributor to *Edinburgh Review*. M.P. 1830. Member of the Supreme Council of India, 1833–8. Secretary at war, 1839–41 (Melbourne). Paymaster-General, 1846–7 (Russell). Author of *History of England, Lays of Ancient Rome*, etc. Created Baron Macaulay, 1857.

MAITLAND, Frederic William (1850–1906). Downing Professor of the Laws of England, Cambridge. Author of *Domesday Book and Beyond*, etc. Most luminous of all English constitutional historians.

MELBOURNE: William Lamb, 2nd Viscount Melbourne (1779–1848). Chief Secretary for Ireland, 1827–8 (Canning, Goderich). Home Secretary, 1830–4 (Grey). Prime Minister, 1834 and 1835–41.

MILL, John Stuart (1806–1873). Philosopher and economist. Son of James Mill, a disciple of Bentham. M.P. for Westminster, 1865–8. Author of *A System of Logic, Principles of Political Economy, On Liberty, Considerations on Representative Government, Utilitarianism,* etc.

MILNER, Alfred; Viscount Milner (1854–1925). Under-secretary in the Ministry of Finance, Egypt, 1890–2. Chairman of the Board of Inland Revenue, 1892–7. High Commissioner in South Africa, 1897–1905. Favoured war against the Boers. Played a leading part in encouraging the House of Lords to reject the budget of 1909. Member of Lloyd George's War Cabinet, 1916–18.

MORLEY, John (1838–1923). Editor of the *Fortnightly Review,* 1867–82. M.P. 1883. Chief Secretary for Ireland, 1886 (Gladstone); and 1892–5 (Gladstone, Rosebery). Secretary of State for India, 1905–8 (Campbell-Bannerman). Lord Privy Seal, 1908–14. Resigned at outbreak of war. Created Viscount Morley, 1908. Author of *Life of Gladstone, Walpole, On Compromise,* etc.

NORTHCOTE, Sir Stafford (1818–1887). Private secretary to Gladstone, 1842. Co-author (with Sir Charles Trevelyan) of the Report on the Civil Service, 1853. M.P. 1855. President of the Board of Trade, 1866 (Derby). Secretary of State for India, 1867–8 (Derby, Disraeli). Chancellor of the Exchequer, 1874–80 (Disraeli). Leader of the Conservative Party in the House of Commons, 1876–85. Created Earl of Iddesleigh. First Lord of the Treasury, 1885 (Salisbury). Foreign Secretary, 1886–7 (Salisbury).

PAINE, Thomas (1717–1809). Author of *The Rights of Man,* etc. In 1790, he was entrusted with the key of the Bastille by Lafayette, for transmission to President Washington.

PALEY, William (1743–1805). Theologian. Author of *The Evidence of Christianity,* etc. His book *Principles of Moral and Political Philosophy* (1785) is said to have stimulated Bentham to publish his *Principles of Morals and Legislation.*

PALMERSTON: Henry John Temple, 3rd Viscount Palmerston (1784–1865). Irish peer, and hence eligible to sit in the House of Commons. Secretary at war, 1827 (Canning). Foreign Secretary, 1830–4 (Grey, Melbourne), 1835–41 (Melbourne), and 1846–51 (Russell). Home Secretary, 1852–5 (Aberdeen). Prime Minister, 1855–8 and 1859–65.

PARNELL, Charles Stewart (1846–91). Irish nationalist leader and leading proponent of Home Rule. M.P. 1875. Practised calculated obstruction in the House of Commons. His career was broken after he was cited in the O'Shea divorce case, 1890.

PEEL, Sir Robert (1788–1850). M.P. 1809. Chief Secretary for Ireland, 1812–18; Home Secretary, 1822–6 (Liverpool). Home Secretary, 1828–30 (Wellington). Created the Metropolitan Police Force, 1829. Prime Minister, 1834–5 and 1841–6. Carried the repeal of the Corn Laws, 1846.

PERCEVAL, Spencer (1762–1812). First Lord of the Treasury and Chancellor of the Duchy of Lancaster, 1809–12. Assassinated in the House of Commons.

PONSONBY, Sir Henry Frederick (1825–1895). Private secretary to Queen Victoria from 1870 until his death.

ROSEBERY: Archibald Philip Primrose, 5th Earl of Rosebery (1847–1929). Lord Privy Seal, 1885 (Gladstone). Foreign Secretary, 1886 (Gladstone). Chairman of the Imperial Federation League. Chairman of the London County Council, 1889–1892. Foreign Secretary, 1892–4 (Gladstone). Prime Minister, 1894–5. Resigned leadership of the Liberal Party, 1896. His horses won the Derby three times, twice while he was prime minister. Married Hannah de Rothschild.

RUSSELL, Lord John (1792–1878). Paymaster-General, 1831–4 (Grey). Home Secretary and Leader of the House of Commons, 1835–9 (Melbourne). Secretary of State for War and the Colonies, 1839–41 (Melbourne). Prime Minister, 1846–52. Foreign Secretary, 1852–3; Cabinet minister without office, 1853–4; Lord President of the Council, 1854–5 (Aberdeen). Resigned, January 1855. Secretary of State for the Colonies, February 1855 (Palmerston); resigned, July 1855. Foreign Secretary, 1859–65. Created Earl Russell, 1861. Prime Minister, 1865–6.

SALISBURY: Robert Arthur Talbot Gascoyne-Cecil, 3rd Marquess of Salisbury (1830–1903). M.P. (as Lord Robert Cecil) 1853. Wrote copiously in periodicals, especially the *Saturday Review* and the *Quarterly Review*. Became Viscount Cranborne and his father's heir on the death of his elder brother, 1865. Secretary of

State for India, 1866–7 (Derby). Resigned in opposition to Reform Bill. Succeeded his father as Marquess of Salisbury, 1868. Secretary of State for India, 1874–8; Foreign Secretary, 1878–80 (Disraeli). Leader of the Opposition in the House of Lords, 1881–5. Prime Minister and Foreign Secretary, 1885. Prime Minister, 1886–92 (Foreign Secretary, 1887–92). Prime Minister, 1895–1902 (Foreign Secretary, 1895–1900; Lord Privy Seal, 1900–2).

SENIOR, Nassau William (1790–1864). Economist. First Drummond Professor of Political Economy, Oxford, 1825–30; and again, 1847–52.

STOCKMAR: Baron Christian Friedrich von Stockmar (1787–1863). Confidential adviser to King Leopold of the Belgians, and of Prince Albert.

VICTORIA ALEXANDRINA (1819–1901). Queen of the United Kingdom of Great Britain and Ireland, Empress of India. Daughter of Edward, Duke of Kent, fourth son of King George III, and Mary Louisa Victoria, daughter of the Duke of Saxe–Coburg and Saalfeld and widow of the Prince of Leiningen. Princess Victoria succeeded to the throne on 20 June 1837. Married, 1840, her cousin, Prince Albert of Saxe–Coburg–Gotha.

WELLINGTON: Arthur Wellesley, 1st Duke of Wellington (1769–1852). Field Marshal, 1813. Entered Liverpool's Cabinet as Master-General of the Ordnance, 1819; resigned, 1827. Prime Minister, 1828–30. Caretaker prime minister, 1834. Foreign Secretary, 1834–5. Cabinet Minister without office, 1841–6 (Peel). Commander-in-Chief of the British Army, 1827–8 and 1842–52.

WOLSELEY, Garnet Joseph, 1st Viscount Wolseley (1833–1913). Field Marshal. Original of 'The Modern Major-General' in Gilbert and Sullivan's *The Pirates of Penzance*. Served in Burma, the Crimea (where he lost the sight of an eye), India, China and Canada. Commanded Ashanti expedition, 1873–4. High Commissioner in South-East Africa, 1879–80. Adjutant-General, 1882. Commanded in Egypt, 1882. Commanded expedition for the relief of Khartoum, 1884–5. Commander-in-Chief, Ireland, 1890. Commander-in-Chief of the British Army, 1895–99.

Index